THE URBAN PRIMARY SCHOOL

Education in an Urbanised Society

Series Editors: Gerald Grace, Meg Maguire and Ian Menter

Education continues to face a range of problems, crises, issues and challenges. Often, although not exclusively, those experiencing the most severe problems are working within an urban context. Such schools face very particular challenges – high ethnic minority intake, pupil underachievement, problems of teacher recruitment and retention, social deprivation and other factors. Teachers themselves need to be prepared for classes with a rapid turnover of pupils, pupils from homeless and refugee families, pupils with English as an additional language.

This series is intended to help education professionals and academics gain a broader understanding of the challenges faced. It examines the problems facing teachers and learners working in challenging and difficult circumstances, with a view to overcoming disadvantage in contemporary education in the UK and Ireland. It explores social and educational developments and provides educational practitioners, academics and policy makers with focused analyses of key issues facing schools in an urban society, examining the interaction between theory and practice. It offers insights into the linkage between education development and wider social, cultural and economic needs and thus contributes to the achievement of social justice in and through education.

Current titles:

Mel Ainscow & Mel West: *Improving Urban Schools*

Pat Broadhead & Chrissy Meleady: *Children, Families & Communities*

Meg Maguire, Tim Wooldridge & Simon Pratt-Adams: *The Urban Primary School*

Jill Rutter: *Refugee Children in the UK*

THE URBAN PRIMARY SCHOOL

MEG MAGUIRE
TIM WOOLDRIDGE
SIMON PRATT-ADAMS

Open University Press

Open University Press
McGraw-Hill Education
McGraw-Hill House
Shoppenhangers Road
Maidenhead
Berkshire
England
SL6 2QL

email: enquiries@openup.co.uk
world wide web: www.openup.co.uk

and Two Penn Plaza, New York, NY 10121–2289, USA

First published 2006

A catalogue record of this book is available from the British Library

ISBN 10: 0 335 20176 8 (pb) 0 335 20177 6 (hb)
ISBN 13: 978 0 335 20176 1 (pb) 978 0 335 20177 8 (hb)

Library of Congress Cataloging-in-Publication Data
CIP data applied for

Typeset by YHT Ltd., London
Printed in Poland by OZ Graf. S.A.
www.polskabook.pl

CONTENTS

SERIES EDITORS' PREFACE

The Open University Press has been the leading publisher of urban education studies in this country. With early texts such as *Cities, Communities and the Young: Readings in Urban Education* (1973) and *Equality and City Schools: Readings in Urban Education* (1973), the Press gave a considerable impetus to urban education study, research and policy discussion in Britain.

This publication initiative was taken because it was recognized that teaching and learning in urban schools constituted distinctive challenges which required close analysis and imaginative and radical responses. It was also recognized that educational and social policy aspirations for equality of opportunity, social justice and community regeneration faced their greatest tests in the context of urban schooling in major cities and in large working class estates on the margins of such cities.

In England, the Department of Education and Skills publications *The London Challenge* (2003) and *London Schools: Rising to the Challenge* (2005) demonstrate that teaching and learning in urban contexts are still high on the policy agenda. While the particular focus on London has current priority, similar reports could be produced for Birmingham, Glasgow, Liverpool, Manchester, Belfast, Cardiff, Newcastle and other major centres. The urban education question has continuing relevance for policy and practice and it involves national and international dimensions.

It was for these reasons that we suggested to the Open University Press/ McGraw-Hill publishing team that a new series on teaching and learning in urban contexts would be very timely and professionally valuable. We were pleased that this proposal received such a positive response, not only from the publishers but also from our colleagues who will be the contributors to the series.

The series is designed to be a resource for:

- students undertaking initial teacher education

- students following programmes of educational studies
- serving teachers and headteachers undertaking advanced courses of study and professional development such as NPQH
- education policy professionals and administrators
- citizens who want to be actively involved in the improvement of educational services such as parents and school governors

The challenge we have set for the contributors to the series is to write texts that will engage with these various constituencies. To do this, we believe that such texts must locate the issue under examination in an appropriate theoretical, historical and cultural context; report relevant research studies; adopt a mode of analysis expected from 'reflective practitioners' – and keep all of this grounded in the realities of urban professional experience and work settings, expressed in an accessible style.

The inaugural text of the series is, appropriately, *The Urban Primary School* by Meg Maguire, Tim Wooldridge and Simon Pratt-Adams. The literature of urban education has tended to give more attention to secondary and high schools than to primary and elementary schools, perhaps because many researchers in the field have been recruited from secondary school backgrounds. The world of critical urban education scholarship has relatively ignored the complexities of urban primary schooling and perhaps this says something about the priorities of both the academy and the schooling system. This book will do much to remedy this situation.

Maguire, Wooldridge and Pratt-Adams write with the authority and perceptiveness derived from their frontline experience in urban primary schools and communities. What they say about classroom realities will speak directly to classroom practitioners. At the same time, because they have pursued their study of urban primary schooling in advanced courses, they are able to relate school-based analysis to wider theoretical, historical, cultural and socio-political analysis. The result is a study that is not only highly readable and accessible but one that makes a brilliant synthesis of reflective professional knowledge, with well-informed policy scholarship. A particular strength of the book is the space it affords for the voices of urban primary school teachers and headteachers to be heard about the dilemmas and rewards of their work. We need more urban education studies of this quality and especially texts that bring urban primary schools to the centre of attention.

In the concluding chapter, the authors state:

> The dilemma for the urban primary school teacher is to be able to recognise the impact of the wider social context and draw on its cultural resources without losing their belief in the power of education to promote and sustain social transformation.

In other words, the often harsh realities of urban life have to be faced (for this is intellectual integrity) while remaining resourceful and resilient in the face of those realities and committed to the educational and social improvement of urban communities and of their children (for this is optimism of the will).

This book makes a powerful contribution to both intellectual integrity and to optimism of the will in urban primary school education. It will, we are sure, become a major resource and inspiration for all those who care about the urban education question, not only in this country but also internationally.

Gerald Grace, Ian Menter and Meg Maguire

ACKNOWLEDGEMENTS

We would like to thank all those who made this book possible.

Over the years the three of us have worked in numerous urban primary schools and our thanks are due to many former colleagues and friends who have helped us to form ideas from discussions and debates we have had. We are also grateful to our university students and colleagues who have discussed ideas and insights with us. The need for this book became clear through these many discussions. We hope that we have succeeded in extending understanding by uniting theoretical ideas and practical applicability in the context of urban education.

We would like to thank our series editors Gerald Grace and Ian Menter for their expertise and advice during the writing of this book. Furthermore, we are indebted to Gerald for establishing in 1976 the MA in Urban Education at King's College London; and which two decades later first brought the three of us together to study this subject.

We offer our grateful thanks to Tamara Bibby, Steve Blum, Rachel Fletcher, Sharon Gewirtz, Ian Menter and Jacqui Pratt-Adams for reading draft chapters and providing critical comments. Additionally, Steve was invaluable in helping us to assemble the final manuscript.

We are indebted to the many teachers and headteachers from six metropolitan education authorities across England for their contributions to the empirical work in Chapters 3 and 4 of this volume. We would also like to express our gratitude to the following urban headteachers for their contributions: Jenny Bruce, Miles Clarke, Barbara Deakin, Alison Flegg, Richard Goodswen and Gill Quinlivan.

Thanks also to Fiona Richman, Melanie Smith and Katharine Metzler at Open University Press/McGraw-Hill.

Finally, love and thanks to our partners Steve, Clare and Jacqui for their support and encouragement during the writing of this book.

INTRODUCTION

This book is written for all those who teach, who will teach and who used to teach in urban primary schools. It is also written for those who influence what goes on in urban education, for those who prepare new teachers for urban primary schools and for parents and school governors. We hope the book will promote an awareness of the distinctiveness of urban primary schools and foster an appreciation of what they accomplish. In a rapidly changing society, our future prosperity will lie in our capacity to recognize and respect diversity and difference, something that the best urban primary schools manage successfully – but something that does not seem to 'count' for much in a time when formal academic attainment seems to be the main indicator of 'good' education.

Our purpose in writing this book is threefold: we want to try to articulate a more complex picture of urban primary schooling that goes beyond some of the negative stereotypes that still drive policymaking in this area; we want to explore the challenges of learning and teaching in urban settings; and we want to reassert some critical urban educational concerns. This book is also about the opportunities and challenges urban primary schools present to those who work in them. In using the term 'urban' rather than 'inner city' we want to signal that we are not just talking about schools in cities. We are talking about schools that serve socially excluded children and their families wherever they are located.

In the United States in the 1960s, there was a 'moment' when concern focused on the need for a different and distinctive approach towards urban schooling. What emerged was a 'greater awareness of and concern for the urban poor – especially the education of their children' (Cicirelli 1972: 31). The debilitating impact of poverty and disadvantage in limiting life chances was recognized and attempts were made to ameliorate these pressures through educational interventions. This concern was also reflected in other industrialized societies (Harvey 1973). There was a concentrated focus on urban schools and urban policymaking demonstrated, not least, by an extensive literature in the area. Since the early 1970s, however, there has been a shift away from egalitarian concerns and a move towards what Gewirtz (2002), Tomlinson (2001) and others have styled the post-welfarist society. Welfarism comprised a 'formal commitment to distributive justice; that is, to the redistribution of social goods on a more equitable basis' (Gewirtz 2002: 1). In contrast, post-welfarism emphasizes the role of market forces, competition and individualism. Although concerns about urban schools have not gone away, the ways in which they are described and many of the policy responses being advocated for them are now differently inscribed. For example, in England, the main concern is now with promoting inclusion for individuals rather than with understanding why exclusion occurs in the first place and tackling it head on (Dyson 2003).

In terms of educational provision, as Tomlinson (2001: 4) has argued: 'The belief that educational resources would be shared more fairly ... shrivelled back to the pre-war belief that a good education was a prize to be competitively sought, not a democratic right.' One outcome of this change in direction is that there is now less concern with issues of the common good and more concern about private, individual interests and advantage. In consequence, urban education is no longer a central part of teacher education and it does not figure largely in in-service education either.

In this book we argue that the complexities of urban education are still marginalized and that questions of redistribution, recognition and other forms of social justice are silenced discourses. It seems to us a mistake to treat everyone and every school as if they were on a level playing field. Urban schools are distinctive, resources are an issue and diversity is frequently not acknowledged in a 'one size fits all' curriculum. Policies that are driven by market forces might not be the most effective way of ensuring that children learn and teachers teach well in urban primary schools.

Our focus in *The Urban Primary School* is not with the broad history and ideology of primary schooling in England. Primary pedagogy with its values and ethos of service, care and the development of the 'whole child' is made up of powerful discourses that position primary schools in particular ways (Nias 1989; Pollard et al. 1994). This approach towards the work of the primary school, teachers, parents and children has sometimes produced a critical stance towards aspects of policy and practice. For example, many early years specialists have been concerned about aspects of the National Curriculum that they argued were not developmentally appropriate. The highly charged and contested area of how to help children to enjoy becoming successful readers is one high-stakes arena where contrasting discourses of childhood and pedagogy are frequently deployed to argue for one approach rather than another. However, these same powerful systems of beliefs and values that make up part of the discourses of primary practice can sometimes work in ways that 'centre' the individual child in a decontextualized, asocial and ahistorical manner. Our concerns in this book lie in an attempt to recover a contextualized and social account of urban primary schooling.

The three of us who have written this book have all worked in urban primary schools in England and we believe that we can identify with some of the dilemmas that face those who still work in these complex settings. In order to test out our experiences and our theories in this area, we wanted to draw on the perspectives of others who are still engaged in this work. One of the problems in some earlier urban theoretical work was that sometimes it became less accessible to classroom practitioners (Saunders 1981). The focus was often with macro-economic theory rather than its impact on the classroom. For this reason, some central concerns of urban theory were less familiar to teachers (but see Bash et al. 1985). We were also concerned that there seemed to be a tendency to focus on London rather than seeing urban schools as part of the fabric of educational provision across the nation, in other metropolitan settings, overspill settings and even some rural locations. Thus, in this book we have tried to incorporate the perspectives of urban teachers who work in schools in other parts of England to flesh out the theory and reflect a broader understanding of the 'urban'. Somewhat inevitably perhaps, since London is where the three of us teach and live, there is still an accent on the capital.

There is another spatial issue that needs to be explained. Sometimes in this book we talk about UK policy and at other times we talk about English policy approaches as if these were the same. Evidently this is not the case. There are important differences between education policy and provision in Northern Ireland, Scotland, Wales and England and these are not directly addressed in this book. Neither are some specific aspects of urbanism, for example sectarianism, that occur in some of these settings. We have mainly focused on the English setting because 'the central dynamic of educational change in post-war Britain, especially since 1979, has been English' (Jones 2003: 3). English education policymaking and its concentration on new managerialism, standards and performativity has tended to silence social justice concerns in its focus on individual choice and the private good. It is these broader issues that frame the scope of this book.

Themes of the book

The book is based around three main themes. First, a major concern is with the need to theorize urban education in a way that engages with wider social issues related to structural disadvantage, poverty, oppression and exclusion. Second, we want to draw on the voices of those who currently teach in and manage urban primary schools. Third, we want to celebrate urban schools and recognize their contribution to our diverse society.

In terms of theorizing the urban setting and urban education, urban education policymaking has too often started with problem(s) rather than starting from an appreciation of and theoretical analysis of urban settings. Grace (1984: 109) has argued that 'no useful discussion of or even formulation of the "real issues" in the inner city or in urban education can take place independently of theory'. To paraphrase his argument, it might seem that standing back to theorize about urban schools misses the point. What is needed is action. Urban primary schools do face many problems, but how these challenges are understood will have a powerful bearing on what practical outcomes are recommended or implemented by policymakers and politicians. This is a point that we have taken seriously in this book.

There are some obvious 'gaps' in this book. We have not dealt at all with the role of trade unions in urban primary schools. We have not explored the perspectives of some key members of staff such as learning assistants, school administrative staff or even deputy headteachers. We have not dealt sufficiently with the implications of our discussions for teacher education. We have not considered the perspectives of those colleagues in urban local education authorities (LEAs) who work to support their primary schools. We have not considered the complexities involved in serving as a governor of an urban primary school. This work will have to wait for another time. To draw on Grace's work again (1978: 3), what we have tried to do is make visible the 'fundamental contradictions within the wider society' that impact on the urban primary school.

Plan of the book

The book falls loosely into four main sections. In the first section, Chapters 1 and 2, we explore what we mean by 'urban' and 'urban education'. We do this by drawing on a range of approaches as well as contextualizing our arguments. The second section, Chapters 3 to 5, considers what it is like to work in an urban primary school through considering data collected from teachers and headteachers in six different local education authorities across England. In this section we also consider the perspectives and experiences of parents, although here we depend on research published by others in this area. In the third section, Chapters 6 to 9, we focus on in-school issues such as diversity and difference, social class, curriculum issues and social justice in theory and practice. The last section, Chapters 10 and 11, explores urban education developments in the United States and then draws together the project of this book.

In this book, we have tried to provide a broad and comprehensive overview of the urban primary school. In this attempt, we have gone back to some of the foundational texts in urban sociology and urban education theory, particularly the work of Gerald Grace. We have also drawn on contemporary urban-based studies that illustrate the complexities and contradictions of urban educational provision, in particular the work of Sharon Gewirtz, Diane Reay and Helen Lucey. The book also contains an account of a small study that we undertook to explore the complexities of teaching and leading in the urban primary school. However, as with most books that strive to provide an outline of a field of study, we recognize that there are occasions when topics appear to have been overlooked, oversimplified or not always fully developed. We acknowledge that lack of space means we have presented a partial picture in some respects. There is also some repetition in some of the chapters. This is so that each chapter can be read on its own.

To describe each chapter in more detail: Chapter 1 lays out our theoretical and conceptual approach towards the urban and the urban primary school. We consider the impact of urbanization and some of its consequences. We review the history of urban schools as well as some contemporary policy responses in this field. We argue that unless the social and material reasons for the 'problems' of urban schools are examined, the challenge of urban schooling cannot be fully understood and, therefore, cannot be fully addressed. In Chapter 2, we look in more detail at the factors that characterize an urban primary school, in particular, we concentrate on the ways in which social factors impact on urban schools.

Chapter 3 explores the perceptions of urban primary school teachers. We explore the skills and qualities required to teach successfully in urban primary schools. We also consider the factors that contribute to a higher turnover of staff in urban schools. In Chapter 4, we turn to the perspectives and experiences of urban primary school headteachers. In these two chapters, we draw on the small study that we undertook. One of our findings was that many teachers and headteachers chose to work in urban primary schools because of a commitment to 'making a difference' to the lives of children in challenging circumstances. A second finding was that teachers and headteachers saw a need to engage with parents and carers in order to promote effective learning. Simultaneously, the same teachers and headteachers sometimes found this a complex and contradictory demand. Thus, Chapter 5 focuses on home–school relationships in urban primary schools.

Chapter 6 picks up some of the key themes from Chapter 2 and explores diversity and difference. Some aspects of diversity, particularly those related to culture and ethnicity, are more likely to characterize inner city urban schools, and these provide the focus for this chapter. Chapter 7 is concerned with the regulating classed practices that construct the urban primary school in distinctive but subordinate ways. The chapter returns to some of the theoretical concerns outlined in Chapter 1 such as space, competition and consumption. We explore the ways in which the classed practices of choosing schools and selection inside schools connect with these theoretical concerns. In Chapter 8, we explore some policy approaches to urban education and we argue that the urban locale can and should be used as a site for promoting and sustaining a different sort of critical learning. Chapter 9 focuses on the ways in which contemporary policies have an impact in schools in relation to decision making and issues of social justice. We concentrate on the practical enactments of social justice in the urban primary school through drawing on a set of vignettes that illustrate the tensions involved in this decision-making process.

In Chapter 10, we turn to some of the complexities of urban education in the US setting. Our intention is to provide another account of the challenges that face urban education. In this chapter, we explore the way in which different urban dilemmas have been responded to over time in terms of policy and practice. We also briefly explore some work in US elementary schools. Chapter 11 draws all our themes together and provides some conclusions.

1 CONTEXTUALIZING THE URBAN

This book is about the distinctiveness of urban primary schools and the opportunities and challenges they present to those who work in them. In using the term urban, rather than inner city, we want to signal that we are not just talking about schools in cities. We are talking of schools that serve socially excluded children and their families wherever they are located. In this chapter, we lay out our theoretical and conceptual approach towards the urban and the urban primary school. We start by considering the process of urbanization and some of its consequences and then examine some key theoretical approaches towards the urban. The chapter then reviews the history of urban schools as well as some contemporary policy responses in this field. Our case is that unless the underlying social and material reasons for the 'problems' of urban schools are examined, the challenge of urban schooling cannot be fully understood and, therefore, cannot be fully addressed.

Urbanization and its consequences

The 'urban' stands as a condensate for the consequences of urbanization, a process that has been and continues to be driven by changes in production. These changes in production are matched by changes in the wider social world; in employment patterns, housing developments, health and education opportunities. As production becomes larger scale and mechanized and moves away from being small scale and localized, it tends to be re-housed in factories, warehouses and mills, for example. These larger scale centres of production are generally located in towns and cities that provide access to transport, larger markets and a ready supply of labour. Thus, people become compelled to move to towns and cities to seek employment, bringing their families with them. Simultaneously, as towns and cities expand, this puts pressure on housing and other social amenities and, in turn, provokes changes in a variety of other spheres such as leisure, entertainment and land use. Urbanization is irrevocably linked with changes in the modes of production and this spills out into other social arenas.

As Byrne (2001: 14) notes: 'The modern urban world became the dominant way of living because people worked in factories and made things.' But, urbanization does not always occur in a linear shift over time from subsistence agrarian production to industrialization, mass production and de-industrialization (signalled by the decline in manufacturing industries and the growth in finance capital and the service sector). Transitions can be, and often are, more complex. There can be significant overlap between different modes of production and in some cases, such as the contemporary Chinese city, these modes coexist. The contemporary Chinese city contains within its spatial setting a variety of modes of production. Rural farmers bring their produce from the countyside to markets in the city early each morning. There are labour-intensive and highly mechanized factories producing cheap goods for sale and export. There is heavy industry, such as coal mining and steel manufacturing. There are also post-industrial forms of production that are synonymous with late capitalism and technological change (Angotti 1993). Urbanization is made more complex by the fact that people not only move from the rural to the urban, they move from one urban context to another: from cities like Madras to London, from Tokyo to New York (Sassen 1994). These moves and production transitions interact with and on social relations and the provision of social welfare goods including, among other things, health, education and housing.

By 1996 over 50 per cent of the world's population was recorded as living in towns or cities (Clark 1996). In Britain, however, by 1861, the majority of the population was already urbanized (Byrne 2001). While economic imperatives lay behind this early transformation, there were distinctive outcomes in the growth of the UK's cities, particularly in relation to housing. It is worth exploring the case of housing in the UK's cities in more depth as changes in patterns of housing and occupancy are useful in illustrating the relationship between changes in the modes of production, urbanization and ultimately, as we shall see, the spatialized politics of the urban primary school.

The early industrializing towns and cities of the UK were characterized by residential segregation. As urbanization and industrialization accelerated in tandem and as more advanced methods of industrialized production were deployed in the UK (the factory system, for example), so more workers needed to be housed near their places of work. Their managers needed reasonable access but eschewed living alongside their work force. In the nineteenth century, a reserve army of unskilled and temporary labour moved to the newly emerging cities, frequently settling in cheap rented accommodation, the 'rookeries' and slums of Victorian London (Fishman 1988). This casualized residuum of labour was feared by the middle classes but was 'essential' to maintain cheap and flexible labour costs. Workers could be hired by the day and competition for scarce employment kept the wages low (Stedman-Jones 1971). Industrialists wished to keep their own families away from exposure to what they saw as the risks of contamination by the poor, particularly from the new urban working classes who were demonized by the middle classes (Fishman 1988).

The separation of middle- and working-class communities was characterized by distinct and separate residential zones throughout the nineteenth century. This segregation was not just about a wish on the part of the middle classes to avoid the urban workers, it was also about a specific cultural turn, a turn away from the city and towards a distantly remembered way of life, the rural idyll. The growth of the suburbs and the spread of housing that was affordable for the newly emerging middle-class urban professionals who desired fresh air, space and gardens, fuelled a drift away from the city, a pattern that continued into the twentieth century. The rise of the suburbs 'emerged from and reinforced social inequality' (Savage and Warde 1993: 79). This 'social inequality' was fuelled by the middle-class exodus from the city centres and was driven (in the UK at least) by the additional 'need' to invest surplus capital in the built environment through house building and home ownership. This move left the poorer residents in the city centres in what was frequently inadequate housing stock.

The details of the long struggle for affordable and better-quality housing for the urbanized working classes is too complex to undertake here. Nevertheless, over time, old housing stock was gradually replaced, the old urban 'slums' were torn down and the state increasingly took responsibility for providing affordable housing for working-class families – a provision that accelerated after the Second World War. However, Conservative housing policy in the 1980s and 1990s allowed those living in council-owned housing in the UK the 'right to buy' their homes, since when the stocks of decent and cheap accommodation for working-class communities have been seriously depleted (Burrows 1999). Thus, those left in inner city social housing (much of which is too substandard to be purchased by anyone, even if it could be afforded) tend to be older and poorer people rather than the skilled working classes of previous generations. The cities of late modernity, in the UK and in northern hemisphere settings more generally, are now formed by the new middle classes who have appropriated specific housing stock in 'rising neighbourhoods', through the process of gentrification (which we discuss later), while the new residuum may live across the road or round the corner in social housing or poor-quality rented accommodation. The skilled working classes may have been relocated to the overspill towns or have relocated to edge-cities (Garreau 1992). The older middle classes and 'respectable' working class have settled in the outer rings of cities or in the suburbs.

During the twentieth century in the UK, particularly in the post-Second World War period, parts of the inner city started to become desirable once more. As suburbanization became entrenched in the outskirts of the cities, a complementary housing pattern of gentrification in some inner city settings started to emerge in the 1960s (Warde 1991). Fuelled by the baby-boomers, who were better educated, more prosperous and had larger disposable incomes than their parents' generation, the city became an arena of conspicuous consumption. The baby-boomers married later and started their families later. They expected to become property owners at an earlier age than their parents and they also expected to have access to a cosmopolitan urban lifestyle. In particular, changes in the lifestyles and expectations of young professional women who continued their career development and purchased their own homes made a significant change to the landscape of the urban world (Rose 1988). Suburban housing was by now too expensive and transport costs too high, so that young professionals and others now turned to look for 'improving neighbourhoods' within the city. Other changes in society fuelled the move towards urban gentrification.

The changes in household structures with higher numbers of young and single professional women, dual-earner households and 'positive images of city-living based on a deep dislike of suburban environments' (Savage and Warde 1993: 85) were part of this particular shift. Gentrification was not just a result of changes in modes of production but also a consequence of a new cultural move – the formation of new middle-class groups, often made up of state welfare professionals like teachers, social workers and media-related professionals, who now occupied particular urban spaces (and schools) (Ball 2003a). 'All in all it (gentrification) is a process of the middle class replacing the working class; increasing property values; alteration in the built environment and the emergence of a new urban style of life' (Savage and Warde 1993: 80).

In the late twentieth century and in the twenty-first century, the UK has continued and continues to move towards a new mode of production: de-industrialization or post-industrialization (Martin and Rowthorn 1986). What this means is that while people in the UK are less likely to be employed in manufacturing goods (which are often made more cheaply elsewhere), they are more likely to provide services. 'In Manchester more people are employed in leisure activities operating after the hour of 8 pm than are employed in manufacturing' (Byrne 2001: 58). Paradoxically, many of these services are provided in locations and buildings once used for older industries: for example, dockland sites that have been converted to wine bars, brasseries and shopping malls. In these new times, what is occurring in some urban spaces is a form of hyper-gentrification alongside a reworking of older urban signifiers. To add further to the irony, places are frequently named on the basis of their older industrialized usage: for instance, candle factories turned into privatized gated accommodation. Warehouses in the dockland areas with brushed-brick walls converted into arts centres and loft apartments signal this particular appropriation. In the post-industrializing city, social segregation has become more complex. Instead of the segregated zones of the nineteenth century, different social classes can now inhabit physically parallel but equally separate worlds.

The new middle-class fractions that move into these older areas, built up in the height of industrialization, appropriate the social space for their own cultural 'divertissement' as well as colonizing local schools (or not, if they do not see them as 'good'). Improvements in local services, for example, in health provision and increased personal services such as organic food stores and yoga classes, coupled with the renovation of local buildings, tend to benefit one section of the population and indirectly enhance the 'value' of the property in these gentrified enclaves. The reputations and 'value' of housing and schools in Notting Hill Gate, in the west of London, were very different in the late 1950s and early 1960s than they are today. This was an old, run-down part of London where large Victorian houses were divided up into small flats or made into bed and breakfast hotels to receive new arrivals to the country. The local schools were regarded as challenging to teach in and it was difficult to recruit and retain teachers in this part of London. In many parts of Notting Hill today, there exists a very different picture: a totally revisioned and refurbished location of private accommodation, outpriced except for all but the very wealthy. In the contemporary city, there are communities of people with 'shared, class-related, consumer preferences' (Savage and Warde 1993: 80) who have displaced the indigenous and poorer groups. In these enclaves, there are schools that certainly are *in* the inner city – but they are not *of* the inner city in the sense we deploy in this book.

In the UK urban context, the consequences of de-industrialization are closely linked to processes of gentrification. While gentrification relates to the movement of the middle classes to locations formerly occupied by urban working-class communities, de-industrialization forces us to ask questions about what happens to these working-class communities once the basis for their employment has disappeared and they can no longer afford to live close to city centres. The effects of de-industrialization, as a later stage of urbanization, are only too obvious in certain parts of the UK where older industries have been closed down or relocated elsewhere, leaving in their wake boarded-up shops and houses. In the inner cities, the gentrification of some of the 'desirable neighbourhoods' has involved a displacement of some fractions of the working-class community (Byrne 2001).

So far, we have suggested that changes in production modes meant that towns and cities expanded to accommodate the rise of an industrialized working class and, over time, new managerial and welfare professionals. The creation of segregated housing zones, through complicated and elaborate movements out of the city (suburbanization), and then back at a later point in time by some fractions of the middle class (gentrification), have contributed to a complex class mix in many urban locales. Urbanization was and is an economic process that is still in transition, shifting from industrialization to de-industrialization in the UK setting as elsewhere (Garreau 1992). Not surprisingly, many features of urban life can be seen in non-urban locales such as the housing estates on the fringes of, or just outside, cities such as Glasgow or Manchester. The process of urbanization is intimately connected with social, spatial and economic segregation as well as changes to capitalism itself (see Table 1.1).

Table 1.1 Modes of production and urban systems in the UK

Modes of production	**Urban housing systems**
Early industrialization	Spatial segregation in the city; slums and middle-class housing zones
Advanced industrialization	Growth of suburbanization and gentrification
Post-industrialization or de-industrialization	High levels of polarization. 'Edge cities', overspills and hyper-gentrification

In cultural terms, the urban has always been a 'problematical phenomenon' (Reeder 1977: 75). Reeder suggested that this was because urban settings could simultaneously be regarded as a place of opportunity and innovation as well as, paradoxically, a setting of debauchery, crime and social unrest. In demographic and geographical (spatial) terms, metropolitan cities include both the most and least privileged and powerfully demonstrate the stark polarization between access to and exclusion from cultural/social patterns of consumption. The metropolitan city contains theatres, opera houses, international cuisine, major art galleries and wide-ranging leisure and cultural provision while high numbers of the homeless sleep in the doorways and shelters of the city centre. Simultaneously, 'the city' has continued to stand for disruption and corruption, at least in relation to the urban working classes. For these reasons, as well as for reasons related to housing systems and access to other social goods such as education, it is appropriate to talk of 'divided cities'.

One final matter: while we have focused on the growth of the divided city, our concern is with the process of urbanization and its impact in terms of segregation and social exclusion. The impact of urbanization for rural communities, housing stock and accessing life chances has been no less dramatic. The movement of middle-class families into desirable suburban and rural settings; second-home rural ownership; the decline of work in non-urbanized settings – all these changes have combined to produce high levels of economic and social disadvantage for the rural working classes, whose experiences we would also include in the condensate of 'urban'.

Theorizing the urban

In the past, urban studies have tended to focus on the 'problems' of the city; 'the decline of inner-city neighbourhoods with decaying housing stock, deserted factories and warehouses, boarded up stores and diminishing and often impoverished populations' (Eliott and McCrone 1982: 1). This focus has inevitably resulted in counterclaims, which argue, correctly, that these experiences are not only typical of life in the city. Poverty, underinvestment and exclusion occur in rural settings as well. As Saunders (1986: 7) has pointed out, in the UK: 'The boundaries between city and countryside, urban and rural are generally indistinct.' He suggests that while location is relevant to any discussion of what is meant by the urban, what is distinctive are questions that are 'basic to the sociological analysis of advanced capitalist societies' (Saunders 1981: 278). Grace (1978) recognized that there are similarities between urban and rural settings; poverty and disadvantage are not just evident in cities. However, the crucial point he makes is that: 'Metropolitan cities provide the arenas for the making visible of fundamental contradictions within the wider society and of the ideological and political conflicts associated with such contradictions' (Grace 1978: 3).

This understanding lies at the heart of the analysis of the urban underpinning the work in this book. It is these 'fundamental contradictions' that need to be recognized, and which are intensified in urban settings. Grace (1978: 3) believes that inner city schools, 'particularly those situated within inner rings of deprivation and powerlessness', provide a setting in which 'issues of power, ideology and control become unusually salient and thus available for examination'. To this we would want to add, 'particularly' but not exclusively.

Grace (1984) characterized approaches to understanding the urban in three main ways: as problems, conflicts or contradictions. This is an approach that still has currency in our view. In many ways, it is the 'problems' approach that has continued to dominate urban policy and practice over a long period of time. This approach sees the key issue in the urban setting as a problem of order and control. This approach was reflected in the nineteenth-century model of seeking moral reform to ensure stability. One-off 'problems' were and still are tackled in a discontinuous manner. Underlying factors that produce disadvantage are not addressed or indeed acknowledged. As Grace points out, this approach does not consider questions of power or politics, the factors that constitute the 'problem' in the first place. To cite a contemporary example: New Labour is concerned about young people who truant from school and has attempted to manage this through threatening to take their parents and guardians to court and fining them. If primary and secondary school students 'truant' it may be because the school only offers them a very partial experience of success, the curriculum may be inappropriate, they may be experiencing financial difficulties in their family circumstances, they may be being bullied and so on. Forcing them back to school and financially penalizing their families will do little to address the reasons that led to the truanting behaviour.

The second major approach, the 'conflicts' approach, takes a more overtly political stance. This approach recognizes that urban locales are places of conflict over scarce resources such as housing or indeed schooling. There are conflicts and struggles over who gets what. The city 'concentrates' the process of social consumption and thus patterns of inequality emerge. A good example of this would be heightened disputes over the provision of state housing, particularly in a context of declining availability. At particular moments, 'moral panics' over the alleged housing advantages of young, single women with children or refugee groups, for example, are amplified to fuel exclusionary and oppressive discourses. This approach sidelines the way in which other policies have contributed towards the shortage of housing and 'blames' a particular group rather than seeing the shortage as a result of inadequate levels in provision or as a consequence of selling off council accommodation. A 'conflicts' approach may miss out on the central political question of why certain resources are in short supply in the first place.

For this reason, Grace (1984) suggested that a 'contradictions' approach is more appropriate and useful in explaining inequality, struggles over power and control, ideological formations and economic projects. Grace (1978: 103) argues that contradictions ('structurally determined incompatibilities within a social and economic formation and the priority of profit over justice') mean that a 'problems' or 'conflict' approach cannot do justice to the challenge of the city. The educational needs of children and their families cannot be fully met while the demands for profit take priority over the demands for social justice.

Savage and Warde (1993: 191) believe that not all urban problems are reducible to 'material inequality'. Their case is that many of the 'urban problems' of contemporary society, such as environmental issues, congestion and crime, are better understood as a consequence of modernity, of what Beck calls 'the risk society' (1992). In an unequal society, risk or 'insecurity is the other side of opportunity' (Savage and Warde 1993: 191). Some of the middle class (the old middle class) may retreat to the 'less risky' suburbs and attempt to reduce risks to themselves and their families through accessing 'better' schools, for example. Schools in these areas are attended (and perhaps staffed) by people similar to themselves. Conversely, the 'gentrifiers' who have colonized certain parts of the city (spawning wine bars, cafes, small theatres, designer residences and popular/successful city schools) maximize their access to and capacity for consuming the city, its fashions and its cultural base. This 'colonization' has also involved the appropriation of particular local primary schools that have a disproportionate middle-class intake. These schools then become 'beacons' that draw more middle-class families into these 'good' catchment areas. This move fuels an increase in house prices, which, in turn, works to safeguard and protect these spatial enclaves and reduces 'risk'. But accessing these social goods can be complex and difficult in certain locales even for the middle classes.

Middle-class anxieties about getting their children into what they perceive to be a 'good' school is a significant feature of the contemporary urban education world (Ball 2003a). Fears of contamination by children less fortunate than their own who might 'hold their children back', coupled with anxieties about the accelerating need for qualifications, fuel current middle-class urban panics about education provision. The process of urban colonization of some housing zones and the anxieties of some middle-class families who seek out 'good' schools for their children can sometimes result in the development of a polarized provision of primary schools. In some catchment areas, there can be well-staffed and well-resourced schools that serve a predominantly middle-class intake. A few streets away, another very different urban school may find it difficult to recruit and retain its teachers and may be serving a very different community. This community may be less able to manage the risks and insecurities of modern life, may have fewer cultural and economic resources on which to draw and may live on the 'wrong' side of the 'divided city'.

Emergence of urban schools

In his 'Notes on the schooling of the English working class 1780–1850', Johnson (1976: 44) claimed that 'discontinuous' and 'geographically uneven' moves led to the provision of mass schooling that was 'sharpened and intensified' by the Industrial Revolution. What distinguished the accelerated drive in the nineteenth century towards mass provision was the intervention of the state and its desire for control and regulation. As we have already indicated, in the UK, the nineteenth century was characterized by a 'great movement of population from the land to the towns, from village to factory'

(Hall 1977: 8). The newly emerging industrial cities were unable to respond quickly enough to the sheer numbers of people moving in and settling down. There was a crisis in housing and this coupled with poverty, lack of adequate sanitation and poor health provision led to a series of 'panics' on the part of the emerging middle classes. They feared the 'risk' of illness and contamination, which they believed was caused by the urban working class (Stedman-Jones 1971). There were other fears: the fear of working-class radicalism from groups such as the Chartists (1830s–1840s) as well as fears about moves towards organized trade unionism. There was also the residual 'fear' of what had happened at the end of the eighteenth century in France, the French Revolution (1789), with all the upheavals that this had entailed. For the middle classes, politicians and the 'gentry' the fear of a revolutionary urban mass was ever present (Fishman 1988).

As a consequence, while the cities had to be improved, they also had to be controlled, and it was recognized that education had a role to play in this. At the same time, it was starting to be more widely accepted that the urban masses needed some form of minimal literacy to sustain the growth and expansion of capital. In the mid-nineteenth century, mass education in other European nations was far in advance. An uneducated workforce was no longer economically viable. For these reasons, Johnson (1976: 51) believed that education, or rather *schooling*, for the urban working classes served a dual role; to maintain the cultural hegemony of the dominant classes through taking 'the child from home and prepar(ing) it for work and loyal citizenship':

> Some way had to be found to create, within the ranks of the urban-industrial masses, an inner attachment to society's goals, a positive commitment to the social order. Respectability, thrift, sobriety, self-discipline were required, to form – as it were from inside – an impulse, a 'formed sentiment', among the masses to adapt to the logic, rationale and mores of industrial capitalism. Thus, education took its place, alongside chapel, tract, self-improving societies, temperance movements, improving popular fiction, as a major cultural force reshaping the inner sentiments and aspirations of the masses. (Hall 1977: 9)

In the towns and cities of the rapidly urbanizing nineteenth century, elementary schools were built specifically to school the urban working class. They were set up to 'gentle' the masses but not to 'gentrify' them. The curriculum was basic and its purpose straightforward enough. The state saw elementary schooling as 'manifested in an emphasis on basic skills, precision and accuracy; a growth in scientific and technical elements in the curriculum and a physical training regime which provided the necessary socialization for the industrial context' (Grace 1978: 20). Even at their inception, urban schools were seen as 'difficult places', which catered for unruly children. They were not seen as suitable for children from more economically privileged families who needed a different sort of provision and who needed more than an elementary schooling.

As Johnson (1976: 52) noted, of the early to mid-nineteenth century: 'It is a fair guess that family and neighbourhood and even place of work were of much greater importance than schools.' In many ways, compulsory schooling (for education it was not) seemed almost irrelevant. When work was plentiful, educational achievement was not important; when work was scarce, schools were used to keep working-class youth off the streets. But while the mass provision of elementary schooling might have attempted to control and mould young minds and hearts, this has never been a straightforward task. Schools also produce forms of resistance. Children and their teachers have always been able to interrupt and subvert (to an extent) some of the intentions of educational policymakers. And, in part, it is this resistance that has contributed towards the demonization of the urban school as a place of disruption, difficulty and distress.

Gardiner (1984: 161) says that while the aim of elementary schooling was 'the promotion of social order by the management of "ignorant" working class behaviour through the medium of provided schooling', the problem was that very few of the 'ignorant' working class attended school on a regular basis. Indeed, as Fishman (1988) points out, schools had to emphasize industrial training to prevent truanting. Where teachers treated children in an unjust manner, or simply provided them with irrelevant or 'boring' material, the children signalled this clearly to their teachers and 'resisted' as best as they could. One of the most famous educational 'strikes' occurred in the early 1900s when elementary school children walked out of their schools all across the UK in protest at being caned by their teachers (Newell 1989).

During the early twentieth century, some scholarships were available for 'clever' working-class children who could then go to the local fee-paying grammar schools attended by their middle-class peers. In many cases, this offer could not be taken up. Working-class children often needed to obtain employment to help support their families. In addition, the scholarships did not include money for uniforms and books. So, the meritocratic 'promise' of education as a force for social mobility was not on offer to every working-class child who worked hard. This would have been apparent to the children and their families and may also have precipitated erratic attendance and truanting. The children may have also recognized that education was not really for them:

> In practice the school unconsciously orientated its teaching to the exceptions among us ... who were going to be lifted up into a higher social class. How many of these? ... Always the pride that prevailed in this working class school was that it succeeded in turning out less recruits for the working class than any other of its kind in the district. (Common 1951, in Hargreaves 1982: 75–6)

In 1870 the state finally agreed to provide elementary education to be paid for through taxation. Then, as now, disputes arose as to how much money should be put into education. The elementary schools of the nineteenth-century cities were aimed at controlling and disciplining an 'ignorant' and dangerous urban working class. Schools were expected to 'gentle' and school this unruly mob and render them up as good and docile workers for an industrializing nation. Their curriculum was designed partly with this aim in mind and their teachers were trained to this task. In consequence, it was sometimes difficult to convince middle-class taxpayers that it was in their interest to provide more resources and make better provision for a service from which their own children gained no benefit.

Provision of state elementary schooling was extended in the twentieth century and finally became universal by the 1930s. Free compulsory secondary schooling for all was made a legal obligation (if not an actual provision immediately) by the Education Act of 1944. The newly emerging middle-class professionals who were paying increased taxes for state schooling had started to move their children into the local primary schools where they lived. They were able to access free education in circumstances compatible with their ambitions and where there were often many other middle-class children (suburban schools, for example) they moved into the state secondary system. Particularly after the 1944 Education Act when many of the old high-status grammar schools were incorporated into the state sector, middle-class families started to become comfortable with using (parts of) the state sector for their children. Gradually, state schooling (although differentiated according to locale and catchment area) became the 'norm' for the vast majority of children in the UK.

What we want to suggest is that some of the dominant ideas that framed the provision of the elementary schools of the nineteenth century have persisted, albeit in slightly different forms, to shape and sculpt the contemporary urban state primary school. Thus, many of the challenges of the contemporary urban school lie in the origins and genealogy of nineteenth-century elementary provision. What is meant by urban schools are the schools that have always 'served' a distinct section of society: the urban working class. Their schools, frequently located 'in and around the inner city stand as beacons and landmarks of working class education' (Hall 1977: 11). In contrast, more privileged schools have, in the main, remained outside the city, although some grammar schools have developed in either the middle-class suburbs or within middle-class areas of urban gentrification. Hall (1977: 11) wrote that: 'There has never been, in England, anything remotely approaching a "common" or "comprehensive" school experience for all classes of children. Each kind of school has been absorbed into its socio-geographic segment, and taken on something of that imprint.'

We believe that it is important for educationalists, teachers and intending teachers to have some appreciation of the history of the struggles around educational provision. This provision was not simply a 'good' bestowed by a liberal and benign state. It was and still is contested, subverted and constantly subjected to the political and ideological imperatives of the day. In the nineteenth century, *de facto* segregated schools were provided by the newly emerging modern state for working-class children in order to promote social cohesion and prepare them for their place in the labour market. But schools and children are more complex and thus, policy intentions are often subverted by the actions of real people. This was as true of the nineteenth-century schools as it is today.

Policy responses to the urban

The urban has always been a focus for middle-class action of one sort or another. In the nineteenth century and into the early twentieth century, while there was always a radical working-class discourse that called for broad emancipated educational provision, dominant ideological perspectives emphasized the formation of a 'gentled' working class, as we outlined earlier. During the twentieth century, particularly in the period of the Second World War, different issues began to emerge. One consequence of the evacuation of many urban children into the countryside was that concerns were expressed about the poor physical condition of some of the children. Concerns were also raised about their alleged lack of literacy and numeracy skills. At the end of the war, there was an egalitarian 'moment' when a desire to make a better world was evidenced internationally. There was a clear policy commitment towards the common good. In the post-war reconstruction of the late 1940s and early 1950s, in the UK as elsewhere, strenuous efforts were made to attend to the health of all children and their mothers through the newly created national health service. More schools were built to house the post-war baby boom. Expectations of a better life increased across all classes in society and education was recognized as central in achieving social and economic progress. Secondary education was expanded, although it was provided on a differentiated basis that tended to favour the middle classes whose children were over- represented in the more elite academic schools (Ball 2003a).

By the late 1950s and continuing into the 1960s, it was recognized that while some real gains had been made, working-class children, particularly (but not exclusively) those who lived in urban settings, were not making as much progress as middle-class children. Much of what was written in this period tended to 'blame' working-class families for not providing enough stimulation or not having enough books in their homes (Plowden Report 1967). The view that these children were 'deficient' in some way continued to persist and shape policy. As Tomlinson (2001: 17) says:

> The left's recognition that children were caught up in cycles of disadvantage ... and cultures of poverty ... sparked positive liberal policies to alleviate the influence of poor home background on children's education but perpetuated the view that family factors were responsible for the poorer educational performance of working class children.

In the USA, attempts at 'compensation' were developed by the government, such as the Headstart programmes (forerunners perhaps of Sure Start in the UK), to overcome early disadvantage through positive interventions and the provision of additional resources that were targeted at poorer families. In the UK, similar attempts were made in the 1960s to ameliorate social disadvantage such as designating some areas as educational priority areas (EPAs). Schools in these areas were given small amounts of additional resources to assist them in their work. These attempts were 'problems based' and displaced any wider consideration of the conditions that support poverty or the 'political failure over redistributive justice' (Tomlinson 2001: 18). Unlike the US strategy, no real attempt at redistribution was made in the UK setting at this time.

By the mid-1970s, the sorts of egalitarian moves described earlier had been eclipsed by an international oil crisis and a massive recession, which led to high levels of unemployment. In the UK, the alleged radical and progressive educational policies of equality and opportunity of the 1960s were partly 'blamed' for economic problems and what was viewed as 'over-permissiveness' in society. In response, educational reform took a rightwards swing (Jones 2003). Perhaps the key signifier of urban educational change was the demolition of the Inner London Education Authority (ILEA) (a citywide unified authority) through the provisions of the 1988 Education Reform Act (Lightfoot and Rowan 1988). The ILEA had taken a lead in the UK in responding positively to working-class communities, to issues of 'race' and gender in particular. It had increased funding to schools in disadvantaged areas. Now it was 'punished' and disbanded. The way was clear for a radical right-wing intervention into education where individual competition and market forces were to dominate until the late 1990s (Lawton 1994).

In a lecture called 'Divided cities: "Dwellers in different zones, inhabitants of different planets"', Maden (1996) provided an overview of research that demonstrated the increased gap between rich and poor that occurred under the Conservative administrations in the UK from 1979 to 1997 (see also Hutton 1995; Smith and Noble 1995). Maden argued that 'what seems to be less well understood or debated is that the most extreme manifestation of this division is in our cities and that it affects children, especially' (Maden 1996: 19). Between 1981 and 1991 the 'degree, intensity and extent of poverty increased markedly in inner London and other large metropolitan areas' (Maden 1996: 20).

Yet, specifically in relation to education policy, any recognition of the impact of economic polarization has frequently been displaced by discourses that mask inequality and injustice. In the current policy climate of New Labour, 'competition, choice and performance indicators remain the unchallenged totems of policy, not in overt policy statements but simply by being left untouched by New Labour reforms' (Fergusson 2000: 203). Fergusson argues that 'markets and managerialism hold sway' and that the only difference between the previous Conservative administrations and New Labour is that 'the commitments to excellence and diversity are softened in favour of raising standards for all' (Fergusson 2000: 203).

The previous Conservative administrations (1979–97) had argued that many schools were failing their intakes. The 'blame' had turned away from working-class children and their families and onto urban primary schools and progressive pedagogy. Not only did 'discourses of derision' (Ball 1990) fuel parental fears about schooling, they softened the ground for the government to move into the control of education in a historically unprecedented manner (Dale 1989). Through the insertion of market forces, competition and an emphasis on narrow measures of performance underpinned by financial consequences where funding followed enrolment, 'good' schools would improve and 'bad' schools would wither on the vine. One problem was that failure and success were constituted in a particular manner (test scores and league tables). In a competitive market-driven enterprise, such as education provision, the downside is that there are losers as well as winners. One of the rationales of league tables is that someone is at the top and someone has to be at the bottom. Even a superficial scan of league table positions will reveal a fairly close correspondence with indices of social disadvantage such as free school meals, higher than average child mobility and higher numbers of children identified as having learning difficulties.

New Labour came into power with an expressed concern about high levels of child poverty in the UK as well as a desire to combat social exclusion. Many of their policies have aimed at tackling these issues. Policies such as family income support have made a small attempt at wealth redistribution. In terms of education, New Labour set up education action zones with the aim of improving education provision in areas of high social deprivation where additional targeted money was allocated (Gewirtz 2000). Policies such as Sure Start were set up to promote childcare and educational support to enhance children's success when they moved into mainstream schooling. Excellence in Cities (EiC) was also set up in order to provide support for schools in areas of recognized social deprivation. Strategies such as the means tested educational maintenance allowances (EMAs) have resulted in weekly payments for students staying on in post-compulsory education whose families are on lower incomes. While many of these policies could be seen as part of what Grace (1984) called the 'problems approach', it could be argued that attempts like some of these redistributive policies do have some potential to go beyond this.

Simultaneously, New Labour has attempted to keep the middle classes 'on side' and has produced policies to encourage them to keep sending their children to urban state schools (Whitty 2002). Policies such as the 'gifted and talented' provision within the EiC policy have led to differentiated provision in schools. Schools in 'disadvantaged' urban settings have been allocated additional funds to provide for socially excluded students as well as make extra provision for 'talented' children. In some schools, the 'gifted and talented' provision has overwhelmingly been colonized by middle-class children (Lucey and Reay 2002). However, in this policy strategy it is possible to read a particular message aimed at middle-class parents who may fear the 'risk' of sending their children to schools with 'disadvantaged' children. The 'gifted and talented' provision may simply operate as a form of internal segregation sending out messages to 'less talented' children that they are of less value. City academies, the new semi-privatized schools currently being set up in urban areas of 'disadvantage', may only serve to heighten and extend polarization and segregation between schools.

All these policies fail to recognize a central contradiction in educational policymaking. It is obviously desirable that all children are able to attend 'good' schools (although what is 'good' is contestable) and these schools will be better placed to support 'disadvantaged' children. But, 'if all primary schools were to improve so that they performed at the level of the most effective, the difference between the overall achievement of the most advantaged social groups and that of the disadvantaged might actually increase' (Mortimore and Whitty 1997: 9).

Conclusion

In this chapter, we have argued that the discourses surrounding urban schools have been historically constructed, in some part, out of moral panics and sets of crises around middle-class concerns to assert control, maintain the status quo and their social advantage. Policy responses to these schools have frequently been couched in a problems-oriented approach that has decontextualized urban schools, sometimes arguing that 'poverty is no excuse', sometimes by refusing to see any need for additional resources. More recently in policy terms, urban schools have sometimes been treated as if they were the same as schools with a disproportionate intake of middle-class and pro-school children, while simultaneously celebrating those urban schools deemed to have 'succeeded despite the odds' (Maden and Hillman 1996).

In 1991 the Inspectorate recognized the distinctiveness of urban schools as places where 'a higher than average proportion of pupils were disadvantaged'. They acknowledged the 'extra challenge' as well as the specific demands of teaching in urban schools. They listed these as follows: multicultural education; language development, including English as an additional language; class management, behavioural problems and absenteeism; low expectations and underachievement. This approach towards the urban school sweeps aside the structural underpinnings that support and frame disadvantage and structural patterns of social exclusion. To continue to focus on the children as the 'problem' or as 'deficit' in some way without any appreciation of the broader social and political context of urbanized life is counterproductive at the very least. By deploying this approach towards urban schools and the families they serve, real problems – lack of access to quality housing or good healthcare or lack of employment opportunities – are just not recognized. 'The urban poor, however they are constituted in ethnic, gender or class terms in various societies, and wherever they are located, are a challenge to established institutions' (Grace 1994: 45).

This 'challenge' is not always straightforward for teachers to understand and 'manage', but without any knowledge or theoretical exploration of the urban context, it is perhaps understandable that some schools may 'blame' (some) urban children and their families for the 'disruptions' they sometimes pose. This 'problems' approach, in turn, fails to recognize the positive contribution that can be made in urban schools and in the wider society by, for example, multilingual children and their families.

Perhaps different sorts of questions need to be asked, questions about social justice. Rather than treating all schools as if they were the same, and rather than providing additional resources to a small number of schools serving socially disadvantaged communities (such as city academies), what might be a better way forward would be an all-out attack on poverty. 'Without a sustained attack on material poverty, any educational gains among disadvantaged groups are likely to be short-lived' (Whitty 2002: 123). Writing of the US urban context, Kozol (1995: 189) says:

> Many of us who came of age during the 1960s, thought that these most blatant forms of residential segregation, and the gross extremes of wealth

> and poverty, of cleanliness and filth, of health and sickness in our nation, would be utterly transformed within another generation. It was a confident, naïve, and youthful expectation, characteristic of that era. Our confidence, we now know, was mistaken.

One of the policy mistakes has been to expect that education on its own could ameliorate the excesses of urbanization – that education could indeed 'compensate for society' (Bernstein 1971). Another has been a failure to appreciate the underlying reasons for the 'problems' of urban education. Without this critical policy approach, the challenge of providing socially just education in a structurally and materially unequal society cannot be fully understood and, therefore, cannot be fully addressed.

Questions

1. Select one current urban education policy. In what respects does it take a problems, conflict or contradictions approach?
2. In what ways do housing and housing occupancy patterns impact on primary schools in your area?
3. What continuities can you identify between early forms of urban schooling and current practices?

2

URBAN PRIMARY SCHOOLS AND URBAN CHILDREN

In this chapter, our intention is to contextualize our theoretical analysis of urban primary schools. We begin by giving three examples of different primary schools that we would classify as urban. These examples are then used to illustrate some of the characteristics of urban primary schools. At the heart of this chapter is a concern to chart the complex social context that mediates the social world of the urban primary school and to argue that this setting provides a distinctive set of challenges for educational policymakers and practitioners alike that need wider recognition.

In this chapter we want to provide a contextualized account of urban primary schools, that is, those schools that serve 'deprived areas' and excluded communities (Power et al. 2002). Some urban schools are likely to have several other key characteristics, most notably greater proportions of children from a minority ethnic background and children for whom English is an additional language (EAL) (DfEE 1999a). Other urban primary schools will serve a more homogenous working-class community. In general terms, however, the urban schools that we are referring to are those that reflect the higher levels of social deprivation, poverty and disadvantage that are usually, but not solely, found in large urban areas (DETR 2000).

Throughout this chapter, we will refer to three primary schools (see following) that we consider to be urban primary schools. Although we have changed their names and have left out any information that could lead to their identification, we have incorporated some details from their Ofsted reports in order to provide a contextualized account of three different urban primary schools. The intention is to provide some indication of the challenges and complexities faced by urban primary schools as well as highlighting some of their distinctive features.

Ranleigh Primary School

Ranleigh is a community school 20 minutes' walk from the business district of a large southern city. The central business district is the most expensive location in the city, however most of the children who attend Ranleigh live at the other end of the housing spectrum. The children's housing is characterized by overcrowded and substandard accommodation, mostly in local authority high-rise flats, without gardens. There is almost no space between the flats for children to play and where there is a piece of land it is covered in signs asking the children to refrain from playing with balls. Few parents or carers have experience of higher education and there are high levels of local unemployment in the area. The school recruits high numbers of minority ethnic children and very few of the children are from middle-class households. The majority of children at the school are of Bangladeshi descent and almost no children come from homes where English is their first language. Some of the children start school with little or no English. Nearly 75 per cent of the children are entitled to free school meals, which is well above the national average, while approximately 35 per cent of the children are identified as having special educational needs at either school action or school action plus of the special needs code of practice. Seventeen children have a statement of special educational needs. The rate of attendance is around 92 per cent, which is low for the borough and the country as a whole, although the levels of attendance are rising steadily. The school is positioned about halfway up the league table for the borough and is viewed as an improving school by the local education authority (LEA).

The headteacher and deputy head have been in post since 1990, although the teaching and support staff are more transient. In the academic year 2002–2003, for example, 14 full-time teachers from a total of 22 either stopped teaching or moved to other schools. They were replaced by four newly qualified teachers, in addition to long-term supply teachers from Australia, New Zealand and Canada. Recruiting experienced staff is a problem for the school.

Mortimore Primary School

Mortimore is a small primary school located in a disadvantaged and run-down part of a northern city. It is surrounded on three sides by housing estates and some wasteland on the other side. The school is housed in an old Victorian triple-decker elementary school building. The school admits children from the age of 3 to 11 to its mainstream classes and also makes provision for children who have special educational needs within its own self-contained unit.

One of the surrounding estates was built before the Second World War and is in need of repair. The other estate was built in the 1950s and is also in need of some repair. None of the flats has a garden and the area is regarded as somewhat 'unsafe' in the evenings due to the high levels of local crime and drug use. There is no private housing in the area at all.

The local community is made up of an old settled white working-class constituency, which has recently expanded to include families of minority ethnic descent. The area is reputed to be a stronghold of the British National Party. Many refugees and asylum seekers have recently been housed in the area and the intake to the school reflects this diversity. The majority of the children live very close to the school. However, some children are bussed in to attend the unit for children with special educational needs.

Forty-five per cent of the children qualify for free school meals. The school makes special provision for highly mobile children (those who move from school to school) and refugees and asylum seekers through two locally funded projects. Additional provision is made for children who have English as an additional language (EAL) in the form of extra classes and specialized teachers. A substantial number of children are at an early stage of English acquisition. Twenty-five per cent of the children are on school action or school action plus of the special needs code of practice. Mortimore has a school liaison officer, funded by a local charity, who works to support parents in encouraging their children to come to school. The school is near the bottom of the league tables for performance in SATs in the local education authority.

The headteacher has been in post for three years. The previous headteacher took early retirement on health grounds. The school is mainly staffed by young teachers in the early stages of their teaching careers and staff turnover is considered to be high. Local parents work as classroom assistants in the school.

Maynard Primary School

Maynard Primary School is situated on a large site on the outskirts of a Midlands city. A busy motorway runs alongside the school, which contributes to continuous noise and air pollution. The motorway also acts as a physical barrier, cutting the school and community off from local resources and amenities available to other schools in the borough. For this reason, the school and community sometimes feel marginalized, isolated and neglected. All the children come from an area of council high-rise flats and small houses in the immediate school vicinity. There are only a few children who attend school who travel some distance. Forty per cent of the children are eligible for free school meals and almost all children are from working-class families. Ten per cent of the children are characterized as having English as an additional language. The school compares favourably with other schools in the LEA league tables for SATs results at both Key Stages 1 and 2.

The school has achieved Beacon status and works in partnership with other schools to develop and support struggling schools in the neighbourhood. The school, led by a very committed headteacher who has worked in the school for over 10 years, has worked hard to overcome a negative reputation and is now recognized in the authority as being successful.

Maynard Primary School has a low turnover of staff and recruiting good teachers is not a problem anymore. The school has a particularly strong commitment to the provision it makes for children with special educational needs, of whom 27 per cent are either on the school action or school action plus scale of the special needs code of practice. The school has nine children who have a statement of special educational needs.

Drawing on these three examples, what we want to do in the rest of the chapter is explore some of the characteristic features of urban primary schools. Although urban schools do face challenging and difficult conditions, children are not predisposed to failure by attending an urban school. If families are entitled to free school meals for their children, there is no guaranteed cause and effect process that means their children will underachieve. What we want to avoid above all in this chapter (and throughout the book) is the suggestion that children in urban primary schools are 'set up to fail'. Equally, we want to take a realistic approach towards these schools. As Grace (2005: 7) says of urban schools: 'Given that the major challenges in this area are social, structural, political and economic, the idea that schools can "do" anything in relation to these challenges seems naïve.'

Poverty and free school meals entitlement

One dominant 'characteristic' of urban primary schools relates to their higher proportion of relatively disadvantaged children. In the literature and policy documentation on urban schools, relative terms like poverty and social deprivation are often deployed when describing urban communities, frequently without explaining what these mean (Whitty 2002). In the UK, the poverty that exists is generally understood as being a lack of resources that would commonly be regarded as necessary for a decent life (Townsend 1970). For this reason, poverty and deprivation are relative terms, relative to common expectations of decency. Oppenheim (1993: 4) explains relative poverty as: 'Going short materially, socially and emotionally. It means spending less on food, on heating and on clothing ... Poverty means staying at home, often being bored, not seeing friends.'

The most commonly used indicator for poverty is the Households Below Average Income (HBAI) statistics that are gathered through the Poverty and Social Exclusion Survey of Great Britain (PSE). This indicator regards households that have an income of below 60 per cent of the national median as living in relative poverty. Using this benchmark, in 2002/03 HBAI statistics showed that 12.4 million people in the UK were living in poverty, of which 3.6 million were children. This compares with 1.9 million or 14 per cent of children in 1979. In the same survey, 35 per cent of the population in inner London were regarded as living in relative poverty (Flaherty et al. 2004).

Education authorities and educational researchers frequently use the number of children who are eligible for free school meals (FSM) as an indicator of poverty and social disadvantage. Children are entitled to free school meals when their families receive income support or family credit. In general terms, half of all people in social housing are on low incomes compared to only one in six in other forms of housing (www.poverty.org.uk) and in areas where there are higher numbers of minority ethnic and EAL children there are higher levels of FSM entitlement. For example, Hackney has 35 per cent and Tower Hamlets 43 per cent FSM entitlement compared to the national average of 14 per cent. Other areas may be culturally less heterogeneous but still have high numbers of families that qualify for free school meals. For instance, 14 per cent of children in Manchester are speakers of languages other than English compared with a national figure of 11 per cent, but 36 per cent of its children are entitled to FSM. The same can be said about many other sizeable towns and cities across the UK. In Scottish schools, the average entitlement to FSM across the country is approximately 23 per cent, but this peaks in urban settings such as Glasgow and Edinburgh and falls off in rural settings (Scottish School Census 2002). At Maynard Primary School (one of our examples of urban primary schools), 40 per cent of the children are entitled to free school meals.

According to Poverty and Social Exclusion (PSE) figures, one-fifth of rural households experience poverty compared to one-third in inner London (Flaherty et al. 2004). In Worcestershire, the eligibility for FSM is 7 per cent, Warwickshire 8 per cent, Shropshire 9 per cent, Devon 9 per cent and Cumbria 11 per cent. Generally, the more industrialized or built up an area, the greater the degree of social deprivation; the more rural, the less likelihood of social deprivation as indicated by both the data on FSM and the PSE survey, although rural poverty and social deprivation do exist and are at high levels in some places (Howard et al. 2001). The key question is to what extent do poverty and social deprivation affect the educational attainment of children and in what ways do they affect the day to day working of schools that serve these areas (Power et al. 2002)?

Low-income families, or those that are classified as living in poverty, often experience a range of interconnected and complex problems that, by their very nature, affect academic performance (Coles and Kenwright 2002). Families with little surplus money may have diets that rely on processed low-cost foods that increase tiredness and illness. According to the New Policy Institute and the Joseph Rowntree Foundation (Hills 1996) more than one-third of adults with manual backgrounds aged between 45 and 64 have a longstanding illness compared to half that number from non-manual backgrounds. In addition, low income has sometimes been associated with low self-esteem and reduced motivation (Whitty et al. 1998). A further factor is that parents on low incomes may, for different reasons, be less able to help their children with homework (Matheson and Babb 2002). There seems little doubt that adverse social conditions get in the way of education (Whitty 2002). For example, turning to the social context of one of the examples of urban primary schools in this chapter, Ranleigh serves a community that is largely unemployed, with high numbers of its children eligible for free school meals. Thirty-five per cent of the children at Ranleigh are identified as having special educational needs, albeit at different levels of need. The local housing is described as 'substandard'. These factors will undoubtedly influence attainment in school. In an earlier small-scale study of urban schooling (Pratt and Maguire 1995: 24) a headteacher put it like this:

> A child comes to school having slept ten to a damp room with no breakfast, telling me the electricity has been cut off and petrol poured through the letter box. How would you feel? Could you concentrate on learning?

The DfES regularly publishes comparative performance data of children at Key Stages 1 and 2 in English schools (HMSO and www.dfes.gov.uk). Their figures reveal that there is a correlation between the academic performance of children and the social characteristics of a school as defined by eligibility for free school meals. As the percentage of children eligible for free school meals increases, the percentage of children attaining Level 2 and above at Key Stage 1 and Level 4 and above in Key Stage 2 decreases. For example, based on the figures for 2004 (DfES 2004), in English at Key Stage 2, in schools where there were fewer than 10 per cent of children classified as receiving FSM, 82 per cent attained Level 4 and above. In schools with over 40 per cent receiving FSM, the figure fell to 57 per cent. This pattern was also reflected in mathematics attainment: 78 per cent achieved Level 4 and above when fewer than 10 per cent of children received free school meals, while only 57 per cent attained Level 4 and above when free school meal eligibility rose to over 40 per cent of the school population (DfES 2004). The concern of many headteachers and teachers is that this sort of information is not published alongside the schools performance data. Teachers and headteachers alike in urban schools sometimes feel there is not a 'level playing field' when it comes to the subject of testing their children at 7 and 11.

It is useful to return to our three 'typical' urban primary schools and consider the additional challenges for schools where higher than average numbers of children are designated as having a special educational need at some level: Ranleigh at 35 per cent; Mortimore at 25 per cent and Maynard at 27 per cent. When these figures are set alongside the percentages of children in receipt of FSM (75 per cent at Ranleigh, 45 per cent at Mortimore and 40 per cent at Maynard), then clearly these schools are not on a 'level playing field' with schools that have a socially advantaged intake.

It is not that this sort of information is ignored by the DfES; in fact the DfES is all too ready to help schools calculate their performance according to percentages of FSM by publishing national value added and national benchmarking information. The intention behind this is to allow schools to compare their performance with other schools with similar intakes. Charles Clarke, when Secretary of State for Education and Skills, delivered a speech in April 2003 in which he said: 'There is a massive variation of school performance in helping children achieve their Key Stage 2 target. It's not a variation between schools in the leafy suburbs and schools in the inner cities. It's a variation at every level of relative poverty' (EducationGuardian.co.uk).

In simple terms, therefore, where there are greater levels of poverty, one might expect to find reduced academic performance. Charles Clarke continued his speech by arguing that while there is a statistical correlation between achievement and poverty, schools within each percentage band of

FSM should all achieve similarly. If some schools are underperforming relative to schools with similar intakes, they need to improve. David Miliband (cited in Brown 2003: 15) when he served as a Minister for Education, agreed that 'the evidence is clear … that schools serving similar types of pupils achieve dramatically different results' and that this needs to be addressed by schools (see also Barber 1996 and Maden 2001). Of course, this begs questions about what is meant by 'similar types' of children as well as 'dramatic' differences in results.

This line of reasoning is intended to urge schools to work to achieve in line with schools with similar intakes, but there are also those who seem to be suggesting that many urban schools, given the right support and leadership, can in fact 'compensate' for social deprivation and attain results far in excess of national averages (Stoll and Fink 1995; Jesson 2004). Jesson analysed the data made available by the DfES from 1998 to 2003 and suggested that the gap in attainment had narrowed: 'The fact that it has occurred through significant additional improvement in schools with the highest levels of disadvantage suggests a need to revise our views about the role of free school meals in influencing performance' (Jesson 2004: 14). To this we would want to add that many urban primary schools, like Maynard for instance, have improved their academic performance, frequently because of 'the dedicated service of many inner-city teachers and headteachers' (Grace 2005: 6). Equally, the schools of the more privileged have also made substantial gains (Whitty 2002). Even if the 'gap' has narrowed, it does not seem likely that differential levels of attainment can be closed that easily. As Thrupp's (1999) work has demonstrated, differing academic attainment is largely related to the social class intake of a school more than to what happens in the classroom.

In a discussion on whether schools are able to counter and overcome social disadvantage, Mortimore and Whitty comment that they 'do not consider that there is any single factor which could reverse longstanding patterns of disadvantage but neither do we regard them as an unchangeable fact of life' (1997: 12). They argue that by far the most significant and influential policy shift required to tackle poor attainment in socially deprived areas are those that address the causes of poverty and seek to deal with the broader issues of social inequality. If this takes place alongside 'dynamic school improvement strategies' (Mortimore and Whitty 1997: 4) then improvements in attainment can be made, as with our example of Maynard Primary School.

However, it is quite wrong to suggest that, because some schools in socially deprived areas can improve, all urban schools can realize similar improvements. Schools are subject to differing influences and conditions, many of which are outside their control, such as high mobility in intake, as with our example of Mortimore Primary School. In addition, and in relation to our example of Ranleigh Primary School, schools can do little to improve housing, enhance employment opportunities or reduce poverty (Bernstein 1971). One teacher reflected on her powerlessness in the face of a number of social constraints:

> I remember finding out things like kids living, eight kids, mum, dad and all eight kids in a one bedroom flat and he's an invalid, water running

> down the walls and you can't get the health visitors to do anything about it. You can't get the housing to do anything about it. And the family where the kids were never all in school because there weren't enough shoes. We actually had that, can you believe, in this day and age! (urban primary school teacher cited in Maguire 2001: 324)

Minority ethnic children and children for whom English is an additional language

Another 'characteristic' of urban schools that is always highlighted in government policy documents is the higher numbers of children attending many urban schools who are categorized as of 'minority ethnic' descent. There are many dilemmas involved in this categorization. However, here we want to focus on some of the distinctive learning needs that occur in multilingual urban classrooms. This in turn will mean that the work of some urban primary school teachers is similarly distinctive.

Each year the DfES asks schools in England to complete the Annual School Census (ASC). This instrument collects data from each individual school about children, teachers and the school more generally. This process is also undertaken in Wales, Scotland and Northern Ireland by the various national education departments. In England the data are organized, analysed and revised by the Government Statistical Services before eventually being published by the DfES (www.dfes.gov.uk). Among the data contained within the ASC, or Form 7 as it is known in English schools, are the numbers of minority ethnic children and the numbers of children for whom English is an additional language (EAL).

The minority ethnic groupings used in the English data collection are the same as those adopted by the 1991 National Census and they are problematic. Bonnet and Carrington (2000: 488) suggest that the 'very process of compelling people to assign themselves to one of a small number of racial or ethnic boxes is, at best essentialist and, at worst, racist'. The condensing of ethnicities into discrete boxes fails to take account of the complexities of identity. This approach overlooks and marginalizes those whose ethnic identities are 'hyphenated' (Bonnet and Carrington 2000: 491) or hybrid, for example Black-British-African. It also fails to take account of the variety of ways in which people see themselves. The data currently collected and used do not distinguish between 'White European' and 'White Other', while the category 'Any other minority ethnic group' is made up of many other separate communities that are not reported. There is no recognition made either for communities who may be second-, third- or even fourth-generation British. However, Form 7 does give us an overview of ethnic grouping in England (see Table 2.1).

About three-quarters of a million children are recognized in these English statistics as belonging to a minority ethnic group, which equates with some 11 per cent, or one in nine, of the children of compulsory school age. However, the distribution across England, and in other parts of the UK too, is extremely varied. For example, in Scotland where 96.5 per cent of children in

Table 2.1 Percentage of children by broad ethnic group in English primary schools

	%
White	88.2
Pakistani	2.5
Indian	2.3
Any other minority ethnic group	2.1
Black Caribbean heritage	1.6
Black African heritage	1.2
Bangladeshi	1.0
Black other	0.9
Chinese	0.3

Source: DfEE Statistical First Release 15/1999a

primary schools are designated as 'white', the majority of children designated as 'minority ethnic' predominantly live in specific locales within Glasgow or Edinburgh (Scottish School Census 2002). Although there are sizeable minority ethnic communities in many urban areas this alone does not tell the whole story either. Within metropolitan areas there are different localized patterns of settlement. For example, there are some schools in the London Borough of Tower Hamlets that recruit almost 100 per cent of their children from one minority ethnic group while the actual number of children designated as 'minority ethnic' across the borough as a whole is approximately 33 per cent (DfEE 1999a).

The data produced by the Government Statistical Service in England (DfEE 1999a) identify local authorities where there are particular minority ethnic groups and illustrates, in general terms, how one borough differs from another. What these statistics on minority ethnicity cannot portray are the complexities involved in teaching and learning in multilingual urban primary schools. In the north London borough of Brent, for example, one in 10 children is classified as being 'Any other minority ethnic group' but this information fails to indicate how many of these children arrive at school speaking little or no English or as having English as an additional language (EAL). It also does little to highlight the challenges involved in reflecting and respecting perhaps as many as 10 or more different language communities in one primary classroom.

When we examine the figures for children who are classified as having EAL, the contrast between many urban and non-urban areas is unambiguous. In rural authorities like Lincolnshire or North Yorkshire less than 1 per cent of children of school age have EAL. In other words, out of a total of 45,000 and 40,000 children respectively in these LEAs, this amounts to fewer than 400 children in each county. These figures are reflected across the country in rural areas, while in more built-up areas the percentages begin to increase. Table 2.2 shows the percentage of children classified as having EAL in some major towns and cities across England.

The towns and cities in Table 2.2 have been chosen to illustrate the relatively low numbers of children who have EAL in some major towns and cities

Table 2.2 Percentage of children for whom English is an additional language (EAL) in England in selected towns and cities

	% EAL
Stoke-on-Trent	6.1
Portsmouth	3.5
Bournemouth	2.5
Darlington	1.4
Doncaster	1.4
Bath and NE Somerset	0.9
Plymouth	0.8
Blackpool	0.7
Barnsley	0.3

Source: DfEE Statistical First Release 15/1999a

across England. There are nonetheless some locales where there are much higher percentages, for example Luton (26.2 per cent), Slough (35 per cent) and Bradford (26.9 per cent). However, it is only when we look at the figures for London and other major metropolitan areas that the numbers increase dramatically. In inner London there are 13 different local education authorities and between them there are 175,000 children in the primary school system. Of those, 43 per cent have EAL. In Westminster, the numbers increase to 57 per cent and in Tower Hamlets it is around 59 per cent (DfEE 1999a). Here it is worth highlighting a finding in the 1990s, when it was revealed that despite high levels of economic deprivation, secondary school students in Tower Hamlets who were of Bangladeshi descent achieved higher results than their white working-class peers (Gillborn and Gipps 1996).

To summarize, more than 45 per cent of all primary schools in England have no children who are classified as having EAL while in 8 per cent of schools there are fewer than 5 per cent of children with EAL. At the other end of the spectrum, in 4 per cent of England's schools a majority of children have EAL (DfEE 1999a). *All these schools are in major cities.* Some of these schools may contain only one minority language group, as with Ranleigh Primary School, while other schools will serve a linguistically diverse school population, as in our example of Mortimore Primary School. Respecting and reflecting this linguistic diversity will have costs in terms of pedagogy and resources and it may be schools with the slimmest resources that have to respond to the greatest demands.

Our point in including these data on children in English primary schools who have EAL is to highlight some of the distinctive factors involved in urban primary schools. When some children begin school they may not be proficient speakers of English and may require additional support. Some children may be less familiar with speaking English because they have been brought up in households where English is not frequently used. Other children may have only recently arrived in the country and English might not be their first language either. Their starting point may be different from children who have been listening and speaking English for several years. When it comes to statutory Key Stage assessments, however, the SATs will compare children who have sometimes had different levels of exposure to English.

There is a statistical correlation between the sets of figures for educational achievement indicated by performance data and percentages of children who are classified as having EAL (DfEE 1999a). Children who arrive at school with English as an additional language generally are seen to 'underachieve' compared with children for whom English is the first language. However, Benn and Chitty's (1996) survey of schools reports that schools with a larger number of children who have EAL also have a higher working-class intake and have higher proportions of children who qualify for FSM (Power et al. 2002: 19). Benn and Chitty (1996) believe that the critical factor is related to socio-economics and not to the factor of EAL.

In terms of policy and practice, there is a need for systems and structures that can be put in place to support primary schools where there are high numbers of children who have English as an additional language. The concern for schools is to identify what positive steps can be introduced to support the needs of their children. Indeed, many urban schools serving children with EAL already have a wide range of programmes and support mechanisms in place (Riddell 2003). These include the development and implementation of general assessment measures and provision for diagnostic forms of linguistic assessment and analysis, the collation of specific teaching resources and materials, followed by specific, targeted intervention (Stoll and Myers 1998).

Mortimore Primary School is a good illustration of the sorts of provision commonly made by urban primary schools. Even when children have achieved oral fluency, additional support is often required to assist in the development of fluency in reading and writing. Schools receive additional funding by way of the ethnic minority achievement grant (EMAG) to support minority ethnic groups and EAL children who may be 'at risk' of underachieving. The grant is designed to 'meet the costs of some of the additional support to meet the specific needs' of children. However, many schools and teachers themselves must meet the remainder of the 'costs' through their own hard work.

School exclusions and attendance

The picture we have wanted to create so far about urban schools is that they are typified by higher levels of socio-economic deprivation and in some locations this correlates with higher percentages of minority ethnic and children with EAL – although the key characteristic relates to the socio-economic profile (Power et al. 2002). Not surprisingly, many urban schools are 'underperforming' relative to schools in wealthier areas (Mortimore and Whitty 1997). But there are other features that are characteristic of urban schools. One is the variation between rates of attendance. In general, primary schools with the highest authorized and unauthorized absence rates have the largest percentage of children known to be eligible for free school meals. Conversely, schools with the lowest rates of unauthorized attendance have the fewest children receiving free school meals (DfES 2001).

There are several explanations that can begin to explain this phenomenon. First, where parents are unemployed or unable to work, it may be easier to keep children at home when they are unwell rather than sending them off to school (Riddell 2003). Second, children from more socio-economically disadvantaged areas often have diets that are less healthy than children from more advantaged families, mainly as a result of having lower incomes. This diet may fuel a greater incidence of illness (Flaherty et al. 2004). Overcrowded accommodation and poor housing provision that may lack adequate heating may also contribute to higher levels of unauthorized attendance. Lower rates of attendance are linked to lower levels of academic performance (Benn and Chitty 1996). As Power et al. (2002: 23) argue: 'Schools serving deprived areas are also likely to have lower rates of participation. Intermittent or interrupted attendance will lower motivation and will reduce access to the curriculum with inevitable consequences.' Consequently, urban schools may struggle to increase the attendance rates to meet targets that have been set for them by their local authorities in an attempt to contribute to improving academic performance. The additional work required by staff in urban schools to meet these twin aims is often overlooked. For example, one of our 'typical' urban schools, Mortimore, has sought and successfully gained financial support to fund a post in order to tackle this issue. A great deal of work in schools goes into bidding for short-term funding like this example that can make a difference to children's attendance in urban primary schools.

A related attendance factor that some urban schools may experience is the need for some of their families to take periods of extended leave to visit relatives overseas. As a consequence of having to miss prolonged periods of schooling, children's learning might be affected and schools may be obliged to introduce catch-up programmes to compensate for absence. Obviously, absence from schooling during the early years, when the foundations of literacy and numeracy are being established, can have long-term consequences for children's future attainment. The DfES is trying to tackle this issue by tightening the attendance legislation and offering guidance to schools on ways to discourage parents from taking their children out of school. However, where there is a serious need on the part of the families to visit their relatives overseas, for example due to bereavement or illness, there is a need to travel.

Higher rates of exclusions are typically reported in urban schools. Recent comparative data (DfES 2003) show clearly that children designated as 'Black-Caribbean' are three times more likely to be excluded than white children, while the group classified as 'Black Other' are just a little under three times more likely to be excluded than those categorized as 'White'. Children with statements of special educational needs are up to six times more likely to be excluded (Power et al. 2002). Primary schools are currently tackling high exclusion rates through the introduction of learning mentors, the involvement of outside agencies, by changing school behaviour policies, sharing policies with parents and having a member of staff whose task it is to work with designated children with specific behavioural issues (Riddell 2003). All this is not to say that urban schools have disproportionately challenging levels of behaviour compared with non-urban schools. Rather, there exists a more complex combination of factors that impact on exclusions, which schools are required to tackle. Overwhelmingly, excluded children come from families who are under stress, who are less likely to have employment and who are experiencing multiple disadvantage (Maguire et al. 2003: 58):

> Some of our children experience great distress in their daily lives, a lot of chaos. Their families are under pressure, maybe there are drugs or alcohol related issues, sometimes there is a lot of violence in their lives. It's no wonder they have anger-management problems is it? (special needs coordinator in an urban primary school)

While permanent exclusion from primary school is still relatively rare, exclusion (temporary as well as permanent) at this stage is especially worrying. Education interrupted at this stage can be difficult to compensate for in later schooling (Hayden 1996). Children excluded from primary school:

> [A]re an especially vulnerable minority. They usually have some level of special educational need as well as disrupted and stressful family backgrounds. Their behaviour illustrates distress more often than 'naughtiness'. (Hayden 1996: 235)

The requirement to respond to these pressures in school are demanding of headteacher and teacher time and consequently may 'pull' resources away from other areas of the curriculum. Ofsted (1993), in its report 'Education for disaffected children', suggests that increased levels of stress in families have resulted in a rise in disruptive behaviour in young children. More of these children will attend urban primary schools rather than schools in more socially privileged areas. Helping these children to understand and change aspects of their behaviour will be costly in terms of time, resources and expertise (Maguire et al. 2003). It will mean that sometimes the urban primary school will have to prioritize emotional support and behaviour management issues, for without this basis, academic progression will be less likely to occur.

Refugees and asylum seekers

Another 'characteristic' of the urban primary school is that these schools will be more likely to receive children who are deemed to be refugees and asylum seekers. Asylum seekers and refugees arrive in Britain at the major ports and airports and are required to apply for refugee status immediately. Short-term accommodation is often provided in major urban centres close to the initial entry point although recent policies of dispersal also mean that these families have sometimes been placed in a wider range of urban locations where there is available housing. For example, families have been dispersed to Glasgow and other Scottish cities and overspill estates. Those who attain refugee status or are awarded exceptional leave to remain in Britain while a claim for refugee status is processed have an entitlement to receive an education up to the age of 16 (Rutter 2004). In fact, not only do all children of compulsory school age have this entitlement, they are required to attend school and have the right to use local authority pre-school facilities. Schools, for their part, are required to admit refugee children in accordance with their published admission arrangements, while it is the responsibility of the education authority in which the child is resident to provide a school place (Hamilton and Moore 2004). However, if the school has an entry policy that demands that children practise a particular religion, then children who are not members of either that religion or denomination will not be able to attend that school. This might mean that in some LEAs, a small number of primary schools will support a disproportionate number of refugee children. (They might also be the same schools that accept children with challenging behaviour who might have been excluded from other schools in the borough.)

Some refugee children, from countries that are wartorn or have oppressive regimes, can arrive with a variety of sometimes complex issues and concerns that schools are required to address (Rutter 2003). Some children may well have experienced trauma or persecution and bring with them the emotional scars, which can sometimes result in challenging behaviour. Furthermore, some children may have an illness or disability caused by conflict or warfare in their home country.

Children who arrive as refugees may also have been schooled in conditions that are quite different from the UK education system. It may take longer for some refugee children to settle and adjust to their new learning environment. For example, the informal approach in early years UK settings might be less familiar to parents and children who have recently arrived. In addition, some children may well have little or no English and, although they are entitled to support from a specialist EAL teacher, this might not always be forthcoming. In all cases, the class teacher will have the main responsibility for the children's educational progress. Other children may be exceptional in certain subjects, for example in mathematics, yet this may not always be recognized as they do not have the English language skills to fully engage with the subject.

Urban primary schools can sometimes be faced with a range of complex problems related to settling children into schools, dealing with emotional problems or introducing children to a new curriculum (Rutter 1994). To overcome this, schools need to dedicate a considerable quantity of teacher time, a high degree of commitment from teachers and schools as well as focused resources to support their teaching. Currently, the legal process for refugee and asylum-seeking families is a complex and contested process that can cause a great deal of anxiety for the families and children concerned. These pressures may well influence progression in school. However, urban primary schools, like Mortimore for example, are also trying to meet other equally complex needs; special educational learning needs; socio-emotional needs; while at the same time respecting and reflecting a wide range of linguistic and cultural diversity.

Teacher recruitment, retention and the use of supply teachers

As we saw in our examples of schools at the beginning of the chapter, there can sometimes be difficulties in respect of the recruitment and retention of teachers in urban settings. Ranleigh Primary School had to replace two-thirds of its teaching staff and has had difficulties recruiting experienced teachers. While the DfES (2002) has been keen to celebrate an overall increase in the number of full-time teachers and the decrease in use of short-term supply staff across England, in some areas of the country the picture is somewhat more complex. For example, in 2002 in London schools, the average percentage of schools with teacher vacancies was nearer 3 per cent but urban boroughs like Tower Hamlets and Hackney had 5 per cent of teaching posts unfilled (DfES 2002).

Unions draw attention to high levels of stress, increasing workloads and rising debts that are driving newly qualified and experienced teachers to abandon the profession (National Union of Teachers 2002). The National Foundation for Education Research (Spear et al. 2000) identifies salary levels and the salary differential between newly qualified and experienced teachers but also the negative perceptions of the status, security and career structure as having an effect on recruitment. While some problems in retention have been experienced across the country as a whole, these problems have always been more acute in urban settings. The difficulties of teacher recruitment and retention, however, can sometimes be compounded by the use of temporary teachers.

An Ofsted report, 'Schools' use of temporary teachers' (2002), sought to identify where supply teachers were most often used and the problems that were associated with the overuse of temporary teachers. Put simply, if there are more shortages in urban settings, then urban schools will be employing more supply teachers. In schools like Ranleigh Primary School, which regularly experiences high levels of teacher turnover, supply teachers keep the school going. But this provision can have consequences for classroom practice. For instance, the Ofsted report (2002) claimed that temporary teachers taught twice as many unsatisfactory lessons as permanent teachers. Not surprisingly, it found that supply teachers were often unfamiliar with the children they were teaching and did not always appreciate the individual needs of the children. It pointed out that supply teachers were sometimes expected to teach age ranges and subjects with which they were less familiar. Ofsted (2002) also suggested that while supply teachers were required to support the implementation of the numeracy and literacy strategies, some had little or no understanding of the format or organization of either the structure or content of the lessons. It is worth pointing out that in the Foundation Stage and in Key Stage 1, where the starting blocks for numeracy and literacy are being established, the lack of a primary specialist may well inhibit children's progression.

Ofsted (2002) suggested that supply teachers were sometimes poorly briefed about what to teach or what to expect from children. Even when supply teachers were in school for longer periods, the arrangements for monitoring their progress in general terms were sometimes inadequate. Induction arrangements for teachers taking up temporary terminal contracts were regarded as insufficient, while on many occasions, there were no formal procedures whatsoever to support the induction of temporary staff. With respect to children's attitudes to work and levels of behaviour, not surprisingly, supply teachers were found to have greater difficulties than permanent teachers in managing behaviour and improving attitudes.

While many of the findings from the Ofsted report might come as little surprise to teachers who are left to support temporary staff, it highlights the complexities that can face schools and urban primary schools in particular. Where there are higher levels of teacher shortages and an overreliance on supply and short-term teachers, the performance of children may deteriorate and the level of unacceptable behaviour can increase. This can lead to greater levels of stress being placed on the permanent staff, thus precipitating further resignations and a permanent cycle of higher than average levels of staff turnover. However, while supply teachers can create difficulties within schools, they provide an important function. Many urban schools are 'held together' by supply teachers or teachers on short-term contracts because of the shortage of permanent staff, as with Ranleigh Primary School, one of our examples in this chapter.

Conclusion

This chapter has highlighted some of the characteristics of urban primary schools and has identified some of the major challenges they face. In essence, an urban primary school is likely to have one or several of the characteristics we have indicated: high numbers of children from working-class families, many of whom will qualify for free school meals or whose parents are on low income. Urban schools in some parts of the country will need to support children who have EAL. An urban school is likely to have lower levels of attendance and higher rates of exclusions than a non-urban school. Urban primary schools may have to deal with higher proportions of children experiencing emotional and behavioural distress. In addition, urban schools may well have a higher than average turnover of teaching staff. Not every urban school will demonstrate all these qualities, but all will recognize aspects that directly relate to these factors. Each of these features requires consideration by schools that can often lead to an increase in workload for staff in a way that would not be experienced in schools with more socially advantaged intakes. However, urban schools will be less able to rely on additional income from fundraising and will have to rely on their basic financial allocations, topped up by some short-term funding from charities or from urban-focused policies, if they are able to successfully bid for or qualify for additional support.

While the features of urban schools offer distinctive challenges, they do not inevitably cause schools to fail. Children will not inescapably underachieve or schools automatically become unsuccessful in urban settings. It is possible to go some way to meet the challenges we have highlighted. One of our examples, Maynard Primary, is recognized as a successful urban school. However, schools like Ranleigh and Mortimore face a series of complex challenges. Some of these challenges are structural such as high levels of local unemployment, poor housing and higher than average levels of relative poverty. Other challenges are school specific. Higher than average numbers of children with learning difficulties, older school buildings in need of repair and higher than average levels of staff turnover make it harder for urban schools to meet the needs of their children and parents. We believe that greater consideration needs to be paid to the unique circumstances faced in urban localities and urban primary schools. Primary schools provide the foundations and the building blocks for educational progression for young children everywhere. Policymakers and practitioners need to work together to improve urban conditions and optimize the opportunities for children who attend urban primary schools to learn and to grow.

Questions

1. How would you characterize the urban primary schools in your area? What dangers can occur as a consequence of some of these characterizations or stereotypes?
2. What factors affect the education of children in urban schools? What are schools doing in your area to overcome any negative factors?
3. What sorts of policies could be set up to provide more support to urban primary schools?

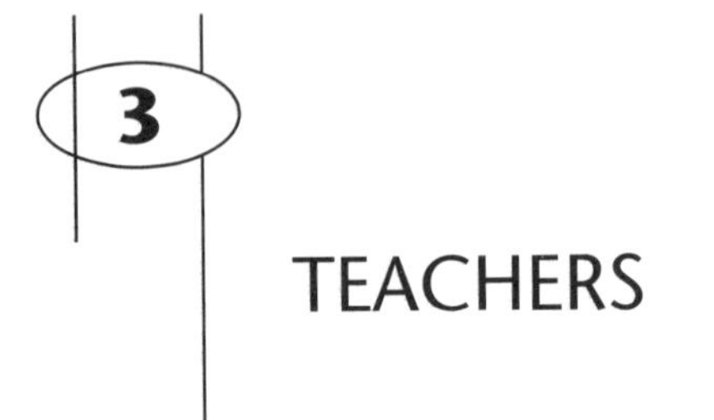

TEACHERS

In this chapter on teachers in urban primary schools, we consider the consequences of this setting for their work. The chapter begins by briefly reviewing some major influences that have shaped primary schooling. We then describe a small-scale study that we conducted with a number of English urban primary school teachers in order to explore their perceptions of what it is like to teach in an urban school. Next we examine what the teachers consider to be the rewards and the challenges of teaching in urban primary schools. We discuss reasons for the greater turnover of staff in urban schools and consider what can be done to encourage teachers to remain in post. We then provide a short account of some of the ways in which beginning teachers can be better prepared for what to expect when they take up posts in urban primary schools. We conclude the chapter by claiming that while the occupation of primary school teaching is shaped by a set of shared ideals and values, urban classrooms are distinctive in framing the work of primary teaching.

Primary schooling and the role of the primary school teacher

In the first chapter of this book, we provided an account of the origins of the primary school when we explored the setting up of the elementary school system. While the elementary schools of the past and the urban primary schools of the present day serve the same constituency, that is, working-class and disadvantaged children and their families, other dimensions of pedagogy and practice have been refined. Although the historical development of the primary school is worthy of a fuller account than is possible here (see Croll 1996; Alexander 2000) nevertheless, what we want to do is identify some of the key influences that produce what we currently know as primary schooling.

A combination of influences from the work of philosophers and educationalists such as Rousseau, Pestalozzi, Montessori and Froebel have left a lasting legacy in terms of the importance of the growth and development of the 'whole child' in primary schooling. The influence of various psychologists such as Piaget, Bruner and Vygotsky have led to a focus on childrens active meaning making in the learning process and a call for pedagogy to respond to these understandings (Pollard 1996). The outcomes of these powerful discourses have shaped a unique approach towards the education of young children in the UK, one that has been described by Nias (1989) as a 'culture of care'. Nias (1989) emphasized the importance of primary teachers' emotional involvement with the children in their classrooms. From her extensive work in primary schools, she has highlighted the ways in which primary teachers take a moral and ethical responsibility for the learning and the welfare of each child in their care. Training to become a primary school teacher still involves some exposure to these sorts of discourses, in theory and also in practice. But there will be other influences at play that shape the primary school teacher:

> Teachers' professional ideologies and their beliefs about classroom practice have complex origins, deriving from a blend of personal biography, training, professional experience, classroom constraints and national culture and professional traditions. (Osborn et al. 1996: 137)

One key tradition that has shaped primary pedagogy, particularly from the 1960s onwards, has been the perceived need for a high degree of responsiveness to children's individual needs. This tradition includes a wide range of related aims and goals including academic progress but also personal, social and emotional development. While this influential discourse might mainly have persisted as an ideal-type set of values, and may sometimes have been less evident in practice, it has provided an ethical orientation towards the work of primary school teaching. However, the 1980s saw an attempt to break with this approach. Partly in response to vocal criticism of what was sometimes seen as too much teacher autonomy, as well as a desire to insert market forces into the public sector to ratchet up standards (Tomlinson 2001), the Educational Reform Act (ERA) (1988) was enacted. This introduced the National Curriculum and national testing at the end of the newly designated Key Stages. At this time, concerns were expressed that a mandated curriculum might be at odds with well-established principles of child development. It was argued that the role of the primary practitioner might be recast as one of a technicist rather than a reflective practitioner (Osborn et al. 1996).

One major study set up to investigate the changes being ushered in by the sweeping reforms of the late 1980s and 1990s discovered that some primary schools were able to 'make a creative response' to the changes (Pollard et al. 1994). 'They felt able to benefit from the structure and guidelines of the national curriculum without letting it drive them or destroy what they knew to be good about their practice' (Osborn et al. 1996: 152). The researchers discovered that this response was easier to manage in more affluent areas. The project warned that:

> As the effects of the educational market continue to operate, and teaching in the inner city becomes a harder and less rewarding job, the eventual outcome might be a flight of teachers from inner city schools to

> 'easier' more affluent areas – as often occurs in France as a primary teacher's career develops. This could mean a considerable loss to inner city children of committed, confident and experienced teachers. (Osborn et al. 1996: 152)

The National Curriculum is now well established. Many primary school teachers have no experience of teaching in a time when there was no central curriculum or testing regime. However, even for primary teachers who may have moved away from some of the earlier child-centred and more 'individualistic' approaches in favour of more socio-cultural constructions of child development (Anning et al. 2004), tensions still persist. For example, primary school teachers who work in challenging schools may well argue that their first responsibility is to provide the foundational supports of emotional care and safety, without which learning cannot flourish. In urban primary schools, teachers will recognize that their children do not necessarily start at the same point as children from more privileged backgrounds. Yet they will be measured and assessed by the same tools. In urban settings, teachers may be concerned about the rights of children to have their differences recognized and respected. Urban primary teachers may also be caught up in a set of tensions and pressures in trying to meet demands that may seem less appropriate for some of the children they teach, in a context that does not acknowledge the distinctiveness of their setting.

All primary school teachers have to balance competing pressures, demands and expectations with their own values and principles as well as pragmatic factors. In this chapter we want to consider the tensions that arise when primary school teachers have to balance competing demands such as the performance demands of target attainments and raising standards with the demands of responding to the socio-cultural context of the urban classroom. In order to explore any tensions in the role of the contemporary urban primary teacher, we decided to collect their views and perceptions about their work.

How the research was carried out

We conducted questionnaire-based research among teachers in ten urban primary schools in six metropolitan education authorities across England, 60 schools in all. In order to ensure that our sample was drawn from urban schools, we asked local advisors, tutors in local higher education institutions and headteachers to identify some schools for us to approach. In this way, we were able to construct a representative sample of urban schools. Some schools were in large cosmopolitan cities, others served all white housing estates, some were towards the bottom of their LEA league table while others were 'successful despite the odds' (Maden 2001).

We initially contacted the headteacher in each of the schools to explain the aims of our research and to attempt to negotiate access. We wanted to gain the schools' consent to participate before we sent out our questionnaires. We hoped that this would increase the return rate. We made it clear that we understood teachers were extremely busy and we did not wish to add to their busy workload. Once we had obtained the consent of the headteachers, we arranged to post a set of questionnaires to each school for the teachers and we included a separate questionnaire for the headteacher (see Chapter 4). All the heads had undertaken to discuss the topic with their staff and return any completed questionnaires to us. Twenty-two schools returned a total of 58 questionnaires. Therefore, this is a small and partial study. It is not possible to make any major generalizations from this dataset. The findings are indicative rather than anything else. Oakley (1997) has argued that small samples are of limited value, although Sikes (2000) believes they can be useful in highlighting and valuing subjective and grounded experience. Thus, what we are aiming for in this chapter is to start to explore some understandings of what it is like to teach in urban primary schools rather than make claims about all urban schools.

Before we attempt this, it is necessary to provide an account of the questionnaires themselves. Initially, we conducted five in-depth unstructured interviews with teachers in two urban primary schools in London in order to elicit their perceptions of what it is like to teach in these schools (Cohen et al. 2000). We draw on these interviews in this chapter. We then constructed a simple questionnaire (Munn and Drever 1995) designed to collect biographical details as well as information about professional experiences. We were interested in the teachers' reasons for being in an urban environment as well as their perceptions of their experiences. We piloted the questionnaire to ensure that the questions were clear (Wellington 2000) and we concentrated on ensuring that the questionnaire could be completed in a short time. This was essential in order to maximize our returns (Munn and Drever 1995). We then sent out a batch of 10 questionnaires with stamped, addressed envelopes, to each of the 60 schools and 58 were eventually returned. Schools are frequently asked to provide evidence about their practice and document their work. We recognize that researchers trying to collect data in schools can sometimes overwhelm teachers so we are extremely grateful to those teachers whose views make up the bulk of what is contained in the rest of this chapter.

About the teachers

Forty-nine of the 58 respondents to the questionnaire were female and there was spread of ages from 21 to 60; however, almost 30 per cent of the teachers were aged 46–50. Length of service ranged from one year to 40 years, with 20 per cent of the teachers qualifying in the last five years. There was a dip in the numbers of teachers who returned questionnaires and who had remained in service between 6 and 10 years. Almost all the teachers surveyed were employed on permanent contracts in their schools, the only exception being five temporary teachers who were all teaching in London.

Why teachers teach in urban areas

From the questionnaires, and from the pre-questionnaire interview data, it was evident that teachers decide to teach in urban areas for a wide range of reasons, such as increased job opportunities, the opportunity to work with a diversity of cultures and the opportunity to rise to a challenge. The most common reason given by the teachers was that many of them returned from college to work in the areas in which they grew up. For these teachers, there was no conscious decision to choose to teach in an urban area. One informant wrote: 'I was born and raised in an urban environment and that's the environment I know the best.' Other people were more forthright: 'I've lived in London all my life and have no wish to move or work outside.'

On the whole, teachers did not actively choose where to teach – that is, they did not weigh up the advantages and disadvantages of one area over another. Teachers simply taught in locations with which they were most familiar. A recent study of teachers in the greater London area (Menter et al. 2002) produced a similar finding. As Anwar said:

> I've spent all my childhood in north London. I still have friends from my own primary school. I really don't think I'd fit anywhere else. And in any case, I know the backgrounds of these kids, it's the same as mine so they can bluff with me [laughs]. (interview)

Although the majority of teachers said they chose to stay in their home areas (and we found that those teachers who were raised in cities tended to work in urban schools), a small number of teachers positively selected to work in urban schools. The questionnaire responses indicated that there were a variety of reasons for this. Some teachers wanted to stay in an area in which they trained, a finding also reported by Menter et al. (2002). Others wanted a change. One respondent wrote: 'I was brought up in a rural area, small village, and wanted a complete change of environment. Also, I wanted to stay in Bradford, where I had trained.'

Teachers reported that they became familiar with specific schools and education authorities while on teaching practices. They had established a good social life in the locality and often entered into relationships with friends acquired at college, joined community groups and had become part of their neighbourhoods. Teachers were often offered jobs while on final teaching practices that they 'could not refuse' and, even after several years, they had not left these schools.

There were a small number of teachers who we would characterize as 'pragmatic choosers' (Ball et al. 2000). In the questionnaires, these teachers wrote that they chose to work in urban areas because they felt they would be able to find work more easily and it was where they were most likely to move up the career ladder most quickly: 'I moved to London because that's where the promotion opportunities are.' Another teacher wrote of her urban education authority: 'It was easy to get a job and that's where the jobs are available.' A teacher in the northeast suggested the lack of employment opportunities elsewhere forced her into an urban school and that it was as if 'the job chose me'. Yet another teacher suggested that she chose a London school because: 'I needed short-term work for a round-the-world trip and was offered work again on my return. There were no permanent jobs in Scotland therefore I took the position.' Some respondents in the questionnaires noted that it was beneficial to their careers to demonstrate that they could teach in the most challenging conditions before then opting to work in more settled conditions. The evidence certainly bears out the facts that there are far more career opportunities and job vacancies in London and other large metropolitan areas than in more rural authorities (Menter et al. 2002). Whether or not the experience of having taught in urban schools advantages teachers in their careers in the end is less certain.

In the questionnaire, teachers were asked to comment on what they found rewarding or enjoyable about the locality in which they taught. Many teachers referred to the level of support that was offered by the local community: 'The school works very closely with the mosque on issues around attendance and punctuality.' Other teachers mentioned how they enjoyed the sense of community that existed around their school. Teachers often referred to the importance of parents in making them feel valued as professionals (Grant 1993). It is interesting to note that, although parents are seen as a valuable resource and the source of much support, they are also cited by some respondents as one of the key causes of discontentment among teachers.

Teachers wrote that the city could be an important resource for themselves socially and as a tool to improve children's learning (Corson 1998). Teachers reported that access to a wide range of museums, art galleries, theatres, parks and zoos was an advantage of teaching in an urban locality. Some teachers also felt that the social life in large urban areas had more to offer than smaller provincial towns (Byrne 2001).

The teachers surveyed were questioned about what they disliked about the area in which they worked. A clear distinction was made here to isolate factors related to the urban geography rather than factors within the school itself. Teachers reported their greatest concern was with the run-down, polluted environment in which many urban schools were located. One teacher commented: 'The general air of neglect about the environment ... litter, broken pavings, people dump old furniture in the streets! The school premises are very well kept and the immediate area is a complete contrast.'

Another teacher recorded that she found 'dereliction, demolition, disaffection and a sense of depression in the area' while others talked of houses boarded up and communal play areas being neglected and vandalized. Some teachers commented that in their areas there were few parks and green spaces for families to enjoy. The teachers in our study felt quite strongly that 'the environment needs to be developed to enrich the residents'. A further concern related to issues around crime and the fear of crime. In particular, the teachers referred to high incidents of cars being vandalized and drug-related problems in the immediate area around their schools. There was also a sense in which some teachers felt unsafe once outside the security of the school premises.

Although some of our respondents were working in urban primary schools for pragmatic reasons, a significant number (20 per cent) of our respondents positively chose to work in an urban environment specifically for what they referred to as the 'challenge' that it offered them. One respondent commented that 'every day is a challenge' while others sought out an urban area as it offered the opportunity to do something new and different. This positive urban choosing was a feature of Riddell's (2003) study in Bristol. One teacher wrote:

> I was looking for a new challenge/stimulus and had enjoyed working in inner city Liverpool in the 1960s. I had always wanted to work in London but had never had the opportunity. At the time [when choosing where to teach after college] I wanted a greater challenge in my teaching.

In a study of urban secondary school teachers, Grace (1978) found that teachers had sometimes made a deliberate choice to work in what they regarded as tough but rewarding environments. Perhaps this choice is related to an ethics of care (Nias 1989) as well as a sense of service to the communities most in need (Grace 2005).

Many teachers said they chose to work in urban authorities because they wanted to make a difference to the lives of children. The reoccurrence of teachers' wish to 'make a difference' is not unique to teachers in urban locations. It reflects some of the ideal-type values that shape the occupation of teaching – that teaching is more than just about earning an income: teaching is rewarding because it is beneficial to society in general. Teachers feel valuable because they are able to give something back to society (Nias 1989; Riddell 2003). What is distinctive about choosing urban locations is the sense in which teachers may perceive the challenges here to be greater and the difference that can potentially be made to the lives of children as greater still, so the emotional remunerations are also higher (Johnson, J. 1999). One teacher chose an urban school because of what he hoped it would offer: 'I wanted to feel I was working in an area where I was making a difference and working as part of a community, where parents are supportive, and appreciative children are responsive and enthusiastic.'

Rewards of working in an urban school

In the questionnaire, teachers were asked to comment on what they found rewarding or enjoyable about their jobs. Teachers took pleasure from seeing children growing and developing academically and making progress. Several respondents spoke in terms of the rewards from working alongside children who, in their words, were considered to be 'deprived or needy' (Donnelly 2003). Teachers in our small survey were all too aware of the social disadvantage that existed and were eager to be seen doing something about redressing the imbalance. One teacher noted that she enjoyed teaching because she was able to 'provide experiences that children would otherwise be deprived of'. Others felt they benefited from 'seeing a number of children succeed despite having a number of problems related to their background'. The responses highlighted not only the 'feel-good factor' of witnessing academic progress; rather, progress was achieved despite a lower starting point than with children in more affluent schools and despite ongoing social disadvantage (Stoll and Myers 1998). Teachers felt that progress resulted as a direct consequence of what they had done in their classrooms; progress was made because of their work. In one of the preliminary interviews we conducted, Eva told us about her experiences with one child in a reception class in north London:

> You know, I had this kid in my class, Anya. Both her parents had learning difficulties and they both had their own social workers. They honestly lived in really appalling circumstances. But Anya was just brilliant. She basically sat down and taught herself to read 'cos there was no one at home to help. One day she came to read with me and the first time she managed a whole book, I think we both just wanted to cry with joy. (preliminary interview)

Several teachers expressed satisfaction and pleasure from working with children from a variety of social and cultural backgrounds. Working in a multicultural environment and sharing in the variety of cultural experiences that an urban environment offers was seen as extremely rewarding. This finding was also highlighted by Riddell (2003) in his Bristol-based account. One teacher wrote, 'I enjoy the ethnic and cultural mix in the borough where I teach' while another commented that she enjoyed: 'An ethnic mix which is very much a reflection of the wider society. There is a balance of religions and cultures.' Many teachers felt these social and cultural experiences were not only of value and benefit to the children but also to themselves, a finding also reflected in a US-based study of urban teachers (Adams and Adams 2003). Teachers in our small study reported that their lives were enhanced and they were continually engaged in learning opportunities. One teacher wrote that: 'Children have a variety of cross cultural knowledge to bring to lessons and I too ... gain experiences of different cultures and religions.' Carlie, a teacher in south London, whom we interviewed as a preliminary for the study, put it like this:

> In my class, we have over twelve languages to draw on. Last month, two parents came into school to help us understand Diwali better. Now, in what other school would we be able to share all these sorts of experiences?

The term 'making a difference' emerged on many occasions in the responses to the questionnaires and in the small number of interviews that we conducted. The teachers clearly felt they were making a positive contribution to the lives of the children in their care in a way they would not be doing if they were teaching in non-urban areas where the social needs of children were not so acute. Teachers believed that the role they could potentially play in the lives of children was greater in urban settings than with children who were more socially advantaged. In answering the question, 'what is rewarding about your teaching?' replies included:

> The children appreciate the things you do for them and knowing that I have made a difference in their lives and attitudes.

> The children are generally eager to learn and I love watching them make so much progress. I like making a difference.

Burn (2001) also identified a desire among urban teachers to improve opportunities for working-class children but she identified a far more radical element: that some teachers wished to transform a class system that they saw as unfair. Other research indicates that some teachers who work in 'disadvantaged' settings may well become politicized by the inequality and social injustice that they see all around them on a daily basis (Grace 1978; Maguire 2001). As David, one of the teachers we interviewed, said to us:

> Our kids have a great deal stacked against them, poor housing, bad health issues, chaotic family life in some cases. It can be wild out there. And schools can be a port in a storm. Life is already unfair to our kids. If we don't provide the best we can, they will miss out on education too.

Despite acute social disadvantages, the academic progression of the children in their care was highlighted by a significant number of respondents. Comments from teachers included 'seeing a number of children achieve despite having disadvantaged backgrounds'. Teachers recognized that they were making a difference in the lives of children and were providing stability in sometimes turbulent lives (Riddell 2003). Adams and Adams interviewed US teachers in urban schools and their findings are similar in many respects to our own study. One experienced US teacher commented that: 'Being a teacher should make you proud but being a teacher in an urban setting is far more challenging.' This teacher explained that 'it feels good when you take a student who obviously needs you and needs your skills and bring them to the point that the student can succeed' (Adams and Adams 2003: 97). Adams and Adams claimed that, in addition to the rewards that can be offered by the children and their learning, there was often a positive community spirit in urban schools. This was spoken about in terms of supportive parents who appreciated the efforts of the teachers, but also in terms of collegial staff who sustained each other under pressure. In our own English dataset, one teacher commented that 'staff are a close team and we provide a lot of support to each other' and went on to say that: 'Parents were supportive and helped the school whenever they could.' Carlie told us that in her urban primary school:

> Some of the kids are extremely challenging. But then you have to remember what's going on in their lives outside school. It is tough on [the local estate] and they see a lot of harsh things that maybe children shouldn't see. So in school, sometimes it's tough too. But, there's a tremendous feeling that we are all together in something special, parents, kids and teachers.

Challenge of urban schools

The teachers we surveyed reported that they faced a wide range of challenges on a day-to-day basis that were more acute and intense in an urban primary school and which added to their general workload. These challenges can be broadly categorized into three main areas. First, the range of governmental and local authority pressures (Ball 2003b), second conflicts about the role and influence of parents (Vincent 2000) and, finally, those challenges that related to the needs of the children and their learning experiences (McMahon 2003). A recurring theme among the teachers was the pressure to meet standardized governmental and local authority targets relating to the children's performance and attainment, despite what one teacher described as, the 'unlevel playing field' that exists between schools. One teacher put it like this:

> All staff work very hard in keeping results in line with national averages. The school caters for a very different catchment area than that of the middle class areas, yet are marked on the same scale.

Teachers felt it was sometimes almost impossible to keep up with national expectations and saw themselves having to 'go further with less'. Burn (2001: 86) reported much the same feelings of anger and frustration in the way that children, teachers and therefore communities were 'named and shamed' due to so-called 'poor' results of children at 7 and 11 (see also Tomlinson 2001).

Many of the teachers in our study referred to the role of parents. In the discourses that shape ideal versions of primary schooling, parent–school partnerships are always seen as vital to 'good' primary practice (Hallgarten 2000). Yet, what these urban primary teachers had to say reflected some ambivalence about parent–teacher relationships. Teachers recognized the key roles that parents play in their children's education and yet, sometimes, they reported feeling a lack of support from some homes. This was sometimes articulated as parents being unsure how to support their children or lacking the skills to do so. One teacher wrote that: 'Parents don't support children's reading at home. They are often willing but not equipped to assist.' Other teachers mentioned the need to show parents how to support their children with reading or homework, a point picked up by the New Labour government (Gewirtz 2001). One suggested that 'We need to educate parents as well as children' and that children 'begin nursery with low abilities compared to children from other areas' because their parents have not been able to give their children the same opportunities and experiences as more middle-class parents.

Along the same lines, some of the teachers identified reduced parental expectations as having a detrimental effect on children's education, thereby creating greater challenges for the school. Some parents, according to one teacher, had 'low or limited expectations which leads to poor motivation for children'. There were other teachers who went much further and alleged that the greatest challenges did not necessarily come from parents who were 'willing but not always able', but from parents who they regarded as being deliberately obstructive or who contradicted the school's approach to, among other things, behaviour management and discipline. Working with parents and families who may be experiencing acute distress and adversity can be extremely challenging and calls for great sensitivity and awareness (Roffey 2002). 'Being positive and non-judgemental with some families might be seen as a tall order' but 'parents who are struggling with their role also need support not condemnation' (Roffey 2002: 64). This might be harder to achieve in an urban setting, perhaps with less experienced teachers who themselves may be struggling with a number of competing demands for their attention. One consequence might be that some teachers start to 'blame' parents, in order to reduce their own feelings of inadequacy and stress. As one teacher wrote:

> There is poor parenting of young children; discipline and coercion is often inconsistent, often the child leads the behaviour of the parents, the child is upset and the parent backs down. So, higher up the school, this leads to serious behaviour issues, e.g. not conforming in class, fighting, swearing etc.

Pratt and Maguire (1995), in an earlier study into teacher perceptions of urban schooling, found that parents were regarded by teachers as vital in their children's education. Teachers were eager for parents to be fully involved but claimed that without high-quality support agencies, the effectiveness of parental involvement could be reduced (Pratt and Maguire 1995). As David said in interview:

> We know we do better when we stand alongside our parents but it takes a lot of time, time that we just don't always have really. And then, some parents, okay a minority, can just be so aggressive.

There is a tension between the extra time that needs to be devoted to issues of parental involvement and what teachers sometimes refer to as the 'social work' side of the job. Campbell and Neill (1994) found that teachers spend around 35 per cent of their time teaching and up to 56 per cent involved with administration and planning. The remainder, around 9 per cent, was spent on professional development or 'other activities' (Campbell and Neill 1994: 71). The respondents in our study made it clear that for teachers in urban schools, the 'other activities' such as working and supporting parents, encouraging greater parental involvement and maintaining the interest, enthusiasm and behaviour of the children presents a huge and challenging task: 'It has to be done, it really makes a difference when children see their parents in school, looking at their work. But it means being extremely flexible about timing, and being open and approachable.'

This point ties in with the third factor that teachers identified as affecting their work: that of the children's needs and attitudes. Challenging behaviour was identified by one-third of all teachers as the single biggest problem they faced and often the cause of this was put squarely at the feet of parents. It was felt that poor parenting skills led to poor behaviour and the failure of parents to deal with issues as they arose further compounded the situation. The language teachers used to describe this dilemma suggests the level of concern. One teacher mentioned children who were 'a danger to themselves, staff and other children' while another referred to having received 'verbal and physical abuse' from children (Troman 2000). Behaviour and discipline problems were seen as a significant cause for concern, but so were the problems posed by 'children who don't see the relevance of schooling to their lives'.

The urban primary school teachers also drew attention to the additional responsibilities they faced. Among these were teaching high numbers of children who had English as an additional language, the disproportionate numbers of children who were designated as having special educational needs, as well as children's intermittent attendance and their extended breaks from school. These aspects were seen as professional challenges that teachers accepted as part of their responsibilities. However, they believed that these responsibilities were not always fully acknowledged by local and central government.

Teacher recruitment and retention in urban schools

Our survey identified three main issues that led teachers to consider leaving the teaching profession. Problems of classroom management could lead to stress and feelings of being 'burnt out' (Ball 2003b). Teachers reported that feeling undervalued and held in low esteem led them to consider leaving teaching. The reduced financial capacity to live in urban areas was also cited as a reason for leaving.

In our small study, teachers claimed that problems of classroom management were the greatest deterrent to continued teaching in urban classrooms. Stress and burnout were, on the whole, brought on due to continuous low-level aggravation caused by disruptive children. Moreover, some teachers reported that they were spending more and more time on managing classes rather than teaching. Some teachers in our study described their jobs as 'more behaviour management than teaching', while others felt they needed 'smaller classes, less stress and pressure, more resources, nicer environment and fewer behavioural issues' if they were going to be able to continue. However, it is not only classroom teaching that affects levels of stress, but day-to-day urban living. One teacher referred to the experience of teaching in an urban environment as being 'too intensive' and described how 'the traffic problems make the day longer at both ends'. The practicalities of urban living are as one teacher described, 'fast, furious and full on' and it is this that can aggravate feelings of stress (Krupat 1985). One teacher in our survey commented that: 'The job itself is stressful and consuming more and more personal time – if this is then added to confrontational situations and unpleasant behaviour, the job becomes unacceptable.'

The second main reason given by teachers for wanting to leave urban classrooms is the feeling of being undervalued and generally held in low esteem. Some teachers claimed that there was no recognition for all the hard work that they put in. One teacher felt that: 'Teachers leave (urban schools) because they don't want to be associated with poor attainment.' They do not want to be 'blamed' in this way and choose to move away as a consequence. One teacher remarked: 'The government do very little to make teachers feel good or better when they publish results, nor do they take into account the challenging circumstances.' As a consequence of feeling undervalued, some teachers either give up or move away (Smithers and Robinson 2003). If there were more appreciation of the complex conditions in urban primary schools, then some in our survey claimed they would be more prepared to continue.

One teacher wrote that:

> There is a lack of appreciation of what we face on a daily basis . . . there is an idea of the 'normal' child and all assessments done are aimed at this. Many children in inner city areas make excellent progress but remain below national expectations. This can be soul destroying for teachers – failed again!

Some teachers thought that teaching outside urban areas was more pleasant and often easier, but this view was dismissed by other teachers. They identified the 'myth of the relaxed atmosphere' that was likely to be found in non-urban schools. However, there was a commonly held view that although teaching may well be equally but differently demanding outside urban areas, living conditions would be considerably more pleasant. It was described as a better place to bring up children, somewhere some teachers would perhaps be happier sending their own children to school and somewhere that offered a better quality of life in some respects. There was less of the 'litter, crime, and feeling unsafe'.

Teachers in our study, when discussing pay and conditions, did not all demand increased financial remuneration for working in challenging circumstances, although there were many who did feel that more money was one answer. Instead, they recommended other forms of enticement such as help with housing costs or gym membership. Some teachers wrote that they would prefer to see an 'urban allowance' paid to encourage all teachers in urban areas to remain teaching where conditions are the toughest. (The London-based teachers, who are already in receipt of an additional allowance in recognition of greater housing and transport costs, pointed out that their allowance was much less than that paid to other public sector workers in the city and was tokenist at best.) Overall, teachers felt the greatest and most meaningful support would be within the schools themselves to reduce high levels of day-to-day stress (Johnson, M. 1999). By far the most urgent request, made by one-third of the respondents, was for additional classroom support. Teachers said that they needed help with individual disruptive children as well as with children who were new to the English language and needed greater levels of support.

What needs to be addressed swiftly, and is perhaps most urgent, is the need to recognize the hard work teachers do in urban primary schools. Grace (2005) has highlighted the need to celebrate the achievements of teachers who work in areas of acute levels of disadvantage, since a belief that you are not held in high esteem can have a negative effect. Fullan and Hargreaves (1994: 71) note that: 'Teachers who are devalued, discarded and disregarded become bad teachers.' From our limited survey it was clear that teachers wanted to be encouraged and supported. They wanted an acknowledgement and acceptance that some schools and some localities face tougher challenges than others. They expressed concerns that sometimes urban teachers are blamed for 'underachievement' and challenging behaviour. They believed that a myth that teachers are somehow solely responsible for reduced attainment and difficult behaviour is perpetuated through the media. Teachers reported that they would like to see more recognition of the efforts that teachers make and the valuable job they undertake. The teachers we interviewed felt that target setting and the widespread use of performance data that did not recognize contextual differences was a divisive tool and one that was being used more and more often to criticize teachers in urban schools. One teacher wrote that teachers should: 'Stop being shamed for what the pupils can't do – [we] should be celebrating what they have achieved from an unequal starting point.'

Preparing to teach in urban schools

Some of the teachers in our survey, who trained in colleges away from large urban centres, but were now working in urban primary schools, felt they had been under-prepared for what to expect when they took up their posts. Teachers believed they needed to spend more time in the urban classroom to gain a clearer understanding of what to expect before they eventually took up their permanent posts. One teacher we surveyed wrote: 'All training establishments need to forge links with urban schools and students should spend more time in inner city schools alongside experienced teachers on a regular basis.' The teachers believed that practical classroom experience in urban schools not only provided an opportunity to experience what these schools had to offer but also presented a chance to observe good practice in these schools. In the questionnaires, teachers wrote that student teachers needed to be exposed to positive role models who could demonstrate effective teaching in urban environments and that it was positive for 'staff to enjoy their jobs and show the rewards that can be had'.

In addition to having practical hands-on experiences in urban primary schools, the teachers in our study felt that students needed to gain a theoretical understanding of the urban. There was no substitute for what one teacher in the survey referred to as 'up-to-date knowledge in order to put an emphasis on strategies to motivate, assess, communicate, counsel and most importantly, strategies to address behavioural issues'. Others highlighted specific areas where they thought they needed more knowledge and professional development; in particular, they identified a need for more support and advice on how to 'help overcome language difficulties'.

Teachers argued that student teachers needed to understand more about the social and cultural context of urban schools. They believed that it was important to appreciate the social background of the children and the effects this may have on learning. They argued that while practical experience is important, it could not exist in a vacuum, independent from more in-depth theoretical knowledge. In many ways these comments reflect what Grace (1984) has argued; that it is only when theory informs and is informed by practical understanding that teachers will be better placed to attend to the challenges that arise. 'An approach which starts with an appreciation of the range of urban theory is likely to produce a more profound formulation of the crucial issues in urban education' (Grace 1984: 110). As Beth, a deputy head in a south London primary school, said:

> The basic problem here is poverty, poverty, poverty. Families are under stress, living in rotten housing, on an estate where there are high levels of crime and violence. We do what we can in our school but we can only do so much. We can sympathize and we certainly empathize with our children. Maybe all we can do is try and push for literacy and numeracy skills. The thing is, sometimes the children are just so worn down, it is hard for them to get more than a respite break in school, never mind learn as well. (preliminary interview)

There are some examples where an urban experience has been offered to teachers in training. One programme in the United States attempted to develop an awareness of urban schools and the communities in which they operate (Black 2000). Courses were designed that included visits to, among other places, Korean businesses and Hindu temples, Islamic centres and Latin American and Asian study centres. Students were expected to engage in individual research related to specific urban communities alongside readings from various perspectives of multicultural education, for example. However, in the UK, there is less space in teacher education programmes (centrally controlled in England by the Teacher Training Agency now renamed the Training and Development Agency for schools) for this type of approach:

> We have seen a concerted effort to render teaching as amoral, non-intellectual and technical. How does the TTA recognize urban contexts? Well, through geographical shortages and recognition of the need for more teachers from ethnic minority backgrounds. (Menter 1998: 20)

Menter argues that the UK government must recognize the contextual factors affecting urban education and 'direct resources to support schools and training providers' (1998: 22). We would argue that it is not solely urban schools and colleges that must consider the training of teachers but teacher training institutions throughout the country, wherever they are located.

Conclusion

We started this chapter by arguing that all teachers have to balance competing sets of demands and pressures alongside their own values and principles that derive from their biographies, their training and their experiences. They also have to manage the pragmatic demands of their work. For example, Jeffrey (2003: 500) reports some Year Six teachers who felt they had to spend time revising with their classes for the standard assessment tasks (SATs), although they 'excused' some children from this process if they thought 'it would be distressing for them if they found themselves failing too often'. This is a good example of juggling competing tensions about appropriate activities and the emotional needs of children alongside their academic needs, as well as a pragmatic need to ensure coverage and preparation for a key moment of performance against which the school will be made accountable.

Our case in this chapter is that teachers working in urban areas face dilemmas where their orientations as primary teachers towards an 'ethics of care' (Nias 1989) and their awareness of the holistic 'needs' of children make greater demands on their professional repertoires. For example, the teachers in our small survey highlighted a number of additional professional responsibilities that they faced, such as higher numbers of children with learning difficulties and children who exhibited intermittent attendance. They also had to support children and families who were struggling with poor housing and sometimes 'chaotic' family lives in settings of higher levels of social and economic disadvantage. Urban primary school teachers have to manage the tensions created by needing to support children's learning in an appropriate manner while responding to demands for accountability. These sorts of tension can produce pressures, stress and 'burnout' and for these sorts of reasons, as well as practical reasons related to housing and income, urban schools experience a higher turnover of staff, which in turn increases the pressure on those teachers still in post in urban primary schools.

Teaching in some of the toughest schools in the country and working in culturally mixed communities can be extremely rewarding. Significantly, teachers in our study, in common with findings reported by Pratt and Maguire (1995), did not lose sight of their ambition to get the best out of the children they taught. One teacher claimed that, 'For all the moans, we do it because we know we can make a difference and have a positive impact on their lives. Children we teach can and do achieve.' Pratt and Maguire (1995: 28) found that: 'Teachers hold high expectations of the children they teach and powerfully reject any view which suggests that inner-city children cannot achieve as much as any other child.' Despite this, there was a feeling among the teachers we surveyed that there is a failure on the part of the government to recognize urban teachers and urban children for what they have achieved. Teachers in our survey claimed that they were constantly reminded of how much further they had to go to catch up the most successful schools and this impacted on teachers' self-esteem and desire to continue teaching.

The data in this chapter demonstrate that teachers in urban primary schools are eager to 'make a difference' but issues such as high turnover of staff, poor teacher morale, community tensions, fragmented and over-stretched public services are outside their control and influence. These are issues that can only be addressed by support and encouragement, genuine improvements in pay and incentives, recognition and respect for the progress children make and an acknowledgement on the part of education policy-makers and government of the value and distinctive contribution of urban primary teachers. As one teacher put it:

> I wouldn't work anywhere else. It's really tough and really demanding but where else would you get the rewards I get? On a good day, I know that I make a real difference to someone else's life. Now, where else would you get that?

Questions

1. What, if anything, do you think is distinctive about teaching in an urban primary school?
2. How do you think teachers can be encouraged to remain in urban schools?
3. What skills and qualities, if any, do urban primary school teachers need above and beyond those required of every primary school teacher?

HEADTEACHERS

This chapter explores what is involved in the role of the headteacher in an urban primary school. Drawing on questionnaire data provided by 16 headteachers, the first section explores their perceptions of the rewards and challenges of urban headship. The section also examines the qualities that these heads identify as necessary for effective headship in challenging schools and highlights their need for support in this demanding role. The second section explores these issues in more detail based on interviews conducted with six urban headteachers at different stages in their careers. All primary headteachers will share similar concerns and experience similar demands. What makes headship distinctive in urban primary schools is the intensity of the demands and the rewards of headship in challenging circumstances.

In this chapter we focus on headship in urban primary schools. Our intention is to explore the distinctions that shape the professional worlds of urban primary headteachers. Before we address this issue, we need to make a number of observations about primary headship in general terms. As Southwood (1998) has pointed out, to be the head of an infant school is not the same as leading and managing a junior school. To have a special unit or a nursery in the school also makes a difference. As Southwood (1998: 59) says: 'Headship in a designated community school or in a denominational school alters the character of the work.' Headship is differentiated by gender as well as age, social class and other differences (Tomlinson et al. 1999). Headship is also a dynamic process. It changes and develops over time.

Primary headship is a differentiated occupation but there are some commonalities. Not least is the emphasis in all the literature on the centrality and power of the head in shaping and leading 'their' schools (Day et al. 2000). Southwood (1998: 61) highlights a sense of ownership that is evidenced in the way in which 'many heads speak of 'my' school, 'my' budget and 'my' deputy'. Southwood classifies the generic role of the primary headteacher as located in three main sets of 'dualisms'. Heads have to manage and lead the school, that is, they have to cope with the day-to-day responsibilities such as budgets and staffing as well as setting and maintaining a culture and professional ethos. Heads are also caught up in responding to internal and external sets of demands, for example, the need to consider attainment and the need to establish good relationships with the local community. The third duality relates to leading from the front while delegating and sharing leadership responsibilities. These dualities are creative sets of tensions that all heads have to navigate.

At the same time, the job of headship has changed and continues to change dramatically. Heads are simultaneously placed in the roles of being the leading professional and the chief executive (Coulson 1986 in Southworth 1998). Particularly in the English context, but in other nations too, primary heads are being increasingly moved away from their more traditional focus on teaching and learning, with being the head*teacher*, towards taking on an increasingly complex set of demands related to changes in the nature of teaching, the primary school curriculum and primary schooling in general. Fundamentally, Gunter (2001: 101) argues that primary headteachers have a central 'commitment to the children they are working with and on behalf of'. This commitment means that sometimes headteachers experience another set of tensions, for example, between what they know is best practice for their children and what may sometimes be demanded by central government.

There are similarities in the demands of primary headship even though it is a differentiated occupation. There is a wide range of literature that analyses generic concerns such as effective management (Davies and Ellison 1994), successful primary headship (Draper and McMichael 1998) and leadership (Riley and Louis 2000; Fidler and Alton 2004). However, there are some gaps in what we know about the work of the primary headteacher. For example, there is a shortage of accounts from primary headteachers themselves (but see Pascal and Ribbens 1998). Many of the texts on primary headship, useful though they are, sometimes say little about the wider social context or what Thompson (2003: 336) calls 'the grubby material reality of most schools'. Thus, until relatively recently, little direct attention has been paid to the complex job of headship in an urban primary school (but see Donnelly 2003; Riddell 2003). Overall though, as Thompson (2003: 342) claims:

> For heads in schools described as 'challenging circumstances' ... theirs is work about which an insufficient amount is known, and where simplistic technical blueprints for change will have catastrophic results.

In the previous chapter, we described how we undertook a small-scale exploration into the working world of urban teachers and urban headteachers. On the recommendations from people such as senior LEA advisors and tutors in higher education institutions familiar with their local schools, a sample of 60 urban headteachers in six different and contrasting metropolitan education authorities across England was constructed. One intention of the research was to gain an insight into the experiences of leadership and management in six different local education authorities (LEAs) from ten urban schools within each LEA. The questionnaire for the headteachers gathered biographical details and explored aspects of their work. The questions asked about what they found rewarding and challenging as well as any specific skills and qualities they thought were needed for effective urban primary headship.

About the headteachers

Only 16 headteachers returned the questionnaires. Consequently, we are not able to make any major claims from this small survey. Twelve of the 16 were women. Eight of the heads were between 51 and 55 years old and all had more than 25 years of teaching experience behind them. None of this group expected to be a head in five years' time. Of the remaining eight headteachers aged under 50, five were not thinking of giving up urban headship, while the remaining three hoped to be running schools in non-urban locations in the future.

At the end of the questionnaire, the headteachers were given the opportunity to indicate whether they would be prepared to be interviewed at greater length about headship in urban schools. Subsequently, we conducted telephone interviews with six of the heads, one from each of the LEAs that we had contacted (Frey and Mertens Oishi 1995). The questionnaires will be examined in the first section of this chapter followed by an exploration of the in-depth interviews in the second section.

Urban pressures, urban rewards

From the questionnaire data we received, it was evident that headteachers in urban schools experienced a tension in their work between the problems and pressures that were great and the rewards which were similarly high. Some of the heads stated that they had never experienced such a high level of professional satisfaction before taking on headship in an urban school. The kinds of pressures identified by our headteachers were similar to those cited by the teachers discussed in the previous chapter, notably the high degree of social deprivation in the local area, sometimes a lack of parental support, high staff turnover and what they saw as sometimes unrealistic government and LEA targets.

For many heads, the rewards of the job characterized their headship. These included a sense of achievement that came as a result of succeeding against the odds (Maden and Hillman 1996), the opportunity to work with a committed and motivated staff and their own continual professional development (Keys et al. 2003). For instance, some commented that they were continually learning about the rich diversity of different cultures and religions. Some headteachers saw their own cultural learning as a reward: 'gaining an insight into the different cultural background of the children' and 'the pleasure of making an impact'.

All the heads in our study said that they deliberately chose to apply for headships in urban schools because of the 'challenge' that these schools presented and the rewards of the job (Riddell 2003). One head stated that: 'I enjoyed working in this borough and knew what challenges I would face and felt that I could meet those challenges.' Headteachers, who have often worked as classroom teachers or deputy headteachers in the same LEA, know what the local schools are like and what challenges they are likely to face. They are familiar with the wider social and cultural issues (Woods and Jeffrey 1996). While some teachers early in their careers may work in schools and locations they later come to regret, headteachers are much better informed and base their decisions to apply for headships on an informed set of criteria about schools and their circumstances. Ofsted information on the internet means that aspirant headteachers can access a wealth of information about any school in which they are interested. The headteachers in our survey positively chose urban primary schools that presented a challenge but where they believed they could effect an improvement.

As well as the challenge, respondents often referred to the presence of a good team of teachers already working in the school as influencing their decision to apply for the headship (Woods and Jeffrey 1996). Some heads praised supportive parents or well-behaved children as well as the broader reputation of the school itself as factors that affected their decision to choose a particular school. What is worth singling out are the similarities in the responses of teachers and heads in our research. Many teachers and headteachers, it seems, desire to work in what they perceive to be the most difficult schools and to somehow transform them into centres of excellence. The urge to test one's own abilities in the toughest circumstances was a driving force behind the desire to work in challenging urban schools, a point endorsed in Riddell's (2003) study of urban primary schools in Bristol. It was also clear that aspects of their own biographies and commitments underpinned their choice of school. Some respondents reported that they came from similar backgrounds to those of their children. Gunter (2001: 100) makes the point that: 'Who headteachers are and their backgrounds is important, and this cannot be written out of the headship practice.'

When asked what was rewarding about working in their particular school, heads referred to overcoming a range of challenges (Day et al. 2001). One head maintained that he felt rewarded: 'When I make a success of what I'm doing and achieve something against the odds.' The rewarding aspects of the job were occasions when either the children or the school achieved something significant and overcame serious difficulties. Heads wrote of 'children operating in English. Switching from code to code and becoming more proficient in English over time' or 'children doing well despite hardship and disadvantage'. A capacity to identify and celebrate success is vital in all schools (Barber 1998), but particularly in urban schools that are frequently demonized both in the media and within local communities (Lucey and Reay 2002). Headteachers reported that measures of success were parents demonstrating 'they are grateful to staff who show commitment and respect to the children – particularly those who last the course' or when the school had 'changed negative perceptions of the [local education] authority'. Some headteachers praised the commitment of their staff and commented on the pleasure they gained from working with them. Others reported enjoying the sense of working in a lively school in which 'no two days are the same' – a key factor in creating and sustaining a 'positive and supportive' workplace

(National Commission on Education 1996: 21). Other headteachers felt rewarded when they were able to 'offer equality of opportunity for all our children' or when the children 'grew in their knowledge of different cultures and faiths'.

The urban challenge

Gunter (2001: 100) argues that there is frequently a 'deep intellectual commitment to headship' coupled with a 'passion for the job and an emotional engagement with children and people'. This passion and commitment were very evident in our small sample. The respondents highlighted concerns that many heads would recognize, notably supporting struggling children, dealing with parental concerns and making the budget stretch through the whole year (Bell 1999). The respondents also identified a number of pressures that were more directly related to headships in disadvantaged settings such as high staff turnover, racial tension, managing conflict, run-down local environments, high levels of social deprivation and crime (see also Hillman in NCE 1996). In addition, they felt that as a regular part of their job they sometimes had to overcome low expectations, some negative parental attitudes, some acute behavioural difficulties and a shortage of positive parental role models for children (Riley 1998). Some of the headteachers were concerned about the high levels of child mobility in and out of their schools (Dobson et al. 2000). Almost all the headteachers referred to the pressure to meet what they saw as unrealistic targets for the children in their schools in relation to Key Stage 2 SATs. In support of this point, Myers and Goldstein (1998) state that it is necessary to contextualize target setting, taking into consideration income and social background. Added to this, heads identified several societal factors that impacted on their jobs. These included crime, vandalism, drug use and the growth of the gang culture in their local communities. They were also concerned about family disruption and the impact this had on children's learning.

In primary schools, it is often the headteacher who will interact with parents. Several heads recounted how parents regularly came to the school for advice and support in dealing with the difficult situations that they faced, which took up a lot of the head's time (Cox 1999). For some heads, the requests for help from parents increased the pressures they faced, but they reported a sense of satisfaction when they could support parents. By way of contrast, several heads reported alienated parents who wanted nothing to do with the school and transmitted this message to their children. Heads reported parents being 'very defensive when asked to talk about their children'. It can be difficult for families who may be attempting to parent in challenging circumstances having to 'struggle themselves to come to terms with the difficulties their children are presenting' (Roffey 2002: 9) and frequently, it will be the headteacher who has to mediate this struggle in school.

School budgetary changes and under-funding were another main worry for our heads, mirroring the major concern of 80 per cent of headteachers in the National Foundation for Educational Research (NFER) survey of trends in education (2004a). Lack of funding and not knowing how much money they were going to have for more than one year made the job more difficult for the heads in our sample. As one head commented: 'I'd quite like to spend everything we've got, but I can't afford to because you don't know what's going to happen next year.' A number of heads reported receiving a basic share of the budget but not receiving additional funding that could enable them to become involved in more exciting, innovative and creative projects that one head referred to as 'all the add-on stuff'. They identified a number of financial disadvantages that urban schools have to deal with. For example, two heads wrote that they had not been included in the local Education Action Zone (EAZ), in spite of their facing the same challenges as other schools that were included. Other heads highlighted the fact that they could not fund raise as effectively as schools in socially advantaged catchment areas.

Some heads expressed resentment at having to participate in a bidding culture in order to attempt to bring extra income into their school in the first place. Many policies require schools to compete for funds to meet all their needs by writing bids (Power and Whitty 1999). Heads reported that they were bidding 'for just about everything'. Some felt that it was unfair as such a culture tended to award funds to schools better at bid writing rather than based on their educational needs. This culture, they argued, resulted in increased inequalities in resourcing and produced greater injustice.

Nevertheless, heads had to provide the best service they could. If that meant an element of 'opportunism' (Maden 2001), of going out and finding some additional funding for a particular project without this being detrimental to the school, then they would do it. However, if they could see that it was going to have a knock-on effect on the school and its ethos, then they would refuse to get involved. Involvement in the bidding culture could mean taking people 'off the timetable' to write proposals and this was something that they could not always afford to do. In a school where perhaps there was less pressure, it would be easier to bid for money.

Anxiety about staffing issues was expressed by many of the heads, with some typically reporting that they had a regular and high turnover of teachers (Menter et al. 2002). This issue was the primary challenge reported in West-Burnham's study (2003). However, other urban primary headteachers reported having built up a core of stable staff. A view was expressed that some staff could stay in the same job for 'too long' and that this was not healthy for themselves in terms of their professional development or for the children. One head put it like this: 'I think it is difficult when you've taught in an area like this a long time, I think you need to move on and even if it's a similar school, a different school is a good idea.'

There were heads who had addressed the problem of staff recruitment and retention by 'growing their own' teachers, that is, training students at their schools, 'spotting talent' and offering them teaching posts on qualification (Maden 2001). Other heads emphasized the need to find appropriate staff for their type of school and the type of teaching and learning advocated in the school: 'I was more interested in getting the right kind of teacher and then fitting them in.'

The administrative burden on headteachers (Cockburn 1996) was a problem for many of the heads in our research, particularly if this detracted from their being effective leaders. Some heads in our sample claimed that a high administrative load was a contributory factor to headteacher stress (Fidler and Alton 2004). An NFER survey (2004a) found that the most time-consuming activities for headteachers were monitoring the children's achievement, implementing new initiatives, strategic planning, keeping abreast of educational developments and keeping informed about statutory changes. Some heads made the point that the process of putting initiatives in place was complicated. They argued that 'initiative over-load' (Power et al. 1997; Riley and West-Burnham 2004) added to the information that heads had to 'get your head round and understand'. It was not always possible for some heads to delegate responsibilities to other staff in the school as might be possible if the management team was bigger (Riley and West-Burnham 2004). One head commented: 'I think one of the biggest issues being a head of a small school is that you can never think, oh right, I can give that to so and so to deal with because there isn't that person. If you have got a lot of staff then yes they do take on a lot of delegation.'

The politicized nature of the job of headship (Donnelly 2003) was highlighted by several respondents who maintained they struggled with the conflict between their own philosophy of teaching and the real-life pressures they felt from outside agencies. One headteacher summarized the point succinctly by noting that: 'The needs of the children do not balance with the government's political needs.' The conflict between the two positions is what may finally tip the balance in persuading some heads to leave urban schools (Menter et al. 2002). Heads in urban primary schools acknowledged that some of the pressures they faced were pressures faced by all headteachers, wherever they were located. One head suggested there existed: 'The myth of the leafy suburb where everything is nice.' She added that urban headteachers were wrong if they thought they could 'escape everything they hated about running a school simply by changing locations'. However, the vast majority of our respondents argued that their job was more challenging in a number of ways that contrasted with schools in more advantaged areas and that people in the 'leafy suburbs' did not always understand the problems that inner city heads dealt with on a day-to-day basis. These problems could be tiring and unpredictable and could result in the job of headship becoming more stressful (West-Burnham 2003).

Qualities required for headship

Being the headteacher on the 'frontline' in an urban primary school is without doubt a tough job. So, how do these headteachers cope and what specific skills do they feel are required to carry out their job effectively? By far the most common response from heads in this study, as well as others (Maden 2001; Riley and West-Burnham 2004), was that they needed energy, resilience, enthusiasm and a sense of humour. The feeling among the heads we researched and in the literature on headship was that it was virtually impossible to do everything that was expected and the ability to laugh and make time for themselves was what prevented these heads from sometimes losing heart (Cockburn 1996; Carlyle and Woods 2002). Added to this, a sense of optimism was seen as essential. Heads referred to how easy it was to feel overwhelmed by the quantity and range of demands they faced on a regular basis. Several heads in our study likened the experience to 'spinning plates' or 'juggling balls' (see also Riley and West-Burnham 2004). They highlighted the need to prioritize what needed to be done. Heads commented on the weight of expectations they felt to achieve and to continually improve what they were doing in school. Complacency or contentment was not an option. Heads felt that if they lost their positive ethos and determination to continue improvement, the schools and they themselves would become very quickly demoralized.

With reference to the specific challenge of managing and leading in an urban primary school, the heads in our study highlighted additional skills and qualities that they thought were important for successful urban headship. They highlighted the need for cultural sensitivity and respect for difference and believed that more training could be provided in this area. They argued strongly about the need to work effectively with a range of community and religious leaders and the skills and additional knowledge that this sometimes required. Some heads identified a need for training in dealing with 'emotionally complex situations' that sometimes occurred in working with their parents. Many simply argued for more recognition of their difficulties, more resources and more support.

Need for support

Headship is a complex and changing occupation. Not only are headteachers having to take on more work, but the nature of that work has undergone profound changes. Headship is still concerned with 'relationships and trying to maintain educational values' (Gunter 2001: 97) but it is also more and more about increased managerial responsibility within the school (Southworth 1998). This change towards self-managed schools has resulted in the development of a different relationship between schools and LEAs, with heads having more responsibility for decision making (Donnelly 2003). Day et al. (1998: 213) suggest that: 'What is needed in these days of high pressure and fast change is a relationship of mutual support where both school and LEA-based staff see their prime purpose as supporting the learning lives of pupils.' They argue that it is crucial for heads to develop good working relationships with LEA colleagues, particularly the advisory and inspection service.

From the data that we collected from urban primary headteachers, it was apparent that some LEAs were clearly doing better than others in terms of proactive support. Some heads reported innovative support initiatives taking place in their LEAs and a number of heads reported 'buying back' into the advisory/consultancy services the LEA offered to support their work in school. However, several heads reported that the provision of support was 'not very good' for individual heads as it tended to concentrate on the school as an institution. Heads wrote that they frequently gained indirect support through involvement in other government initiatives and in networking with other headteachers, a situation that is reported elsewhere (Southworth and Lincoln 1999; Fidler and Alton 2004).

However, support is not a one-way process. Heads added that if their school was going to get support from external agencies, then it was necessary for these individuals to have credibility in their school setting. This meant an awareness of, and being able to work in, a challenging context. As one head commented: 'It really is no good for somebody to come in and say, well we'll twin you up with some school and they'll tell you how it's done. They may have no experience of dealing with what we have to deal with.' Another head claimed that in the past there had been a history of a 'blame culture' (Power et al. 1997), where their LEA had held heads of urban schools responsible for underachievement, but that this was beginning to change.

In a system where competition between schools is intended to fuel improvement, it might be expected that schools refuse to work together or share ideas. However, many of our heads, as in other studies (Day et al. 2000), referred to the supportiveness of other heads and maintained that without that assistance and understanding they would feel cut off and isolated. The heads we questioned cited the importance of being able to support their 'whole team' within the school. Among the key skills they identified was the ability to say 'thanks', to 'always be available to everyone' and the capacity to 'inspire, motivate and stimulate'. This reflects a style of leadership identified by Grace (1995a) as 'headteacher–professional' where strong emphasis is put on collegial relationships and pedagogy in the school. A number of the heads agreed that where there was a failure to effectively communicate their vision and encourage their staff, they would quickly lose their backing in the future (Davies and Ellison 1994; Wallace and Huckman 1999).

Several heads noted that being part of a network or cluster group of local heads was helpful. Initiatives such as Excellence in Cities have, in some instances, brought schools in urban settings together into support groups. Riley and Louis (2000: 213) maintain that effective leadership is based on:

> A network of relationships among people, structures and cultures, both within, and across organisations which extends beyond the immediate school community, embracing those many actors on the wider leadership stage – governments, trade unions, school districts and businesses – acknowledging the diverse roles which they play.

Bell (2003: 8) recognized that: 'The increasing evidence of effective collaboration between groups of schools shows that there is widespread recognition of the added value of seeking solutions to the most entrenched problems.' As one headteacher told us:

> We had a range of schools in the network, from your really affluent 'well-to-do' areas to areas like mine and schools that were in an even more difficult situation than me to be honest. And we talked about that openly. And we agreed that that was not going to get in the way of the work that we were doing and I think we had that openness and that kind

> of trust between us that we wouldn't be competitive with each other. Because actually we were all working for the same cause, if you like.

While well-established heads seemed to be supportive of each other, there appeared to be mixed support for new heads at a local level, from advisors for instance. This was an area that several headteachers suggested could be improved on, particularly for heads working in difficult and challenging circumstances. When a head went into a new school, they had to 'put their heads down and stay in the school' as one head told us. There was some evidence of personal mentoring schemes for new heads in some LEAs and some of our informants had completed mentor training (Kinlaw 1989; Davies and Ellison 1994).

Experienced heads reported that they could provide support for other urban heads in terms of leadership, management and planning. Yet, Thompson (2000) claims that much of the educational management literature sidelines the knowledge and experience of headteachers. One head described her experience of using a coaching model (Kinlaw 1989) to support a less experienced headteacher colleague: 'It's the first time anybody's ever gone to him and said "OK, you tell me what you need to do to improve and let's look at how we might do that" and he said "he found that quite refreshing".'

As we found in our research and as reported elsewhere, a strong, committed and hard-working supportive staff team was essential to headteachers (Maden 2001). Several heads described actively building a team of the 'right' people who were happy to work together in a, sometimes, difficult school environment. This team included teaching and non-teaching staff as well as governors (Davies and Ellison 1994; Fidler and Alton 2004). Heads also stressed the need for competent administrative officers who could help deal with some of the finance issues. Some heads stressed the importance of having the support of staff colleagues who were excited and committed about getting involved in new school initiatives. As is probably the case in all schools, the deputy head was identified as an important colleague in the management of the school (Wallace and Huckman 1999).

In all schools where headteachers now have responsibility for site-based issues of performance management, the roles and responsibilities of headship have moved away from teaching towards management and leadership. Heads are the leaders in schools; that is their distinctive role. Yet headship is an 'ongoing experience of contradiction and dilemma' (Gunter 2001: 104). Heads have ultimate control and responsibility for their school but they also have to build and sustain good professional and personal relationships with staff, parents, governors and LEA personnel (Day et al. 2000).

The heads also identified other organizations and agencies with which it was necessary to work and receive support from, particularly health, welfare and social services, and the frequency and intensity of these contacts in urban settings has been identified in other research (Riley and West-Burnham 2004). Some heads reported sometimes needing to involve the services of the local police force, although this support was not always forthcoming as their schools were located in high crime areas. Some heads suggested that the depth and complexity of the issues they faced in their schools required a multi-agency and community-based approach (Maden and Hillman 1996). One headteacher talked of the health support that her school needed:

> Our children have more illness than children in some other areas and that's a health issue and we need to work more closely with health. Some of our children have very, very difficult home lives which is a social services issue.

Staying power

The headteachers all recognized that urban schools presented an increased challenge. They were aware that some of their peers in their LEA had found it hard to cope, but most heads in our study had a realistic approach towards their work. They were committed to their schools and planned to stay in the job. Donnelly (2003: 14) has commented that: 'The greatest challenges in life bring the greatest rewards. This applies to all headships, but particularly those of urban schools.' Brighouse (in Riddell 2003: x) says that there are many things that are similar in teaching anywhere, 'but there are also differences, particularly in urban schools'. He argues that with:

> Outstanding urban teachers you see teachers whose capacity to learn and improvise from their learning is formidable. So too is their skill in getting their youngsters ready for learning – a vital factor when the 'baggage' some bring to the school makes it a triumph of will over adversity that they get to school in the first place. (Brighouse, in Riddell 2003: x)

Heads in our study felt that more could and should be done to encourage urban heads to remain in post for longer. There were very few examples where heads demanded early retirement opportunities, more pay, more personal support, better training or even regular sabbaticals, although these were all mentioned. What heads did demand was more money for their schools to reduce class sizes or to buy in additional teachers to support struggling children or those with emotional and behavioural difficulties. Heads also wanted additional funds to pay their staff more so that their teachers would remain in post rather that give up altogether or move to more advantaged neighbourhoods. Heads recognized a plea for more money in their budgets as being a wholly unrealistic expectation but were eager to stress that there were many examples whereby heads could be encouraged to stay that would not cost huge sums.

The most common request was a desire by heads for recognition, by both LEAs and central government, of the difficulties of urban headship (Whitty 2002). Difficulties were caused primarily by unrealistic target setting and benchmarking but also by the culture of league tables and direct comparisons made between schools. Urban heads felt under pressure to consider the place of their school in league tables for attendance, exclusions, attitude (conducted using the Pupil Attitude Survey) and attainment. Heads saw the use of league tables as damaging and demoralizing and almost unanimously demanded their wholesale removal if heads were to be actively encouraged to remain in challenging schools. One head, who at 55 years of age had already announced her retirement, simply wanted the school to be less demanding: 'I'm going to be very honest and say that if I were in a less challenging school or area I would probably have worked for another 2–3 years.' For this head, it is too late, but she concludes: 'Recognition of the real day-to-day issues we face would be nice.'

The heads in our study were vociferous in their belief of the need to create and maintain a good work–life balance and the importance of this has been highlighted in other research (Riley and West-Burnham 2004). However, as one head put it: 'If you're working in a chaotic situation then the work's not going to be finished is it?' Another head maintained that every so often headteachers need some kind of break from the job, whether it is a secondment or some kind of sabbatical in order to energize people and 'recharge their batteries' (Riley and West-Burnham 2004: 34). One head put it thus: 'Colleagues certainly often begin to get worn down by it all and I do think that that's perhaps something that's not taken into account when people just compare schools of similar sizes and so on, they don't see the context.'

Celebrating the school's successes was also seen as a vital ingredient (Stoll and Myers 1998; Day et al. 2000). This suggestion was not about 'teacher of the year'-type awards but a celebration of all that urban primary schools have achieved. Headteachers in our study stated that 'children gaining a sense of achievement and control over their lives' was a cause for celebration. As Rogers (2001: 99) urges: 'The many schools which are quietly succeeding to add significantly to the life chances of their pupils need to be recognized and praised.' One head in our study wrote about a letter she had received from a school inspector:

> It read 'I couldn't help but be enthused by the classroom environments, quality of work, displays and activities you described that your staff engage in and I would hope to support the school in developing its work. Well done to all involved' ... Now that made a lot of difference!

Nonetheless, the pressures can be relentless for school leadership in challenging urban contexts.

Changing the culture – towards success in urban primary schools

In this second section we turn to the in-depth interviews that we conducted with six urban primary school headteachers. Southworth (1998: 60) claims that: 'Headship is differentiated by experience, an idea which relates to the notion that there are phases in headship.' This was an issue that we wanted to explore in relation to urban headship. We selected six heads from different LEAs who had different lengths of experience and who had indicated their willingness to be interviewed. We wanted to explore their approaches to developing and sustaining successful urban primary schools over time.

The headteachers had taken up headships in schools that had been regarded as 'the worst in the borough' or as presenting an extreme challenge. In some cases, these headteachers were committed to staying with their schools until they retired, and some had already spent much of their professional lives in their current headship. The less experienced heads in our sample were planning to move on eventually – but to similar schools. All the headteachers relished their work and the differences they could make in urban schools. They talked of 'improvement', 'transformations', 'quality', 'high expectations' and 'making a difference' – these expressions typically framed their discussions about the challenging role of headship in urban schools. They saw themselves as making a difference and, in many cases, this meant establishing a culture of 'the way we do things round here' (Maden 2001: 26). This they did in a variety of ways including developing strategies with children, parents, teachers and in local religious, cultural and political community contexts. From what they said, however, it seemed that heads had different imperatives in different phases of urban headship.

The new urban headteacher

Belinda and Mike have been teaching for 10 and 14 years respectively and have each been head for two of those years. They began their teaching careers after the implementation of the National Curriculum and the use of national testing to assess children's performance in Key Stages 1 and 2. They are both eager to complete the job they started at their current schools before looking for bigger schools in equally challenging conditions. Both Mike and Belinda sought to change the culture of their school largely through their work with children. The two most significant areas they highlighted were the need to set and maintain high standards of behaviour and to develop a curriculum that matched the needs of their children.

One of the distinctions that came out of the interviews with the new headteachers was that they both took very firm attitudes towards inappropriate behaviour (Draper and McMichael 1998). In their first year of headship, these two new headteachers permanently excluded children and used exclusions to signal the unacceptability of some behaviour. They took a 'tough love' approach and wanted the local community to know they meant business. In some ways, it might be argued that they 'massaged' their intake to a degree – excluding the most difficult children who had to go elsewhere (Gewirtz et al. 1995; Day et al. 1998). From another perspective, they saw it as tackling bullying, aiming high and having high expectations. Both heads were eager to stress the importance of identifying the causes of inappropriate behaviour while maintaining their 'zero tolerance' attitude towards misbehaviour:

> We've got quite a lot of challenging children, challenging in terms of behaviour and our attainment is below the national average. A lot of our children don't have a range of strategies to deal with frustrations. There can be a big flare up and that can take a long time to deal with ... I think one of the frustrations, but it's got lots of potential and I think it's

> different to working in other kinds of schools, is the need to work with a whole range of agencies and people, lots of professionals, we have lots of contact with social services. (Mike)

Mike recognized that children who 'acted up' in school would be more likely to achieve less well and would need time to work through their emotional flare-ups (McCurdy et al. 2003):

> If a child does something, they know it will be dealt with but not necessarily straight away and not in the severest way because actually the worst time to try and deal with it is just when it's happened. But the next day if they know it will be followed up, and you can actually talk through it and talk about how it might have been dealt with differently, which might be a much more effective way of doing it. The kind of consequences we use, they must conform to the three Rs, that they're related to what the child's done so it's not just sitting there doing pages of lines. It must be reasonable and respect must be maintained intact for everybody concerned so we're not out to humiliate children and we have quite a lot of reward systems in place. (Mike)

Belinda also placed great emphasis on establishing her own credentials through the behaviour she expected of her children. She wanted to impose herself on the school (Southworth 1995):

> Those children were compromising the education of other children and I wasn't prepared to let that happen. We did short-term exclusions, masses of short-term exclusions because once children realise that you're serious, 'Oh my God I'm going to get excluded if I behave like this', they do stop. It's fairly utilitarian in viewpoint but I think it's important. You've got 200 children in the school and I wouldn't be prepared to compromise their chances because a certain number of children simply can't behave themselves ... Gradually parents began to see that this was a school where their children were safe because that was a concern for them because bullying had been an issue, that their children were going to be made to get on with their work and work harder than they were and our results went through the ceiling. (Belinda)

Challenging behaviour was repeatedly an issue for many of our urban heads and although exclusion was seen as an easy and sometimes essential short-term solution, the new heads recognized their management responsibility to develop the right conditions for children to learn (Hopkins et al. 1997):

> We introduced a programme ... which was a programme for those children who were persistently poorly behaved. You know constantly distracting other children from their work, that kind of thing. The system that we put in place absolutely worked wonders for that group of children. It was quite punitive actually because it was based on the fact that they'd reached the point, they knew that this system was in place and they knew that if they overstepped the mark, you're going to get put on the ... programme. (Belinda)

Both headteachers believed that, over time, the school sets a culture of what is expected and children tend to adhere to these expectations (McCurdy et al. 2003). Positive behaviour could be 'caught and taught' through modelling, coaching and peer support (Espinosa and Laffey 2003). The heads believed that it was crucial to involve and support their parents in this process (Pascal and Ribbens 1998).

Having implemented behaviour policies, our new heads moved their attention to the curriculum. The heads were prepared to be adventurous and innovative and take as a starting point the needs of urban children (Riddell 2003):

> Well, we based the curriculum on first-hand experience and we do things like visits and residentials. There was a residential that used to happen of long standing but we introduced an additional residential to the kind of topics that we were doing. We had things like arts weeks and poetry weeks. There was a lot of bid writing and attempts to get quality people into school to come and do that but it was worth it because the children needed the first hand experience. A good example is this. You expect children's writing to improve, that's fair enough, you give them the skills to do it but if they haven't got anything to write about, a lot of children can't do it. You're talking about children who didn't go anywhere because their parents haven't got any transport so they only ever go to places in their own locality. It doesn't give them a great deal of experience of the world and it puts them at a disadvantage compared to children in more affluent areas who get taken off on aeroplanes to places in other parts of the world. (Belinda)

Mike, while also tailoring the curriculum for his school, was keen to explore different approaches to learning and teaching (Egan 2005):

> We spend a lot of time looking at learning styles, intelligences and accelerated learning because I don't feel that we can actually improve our children's attainment just by working hard on what we've already been doing. Literacy catch up programmes aren't going to be what turns our children round but a lively, stimulating, challenging curriculum is. So we've adopted this thing where we try and have what we call a unifying feature every half term so if a class is doing Egyptians, they don't just produce a book at the end of their topic. They might have a feast. (Mike)

In what he said, it was evident that Mike was prepared to take risks but overwhelmingly, he was committed to putting the children's learning at the centre of the school (Desforges 2001). He explained:

> We've gone quite heavily into the learning styles that children have whether they're visual, auditory or kinaesthetic ... The kinaesthetic children are often the children that play with things, tap their fingers, prod people and, of course, 70% of special needs children are kinaesthetic. So actually when you give those children something like a gardening project to do, that completely absorbs their interest and the amount of learning they do there is greatly increased. So we have quite a

> lot of disaffected children on gardening projects who spend their lunchtime weeding, watering and we grow a small amount of things like rhubarb, strawberries that are then used to prepare food and they actually eat it. (Mike)

One of the other key ways in which heads began to change the culture of the school was to make an immediate impact as quickly as possible. Time was important and both heads talked of starting 'immediately' on changing the environment. Sometimes they had been given a little extra money to start with, in recognition of the pressing needs of their school. Belinda highlighted the way in which changing the environment was tied up with a change in school culture and ethos (Maden and Hillman 1996; Whitty and Mortimore 2000):

> I think if you change the culture then you change the perception of the school and for me, one of the key things was to improve ... to transform the learning environment. It [the school when she took over] was a cesspit. It was the nastiest looking environment you've ever seen. Like the corridor was the tunnel of doom, full of old wardrobes and chests of drawers with ants in them. I managed to get the probation service to come in and paint the whole school inside ... which just made a huge difference. (Belinda)

These heads referred to the pressures of testing and the publication of results but revealed a determination not to let it affect what they recognized as good practice (Gunter 2001):

> The outside pressure and perception of your attainment and position in the league table is quite hard to deal with at times. At my previous school the first year that the SATs league table was published, we were bottom of the LEA league table and we had the press outside the gates interviewing parents that came in, you know, 'what's it like to have your child at the worst school in the LEA?' I think that sort of climate has changed a bit now and there's more acceptance that it isn't just a level playing field. How you are understood by people outside can be quite difficult at times. (Mike)
>
> When I took over the school, we were bottom of the league table literally ... and then last year the school was the highest in the authority for value added and this year it will be high again and the SATs results are in the 80s now. Which is a real transformation but I have no time for league tables at all. I think it's a complete waste of time and it does cause problems between schools. (Belinda)

The new heads we interviewed were fiercely ambitious for their schools, single minded and determined. These heads have a clear vision for their schools and they are not afraid to make unpopular decisions if it will benefit the school in the long run. They are also prepared to take risks and offer child-appropriate learning contexts for social and emotional learning as well as intellectual growth (Sharp 2001; Jones and Wyse 2004).

Established urban headteachers

In our second category of established urban heads, Andrea and Glynis had been teaching between 20 and 30 years and had been in urban headship for 5 to 10 years. Their priorities were somewhat different from those of the new heads. The established heads were eager to focus on extending the curriculum offered in their classrooms. They had a desire to move their staff beyond the literacy and numeracy strategies to what they regarded as 'proper teaching' (Egan 2005):

> You know when you used to write a book and things like that, they (the children) were much better, much more enthusiastic. I'd say to my class this afternoon we're going to write. Whoopee, oh yes fantastic and we'd be away. You say that to a class now. What are we going to write? Hang on a minute. And here we do have children who say oh good but it's not quite the same. So, we don't do the strategies. We've never done the literacy strategy. (Andrea)

However, although there appeared an eagerness to challenge the uniformity of strategies and introduce more flexibility, in reality there still exists a fairly rigid structure and, in some ways, our sample of more established heads could be seen as less risk-taking than our new heads.

> At 9 o'clock we start maths 'cos everybody does maths and then everybody does English and then everybody does phonics and then everybody does two lessons in the afternoon. Everybody does circle time. So it's consistency, so children wherever they are in the building, whatever age, it's always going to be the same routine. (Glynis)

> Our standards were not above national standards for literacy, no actually we've been doing the literacy hour for a long time and we now do First Steps and this is what we're doing and standards are rising. (Glynis)

The established heads were very familiar with the workings of the National Curriculum. They had the expertise and confidence to be able to take 'ownership' of the curriculum and make it their own (Pollard et al. 1994b). They were actively working to ensure that they were supporting their teachers while simultaneously extending the curriculum offered to the children in their school.

> We've now got the creative curriculum; we're doing our best to give the enrichment activities. Now we're having to work on some of the really key areas like assessment and pupil tracking and target setting and all those things. It's all in place but it's done with staff well-being in mind. It's all on disk, you know, none of our planning is laborious; it's all on the system. Everybody's got access to laptops and we do our utmost to make sure that life is balanced. (Glynis)

To effectively change the culture of the school, established heads recognized the need to work closely with their teachers. From what the heads said, it was evident that they valued teamwork and were determined to work hard with and support their teachers (MacBeath 1998). They moved swiftly when uncomfortable decisions had to be made. They saw a culture of high expectations, teamwork and support as effective in recruiting and retaining staff. What came across from their comments was the centrality of the school as a site for learning – for the children, the parents and the teachers.

> Since I've been here, I've had to do a lot. I've had to get people to change the way they do things. We've had to do an awful lot of changing to move into, you know, beyond 2000 because my predecessor had run a very successful school for 18 years but it wasn't the school that you need it to be now and I think he would admit that. Teachers want to teach here because I think we have worked to make it a good place to be. (Glynis)

Experienced urban headteachers

Ralph and Jackie have been teaching for between 30 and 40 years and have worked as headteachers for almost half that time. What distinguished their approach from the other two groups was their strong emphasis on the importance of working well with the community they served. They worked hard to reduce any 'divide' that parents have sometimes spoken of in terms of home–school relations (Dyson and Robson 1999; Donnelly 2003). An enormous amount of their own time and effort was put into this aspect of their work. These heads were innovative and welcoming to parents. They set up groups, classes and support centres for their parents. They offered parents help and support with learning and with challenging behaviour. In some cases, they offered help with promoting self-esteem and finding employment.

Ralph and Jackie discussed the ways that they approached working with their parents. One of the key aspects they both highlighted was the need to develop and maintain positive relationships and this involved a consistent approach on a regular basis.

> Every morning I would go outside and talk to the parents. Every single day and at the end of every single day as well . . . just making that personal contact is what they appreciated. Learning parents' names. Being a bit more personable with them and not patronising them. (Ralph)

These experienced urban heads invested a great deal of time in empowering their local communities and in using the expertise and resources of the school to work with parents and carers (Davies and Ellison 1994):

> We were able to then offer at least four different parent courses but unfortunately the targets that they have to achieve don't match with what parents want to achieve so having had access to the building . . . we do offer parents workshops about how they can help their children and things to make for their children and that obviously helps to build up relationships with them. (Jackie)

While being able to offer education and training for parents is important, our heads recognized that parents needed uncomplicated opportunities to meet other parents and talk. Jackie had set up a number of additional coffee mornings for parents who shared languages other than English. She also spoke about the need to ensure that parents understood the reasons for the approaches to learning in her school:

> Because, for instance, African parents have very often learned themselves in a very different way to their children and certainly in our school we do have parents who trust us now but you often get parents challenging you as to why they are allowed to play and we have to sell ourselves as learning through play and I think we do that but that's because we do have quite a lot of opportunities for parents to meet with staff. (Jackie)

The experienced heads we interviewed had developed a more pragmatic and matter-of-fact attitude to testing. They were not going to be governed by the tests or any requirement to 'climb the league tables':

> They're not particularly helpful to us in terms of, you know . . . as I say we can go from where we seem to be doing quite well to not doing terribly well in one year because our cohorts do vary quite a bit. There's no objection to testing children. I think the objection is to what's made of the information and there's almost a kind of, some of those things are beyond our control. Some of the journalistic phrases that are used are perhaps more suitable for reporting the fortunes of football teams rather than schools. The bottom of the table kind of thing, relegation and many of the measures that are used are relatively crude although value added is becoming more important. What concerns me is that schools doing a good job in a difficult context sometimes end up being reprimanded. (Ralph)

Conclusion

This chapter has attempted much. We have outlined the intensity of difficulties, challenges and pressures faced by headteachers in urban primary schools, but we have also been eager to identify the rewards and benefits. Urban headteachers, like headteachers elsewhere, are highly motivated and work hard to make a difference to their schools despite the challenge of social disadvantage. In this chapter, we have detailed some of the ways in which heads have sought to tackle and overcome these difficulties through a variety of approaches (see also Keys et al. 2003). For some, this meant focusing on improving the school environment; for others, the priority rested with, among other things, the introduction of curriculum changes or ensuring greater involvement of parents. Heads at different stages of their careers felt more able to tackle some issues rather than others.

Although some heads were able to make a success of turning around failing schools or achieving improvements within their schools, significantly more help and encouragement needs to be provided by LEAs to sustain and assist heads who are struggling in what are sometimes very demanding circumstances (Southworth and Lincoln 1999). One head highlighted a practical step that she thought would make a significant difference to urban primary schools:

> Stop wasting money on massive national initiatives because it's like a job creation scheme. There's millions and millions of pounds that have been put into redeveloping the curriculum and paying for people to do external assessments of threshold applications and so on. That money could have gone directly into urban schools where they haven't got rich parent teacher associations who can raise £4,000 at a summer fair, to improve the learning environment; they can all have new furniture or recruit good teachers. (Belinda)

Above all, the urban primary school headteachers in our sample believed that they would benefit from a quiet period without the ceaseless introduction of new initiatives:

> One of the things that amused me recently was the initiative 'Beating Back Bureaucracy'. You can send away for a 'Beating Back Bureaucracy' toolkit, which is another set of things. You know it's fine, it's great, there'll be a website that you can look at and people will say 'oh there's this website'. It's fine if you've got the time and energy to go through it and I think many heads just don't have the time and energy to even look for things that might be helpful to them because there's so little slack in the system, there is so little room for manoeuvre. (Ralph)

What came across powerfully from the interviews with the six headteachers was their passion and commitment to making a difference for their children and families who already faced a number of disadvantages. Some of the heads were concerned that the context of their school was not taken into consideration. They recognized that they could help their children to achieve well, but, in a hierarchic system, schools like theirs would always look less successful than those in more affluent areas (Mortimore and Whitty 1997).

All the headteachers who returned questionnaires and took part in interviews recognized that their families faced more difficulties and dilemmas than parents in more affluent areas. 'People who live in severely disadvantaged areas are proportionally more likely to have poor educational outcomes' (Power et al. 2002: 2). They acknowledged what Riddell (2003: 68) calls the 'concentration of learning disadvantage' in urban primary schools, but the heads believed they could counter this to some extent. In what they said, they demonstrated that they possessed many of the key characteristics of effective school leadership:

> The importance of a leadership stance which builds on and develops a team approach: a vision of success which includes a view of how the school can improve: the careful use of targets; the improvement of the physical environment; common expectations about pupils' behaviour and success; and an investment in good relations with parents and the community. (Whitty and Mortimore 2000: 164)

However, the need to keep dealing with unpredictability, conflict and frequent shifts in policy typifies the professional world of the urban headteacher (West et al. 2005). In situations of high mobility in staffing and sometimes in the intake of children coming to the school, it can be extremely difficult to sustain and extend the achievements of an urban primary school over time (McMahon 2003). It is the intensity of the demands and the rewards of leading in challenging circumstances that distinguishes headship in an urban primary school.

Questions

1. What are the challenges and opportunities of headship in the urban primary school?
2. What leadership strategies do you think are most effective in urban primary schools?
3. What qualities do you think are essential for effective urban headship?

5

PARENTS

The focus of the chapter is the contested issue of home–school partnerships in urban schools. In the two previous chapters, headteachers and teachers in urban primary schools highlighted the importance of parent–teacher relationships in supporting children in school. They documented the strategies put into place to welcome parents into their urban primary schools in order to facilitate communication and partnership. Yet, at the same time, they expressed concerns about what they saw as some unresponsive and sometimes antagonistic parents. In this chapter, we want to explore parent–school partnerships in more detail as well as the contradictions this sometimes provokes in the urban primary school.

We start by providing an overview of the changes in relationships between schools and parents in order to highlight the conflicts and struggles that have always characterized this area. We then focus on the movement towards empowering parents through extending parental rights in education. We explore some of the responsibilities that parents are now routinely encouraged to take on in order to support their children's progress in school. Finally, this chapter argues that while parent–school relationships are sites of struggle, more can be done in urban primary schools to include parents in working with teachers to support their children in school.

Parental involvement: an overview

From the very start of the provision of state schooling, relationships between parents and teachers have often been 'highly charged' (Lysaght 1993). Then, as now, conflicts and struggles took place over issues such as discipline, parental rights and children's needs (Grace 1978). Some key 'positions' or discourses were asserted in the nineteenth century that have proved difficult to dislodge, despite contemporary shifts in government rhetoric about the desirability of parental involvement and empowerment in the twentieth and twenty-first centuries. For example, in the nineteenth century, schools and teachers were expected to 'gentle' the unruly masses of working-class children that they worked with. Their parents were seen as part of the problem of moral decadence and a threat to social order that elementary schools were exhorted to hold at bay. Teachers were the 'professionals' and parents, particularly the urban working-class parents of the late nineteenth century, were pathologized as part of the wider social 'problem' of order and control, degeneracy and decay (Fishman 1988). Grace (1978: 42) argues that in the nineteenth century, while some teachers developed 'unsympathetic' typifications and saw 'dirty underfed children' as 'evidence of the social disorganisation of the poor working-class families, others saw them as victims of an oppressive economic system'. He adds that the social condition of 'the inner-urban school was often the context for the radicalising of teachers' (Grace 1978: 42; see also Maguire 2001). Overall though, many elementary school teachers set their professional expertise above and against the practical experience of parents and carers, a struggle that has persisted over time, albeit in different forms.

Vincent (1996) identified the 1960s as a key moment when substantial shifts in parent–teacher relationships started to occur. Before this, schools and teachers were in the ascendancy and parents of primary-aged children were frequently not permitted to come into the school unless for a formal occasion such as the traditional Christmas nativity play. It was commonplace to have a line painted in the playground to mark out the border between parents' and teachers' zones of responsibility. In the twentieth century, teachers struggled to assert their professional expertise and were not easily going to accede their hard-won authority to parents (Ozga and Lawn 1981). In some urban areas, however, the welfare state had not been able to replace 'the slum school, and the deprived area' (Jones 2003: 41). In central Liverpool, for example, there still existed 'closely-knit pockets of resistance' to what Jones calls the 'dominant culture' as well as a gulf 'between the ordinary teacher and the child in the down-town school' (Mays 1962: 92, cited in Jones 2003: 41).

By the 1960s changes were taking place in education policy and practice. Vincent (1996: 23) explains that this was the decade that 'witnessed the switching of emphasis by policy-makers from secondary schooling to primary and early childhood education'. It was in this decade too that independent parental pressure groups were formed such as the Advisory Centre for Education (ACE), which still continues its advocacy work today. Vincent (1996: 23) adds that although teachers in the 1960s still tended to view 'parents as inconvenient distractions', concerns about the quality of public services and demands for more participation and accountability were starting to impact on the politicians of the day, who recognized a need to respond to parental concerns (see also CCCS 1981). This shift was also reflected in a key government report of the day into primary education, the Plowden Report (1967), that highlighted the significance and importance of parental involvement.

The Plowden Report (1967), devoted a whole chapter to the value of parental participation and concluded that there was a link between the contribution of parents to their children's education and the level of achievement of their children in school. The Plowden Report recommended greater parental involvement in school activities, including classroom activities. However, as Vincent (1996) notes, Plowden was judgemental of some working-class parents. Plowden argued, for example, that working-class families tended to have fewer books in their homes and were less supportive of education generally. Thus, schools in challenging circumstances had to 'compensate' children for deficiencies in their homes. This deficit approach was hardly a recipe for empowerment and partnership.

In the years following the publication of the Plowden Report, a series of articles began to appear that became known as the Black Papers (Cox and Dyson 1969). These critiques of state schooling were written by New Right educationalists, academics and politicians of the day. Among the many issues that the papers highlighted as causes for concern were what the authors claimed to be increased levels of violence, truancy, and the growth and development of progressive and permissive methods of teaching in primary schools. The authors sought a return to traditional methods of teaching, a raising of moral standards in schools and a curriculum that identified the pre-eminent position of British culture. The Black Papers also sought to encourage more parental involvement both as choosers and participants in their children's education. Academics and politicians such as Rhodes Boyson (1974) and Antony Flew (1976) continued the themes of the Black Papers and urged the government to increase parental rights and responsibility. They argued that this involvement would ensure that schools became more accountable.

Simultaneously, educational research was also highlighting the way in which primary schools, even self-styled progressive schools, were less responsive to the working-class child and his family (Sharp and Green 1975).

Just when the Black Papers and the media more generally were claiming that progressive child-centred education was failing and that there was reluctance in schools to attend to the understandable fears and concerns of parents, one key event occurred that combined these themes. At William Tyndale Junior School in north London, some parents and teachers united to express their concerns about progressive education and what they saw as a lack of discipline in the school. The 'crisis' quickly escalated to hysterical proportions, all the time being fuelled by the ever-present media. The William Tyndale 'affair' was a complicated and protracted concern that we cannot deal with in much detail here (but see CCCS 1981). It eventually led to a public enquiry (Auld 1976) being established and some of the teachers at William Tyndale being dismissed. It seemed that parent power was now firmly on the agenda.

The increasing influence of the Black Papers and the crisis of confidence brought about by the Tyndale affair helped put pressure on the Labour government of the day. The direction of education policy including the precise role and nature of parental responsibility and involvement needed to be clarified. Prime Minister James Callaghan began with a speech at Ruskin College, Oxford, in 1976, in which he called for a great debate or a national discussion on the future of education (CCCS 1981). This was supposed to be a turning point in how schools were to function. The Taylor Committee, which was set up in response to the speech, made a number of significant recommendations regarding the need to expand the participation of parents in schools. However, before the suggestions could be put before parliament, the Labour government suffered an election defeat and was replaced by a Conservative administration led by Margaret Thatcher. What began in 1979 with a new party in government was a comprehensive shift in the distribution of power and responsibility in education towards parents and away from teachers (Dale 1989). In this shift, parents were generally cast as a homogenous group, white, middle class and pro-school, who were best placed to make decisions about their children's education. They were often set against teachers who, it was argued, needed to be more responsive to parents' concerns (DES 1985).

It is not possible here to provide a full account of the complex interplay over time between schools, teachers and parents in a search for better parent–school relations (Vincent 1996; Hallgarten 2000; Crozier and Reay 2005). What is important is that currently, as Reay (2005: 23) argues, active partnership has become 'enshrined in educational policy'. We are now at a point where parental involvement is a necessity for all schools. It is explored and assessed by Ofsted school inspections. It is part and parcel of the contemporary discourse of primary education.

Rise of a parentocracy

When Margaret Thatcher was elected to power in 1979, she was determined to overcome what many saw as the problems of 1970s Britain: notably high unemployment, a perceived failure of social democratic policies and a general decline in confidence in the welfare state and the education system (see Ball 1990). Whitty (2002: 19) believes that Thatcherism in education 'was partly successful because whole constituencies felt excluded from the social democratic settlement of the post-war era'. The attempt to ally parents with government concerns, while displacing key state professionals such as teachers and educational bureaucracies, was part of a new alignment within the welfare state.

Between 1980 and 1986 much of the legislative action concentrated on increasing parental rights such as choice of school, access to information, as well as developing a greater role for parents on school governing bodies. For example, the 1985 White Paper 'Better Schools' (DES 1985) argued that schools and parents had shared interests and that 'schools should explain their aims and policies to parents and associate parents with their work' (Reay 2005: 23). The Education Act 1986 sought to continue the trend of shifting power and responsibility gradually towards the parent and away from the LEAs. This legislation increased the proportion of parents on the governing bodies of schools. It is worth pointing out that research into the constitution of school governors has repeatedly found that governing bodies are overwhelmingly white and middle class (Deem 1989). Nevertheless, even by the end of 1987, parents were still peripheral participants until, that is, the introduction of the Education Reform Act 1988. This marked the point at which the role of the parent would change substantially and would take on the look it has at present.

The Education Reform Act (ERA) 1988 guaranteed that parents would have a choice of school. Put simply, the argument was that the market 'works' best because individuals make choices that 'provide the discipline of accountability and demand that the producer cannot ignore' (Gewirtz et al. 1995: 1). In the education market place, the role of the parent 'shifted from that of a local taxpayer to that of client' (Ball 1990: 97). It was argued that individual parents were best placed to make choices on behalf of their children. Their choices would drive provision; unpopular schools would have to change and become more responsive to parental concerns or they would close because parents would not choose them.

The publication of the Parents' Charter (1991) gave clarity to the rights of parents. When their children were aged 5 and again at 11, parents were able to indicate a choice for a particular school for their children based on whatever criteria they decided. It is interesting to note that the revised Parents' Charter (1994) substituted 'choice' for 'preference'. The distinction between choice and preference highlighted that parents did not have an automatic right to the school of their first choice. Despite this, the DES insisted that exercising a preference was important because the 'choice of school directly affects that school's budget – every pupil means extra money for the school. So, your right to choose will encourage schools to aim for the highest possible standards' (DES 1991: 14). It was argued by the DES (1992) that parents not only had a right to choose an education for their children but also were considered to be in the best position to do so. The 1992 white paper 'Choice and Diversity' asserted that: 'Parents know best the needs of their children – better even than our educational theorists or administrators, better even than our most excellent teachers' (DE 1992: 3). The key question that arises here is what sorts of parent and what sorts of school were envisaged in the rhetoric of this White Paper. To borrow from Crozier and Reay (2005: ix), in this discourse of parents' rights: 'Parents are treated as a homogenous group; no account is taken of gender, social class or ethnic differences.' Neither is there any recognition of the complex circumstances that some families, and mothers in particular, have to face; factors such as poor housing, reduced income, lack of wider support and possibly related health problems too.

The Conservative administrations between 1979 and 1997 oversaw a massive reorienting of educational policy and practice (Tomlinson 2001). The insertion of quasi-market forces and the emphasis on competition as a lever for raising standards was reflected in reforms in curriculum, pedagogy and assessment (Whitty 2002; Jones 2003). These reforms repositioned parent–school relationships. Brown termed this shift as a move towards a 'parentocracy': 'the ideology of parentocracy involves a major programme of educational privatisation under the slogans of "parental choice", "educational standards" and the "free market"' (Brown 1997: 393). What this version of a 'parentocracy' asserts is the rights of individual parents: 'the opportunity to get a "good" education lies with how "powerful" the parents are, in the sense of being equipped with educational knowledge and the ability to act on it' (Crozier 2000: 4). However, in the later phases of the

Conservative administrations, the responsibilities of parents were also addressed.

The Conservatives were keen to involve parents in educational processes. This would ensure that schools and teachers were kept accountable. It would also mean that parents would have to take on more individual responsibilities; responsibilities for choosing on behalf of their own children and protecting their own interests. If the state were responsible for providing education, schools, curriculum, assessment mechanisms and teachers trained to 'deliver' all this, parents were now individually responsible for 'choosing well' and ensuring that their children were successful within the educational system.

Responsible parents and home–school partnerships

With regard to parent–school relationships, New Labour has continued what Crozier (2000: 7) calls a 'two-pronged' approach. One aspect of this is to continue to make schools and teachers accountable to parents through monitoring and reporting on their work and the second prong is an emphasis on parents taking on more responsibility for their children's learning (Whitty et al. 1998). Crozier (2000) and Reay (2005) have summarized these New Labour policy imperatives that include: ensuring that parents make their children attend school regularly, ensuring that parents make their children do some homework, ensuring that parents support their children's academic progress and ensuring that parents take on more responsibility for their children's behaviour. For example, Jack Straw (when Home Secretary) advocated that parents whose children were continually disruptive might need to attend compulsory parenting classes. Gradually, a different 'tone' started to creep into parent policy. Research was suggesting that 'problems' of social order, control and even 'degeneracy and decay' were still evident in urban settings. Concerns about drug and alcohol related offences, high levels of school truancy, high teenage pregnancy rates and even so-called 'feral' youths, for example, combined to produce a 'moral panic' about (some) working-class parents (feckless, lazy mothers and absent fathers) and their children, reflecting some of the typifications of working-class families that had been generated in the nineteenth century. In consequence, parental policy took a new turn. David Blunkett, when Secretary of State for Education, argued that:

> When there is a problem it is all too often because parents claim not to have the time, because they have disengaged from their children's education or because ... they lack even the basic parenting skills ... So far from being a nanny state, we must become an enabling state, which ensures that parents and families have the backing when they need it. (in Carvel 1998, cited in Crozier 2000: 8)

One immediate consequence of this speech was that New Labour set up classes to support parents in supporting the literacy and numeracy strategies in primary schools. Another outcome was the development of statutory home–school agreements that laid out roles and responsibilities for both sides as well as sanctions if relations broke down (DfEE 1998a). Implicit in all these policy enactments was the construction of the 'good' parent and the 'bad' parent. The 'good' parent would be seen by the school as the parent who fell in with their suggestions and became active and responsible in supporting the work of the school. The 'bad' parent would be 'uncooperative' or 'demanding'.

It is widely accepted that good home–school relations enhance children's progression in school. However, what is contentious is the nature of these relationships or 'partnerships'. It is evident from our earlier chapters and much of the published research (Vincent 1996; Crozier 2000; Vincent 2000; Crozier and Reay 2005) that although educational professionals recognize the need to involve parents, this relationship is not always straightforward. Schools may appear to parents to be 'full of adults, with their expertise and incomprehensible jargon, apparently waiting to make judgements of their child and implicitly on their parenting' (Beresford and Hardie 1996: 140). Parents might seem to be 'difficult', elusive, disorganized and sometimes antagonistic to the school. And yet, individual parents have to assume greater responsibility for choosing, for supporting their child and for working with the school. As we have already suggested, some parents might have less capacity to take on these additional responsibilities. What are the consequences of a culture of individualism and consumerism and a 'strategy of responsibilisation' (Crozier 2000: 6) for the parents of children who attend urban primary schools?

Parents as consumers

In terms of patterns of consumption, the research into parental choice of secondary school shows a strong relationship between social class and the ability to gain educational advantage through the opportunities that the free market has to offer (Butler and Robson 2003). Parental choice has emerged 'as a major new factor in maintaining and indeed reinforcing social class divisions and inequalities' (Gewirtz et al. 1995: 55). Parental choice research has highlighted another classed difference: that is, the choices made by working-class families and their children tend to be localized. As Gewirtz et al. (1995: 47) found in their study, working-class parents tended to be more concerned with 'facilities, distance, safety, convenience and locality' rather than selecting a school with 'good' examination results. Working-class children themselves tended to have a greater say in choosing their secondary school (Maguire 1995; Wooldridge 1997). Reay and Lucey (2003), in their research into children choosing a secondary school, found that 'educational destinies are tied to geography' (2003: 123). Children want to be with their friends, remain with their peers and therefore they go to the local secondary school. Reay and Lucey (2003) argue that for many working-class choosers '"good" schools were seen to be beyond the horizons; out of reach both physically and psychically' (2003: 125). Thus, parents whose children attend urban primary schools are substantially more likely to select local urban secondary schools for their children. Localism rather than market-driven 'choice' is more likely to typify the consumption patterns of working class urban parents.

Parents as partners – factors of class

The opportunity to choose a primary and secondary school is one key area of involvement but it is only one element of how parents act as participants and decision makers in the education of their children. Reay (1996; 1998a) conducted extensive research into how parents from different social classes engage with their children's education on a day-to-day basis. She carried out in-depth interviews with two sets of parents from very different urban primary schools in London. One of the schools, Milner, was a multi-ethnic school with a majority of working-class parents while Oak Park, only three miles away, was predominantly white, serving a largely middle-class community. What Reay discovered was that the contribution of parents to their children's education varied enormously along class lines between the two schools. Middle-class parents from Oak Park spent a great deal of time and money supplementing their child's education through private tutors and music teachers.

Working-class parents, by way of contrast, had different considerations. One parent described how she found it difficult to hear her child read in the evenings when she was so depressed about her financial situation. Reay (1996) summarizes the situation succinctly by concluding: 'Relative affluence provides the freedom not to be preoccupied with how each £10 is spent' (1996: 583). When it came to out-of-school activities, in some cases, middle-class parents were spending up to £100 a week for their primary-aged children to attend classes in dance, drama, music, art and poetry as well as maths and English. Reay (1998a) notes that some middle-class parents were spending almost as much on extra tuition for their children as some working-class mothers were receiving in total (1998a: 15). Reay noted some examples of working-class mothers organizing and arranging supplementary tuition; however, these were far less frequent and in some cases had to be abandoned when these mothers realized they could no longer afford the fees.

Middle-class parents have a distinct advantage over their working-class counterparts and better-off parents have always had the capacity to buy educational advantage for their children by providing additional tutoring while also being able to spend more time assisting with reading and homework. Reay (1998a) argues that, more recently, middle-class parents have been far more adept at exploiting enhanced parental rights under recent legislative changes described earlier. This is not to say that working-class parents were unaware of their role as consumers. Rather, they felt they were unable to use it as effectively as middle-class parents. For example, the mothers at Oak Park often approached teachers or sent letters asking for explanations of why things were taught, demanding that more homework be set, lessons be delivered in a more formal style or more computation occur in maths lessons. Meanwhile, at Milner Primary School, Reay found no examples of parents writing letters, although there were a few examples of parents who had asked teachers either to teach a more formal curriculum or to set homework. However, mothers at Milner did not have much success with this while those at Oak Park succeeded in radically altering the way their children were taught.

Not only were middle-class mothers at Oak Park able to affect the content and delivery of the curriculum, they were able to determine the future of one of the teachers. Reay notes that 'middle-class parents in the school had already mobilized successfully as a pressure group to remove a teacher who they felt was not offering a sufficiently academic curriculum' (1998a: 22). This example highlights the way in which middle-class mothers were confident, skilled and effective in supporting their own individual children in the educational race. So at Oak Park, 'partnership' tended to mean that parents had more capacity to control the relationship; 'the power to define lay more often with the parents than the teachers' (Reay 1998a: 123). At Milner, parents were only viewed 'in terms of their "nuisance factor" not as a threat' (1996: 585).

What seems certain is that middle-class parents are more able to exploit their rights to directly influence their children's schooling. Indeed, according to Vincent and Martin (2000: 465), it is almost as though middle-class parents recognize 'the monitoring and surveillance of their child's progress as a key part of their relationship with the school'. Vincent (2001) summarizes the situation by stating that:

> Middle-class parents can call on resources of social, cultural and economic capital in order to exercise their voice over education issues. Working-class parents, often lacking the sense of entitlement to act, and often the same degree of knowledge of the education system are more likely to be dependent on professionals. (2001: 21)

In relation to parents of children at urban primary schools such as Milner, it seems that they may be less likely to become involved in the work of school, sometimes because of lack of time and the demands of managing their circumstances. Even where they do become involved, they may be more prone to being 'fobbed off' by teachers (Reay 1998a: 118) or to being regarded as uncooperative and a 'hindrance rather than as partners in the process of education' (Roffey 2002: 18). They may even find themselves being 'blamed' for some of the consequences of living in circumstances of relative poverty. They may also have had less than positive experiences of education themselves and they may have less knowledge of and confidence in dealing with educational professionals (Hillman 1996).

Parents as partners – factors of 'race'

When we come to explore the experiences that black and other minority ethnic parents report of their relationships with mainstream schools, Crozier (2005) claims parental anxieties about schooling often start long before the children go to school. Parents in her studies reported being worried about the possibilities of racism and the impact this could have on their children. Many parents were aware of reports about black underachievement and higher levels of exclusion from school. All this fuelled their concerns. When their children started school, they invariably reported perceptions that their views were not taken into account. Some parents reported that schools held lower expectations of their children. For these reasons, some parents in Crozier's studies (2000) reported that they had struggled to pay for their children to go to private schools. Many of the parents 'expressed anxiety regarding the treatment of their primary school aged children' (Crozier 2005: 44) and were anxious that racism and discrimination might not always be recognized, understood and dealt with. Blair (2001: 38) states that 'parents talk about being "talked down to" by teachers, and generally treated, on the basis of their colour and class, as second-class citizens'. It is worth reporting the views of a black supplementary school teacher in the study undertaken by Reay and Safia-Mirza (2005: 149):

> Our parents feel very strongly that they are not listened to. The education system has a very long history of keeping parents out . . . I think it's part of that history, you know, 'We're the teachers, we know best.' It's partly to do with class but it is also because whenever they see Black parents opening their mouths they see them as creating discord or problems.

As Blair (2001: 37) has commented: 'Teachers sometimes assume that black parents are aggressive and this makes them feel intimidated, thus hindering their ability to relate to black parents.'

Wright et al. (2000), in their study of black exclusions in secondary schools, point out that policy changes that emphasize attainment in national tests, for example, can mean that other questions such as curriculum appropriateness, or even pastoral care issues, can get sidelined. In these managerialist times, schools may come to see some children as more or less 'deserving' of teacher time and attention. Some children may be harder to reach and harder to teach. These children, predominantly white and black working-class boys, may, therefore, be more prone to exclusions from their schools (Wright et al. 2000). In cases where primary school-aged children are permanently excluded they may well find themselves placed in another local urban primary school that has vacancies. In consequence, some urban schools may well be attempting to deal with a higher than average number of children with complex social, emotional and behavioural needs. In a context with higher staff turnover and less income flow, it might be more difficult to respond appropriately to parents and children – particularly in a school that has a great deal to do in terms of meeting its learning targets as well. Parents who have already experienced one breakdown in home–school partnerships through exclusion may now find themselves being 'blamed' by a second school that could perhaps be less well resourced (both financially and in terms of human resources) to respond in a sensitive and supportive manner.

New Labour and parents

When New Labour was elected to power in 1997, it immediately set about promoting social inclusion and what the then Secretary of State for

Education, David Blunkett, called 'excellence for the many not just the few' (cited in Gewirtz 2001: 365). New Labour produced a set of reforms focused on disadvantaged areas. These included the expansion of pre-school education and the setting up of Sure Start (DfEE 1999b), which concentrated on helping families with young children. It included parental advice and support, as well as services to support play. In addition, New Labour reduced class sizes in the early years of compulsory education and introduced the literacy and numeracy strategies. New Labour has also attempted to reduce structural inequalities through policies such as the reinsertion of the minimum wage and family tax credits. As Whitty (2002: 120) observed of these policies: 'Schools matter but so do families and communities and it is encouraging that the problems that many poor families encounter in providing appropriate educational support are at last being properly recognized.'

New Labour launched a 'Parents' centre' on its website and also publishes a magazine called *Parents and Schools*. Gewirtz (2001) argues that New Labour parental policies stem from a position that sees working-class parents as having less knowledge of the educational system and fewer material advantages than middle-class families. Their policies are, therefore, aimed at providing more knowledge, which Gewirtz believes is a reasonable ambition, but are also aimed at 're-socializing working-class parents'. She believes that this second part of the project continues to pathologize working-class families while also oversimplifying the values and parenting of middle-class families.

Gewirtz (2001) examined a wide range of DfES advice and recommendations to parents and maintains that there is a strategy that 'aims to eradicate class differences by reconstructing and transforming working-class parents into middle-class ones. Excellence for the many is to be achieved, at least in part, by making the many behave like the few' (2001: 366). She argues that working-class parents are being urged to be more active choosers of their children's schools. Advice concerning what to look for in a school and how to evaluate performance tables is given prominence on websites and in official literature and is clearly aimed at those parents who are not yet fully involved. Gewirtz identifies the drive to 'promote' and extend the social capital of working-class families as deeply woven into these parenting policies. The social capital that is extended in community and family networks can support and 'at least to a limited extent, counteract material disadvantage' (Whitty 2002: 116). 'Sure Start aims to build for parents in areas designated as disadvantaged the kinds of intra-famility and community social capital that middle-class parents are assumed to be able to exploit' (Gewirtz 2001: 271–2).

Gewirtz argues that the current approach towards improving parental participation by New Labour, as contained in its policies, and as reflected in its publications and on the DfES website, seem to be shoring up a simplistic and polarized view of working-class (and indeed middle-class) parents. In relation to working-class parents, she argues that there is at least one alternative viewpoint: that is to recognize the activism of many black and white working-class parents, who have struggled and campaigned for better resources and against the 'racist assumptions of a white-dominated education system' (Gewirtz 2001: 376). One of the dangers of the 'oversimplified view' of working-class families that is reproduced in New Labour's policy lexicon, is that it fuels a 'deficit' approach that may be then unwittingly reflected in teacher education programmes or taken up uncritically by those who work in urban primary schools. A second major point made by Gewirtz is that the factors that prevent parents from becoming more involved in their children's schooling, 'poverty, stress, ill-health and poor living conditions' (2001: 36), are simply not mentioned in many of the New Labour approaches towards enhancing 'partnerships' in schools.

Towards better partnerships

Crozier and Reay have offered a number of suggestions as to what teachers could do to improve relationships between home and school. As they put it, although home–school relationships 'do not lend themselves to a wish list of quick fixes ... there are still things schools can do to lessen inequalities' (Crozier and Reay 2005: 158–9). These include 'developing forums in which less privileged parents have a voice' (2005: 158) and becoming involved in 'lifelong learning' programmes to provide support for parents wishing to be more involved in their children's learning. In addition, they suggest that teachers should write newsletters and provide a regular time each week to talk to parents. Schools need to train administrative staff to deal appropriately with parents, and schools need to ensure there are always adequate bilingual assistants available to translate. Blair (2001: 38), drawing on a case study of one school that was 'successful' for black children, identified similar strategies. She stated:

> The most effective ways of gaining the parents' support and cooperation was to listen to their concerns, consult them about and give them a voice on important issues, both pastoral and academic, and perhaps most importantly, show them respect by acting on their concerns and not merely involving them in a tokenistic way.

In this chapter, we have started from the assumption that good home–school relationships, or partnerships, are important in children's development. In the early years of schooling and during the primary phase, parents will tend to be more directly involved, delivering and collecting their children to and from school on a daily basis and participating in various home–school curriculum partnerships. In some ways, these 'easy links' might lead to a sense of complacency that all is well.

In contrast, what has been argued in this chapter is that the rhetoric of 'partnership' can sometimes mask uncomfortable dilemmas. Some parents find it harder to approach the school and may feel that their concerns are 'fobbed off' or ignored. Parents might not understand why certain practices are being employed, for example, learning through play, and may not feel confident or assertive enough to question the teacher. Some parents might not feel comfortable or even welcome in their child's school. For example, black parents in Birmingham reported that they were more often involved in conversations with teachers about their children's behaviour than their school work (Cork 2005). Simultaneously, teachers might feel threatened by some parents and might misinterpret interest as aggression. Teachers may want to feel that they are in control in their classrooms and that their expertise is not being called into question by parents who have not completed any specialist training in education. For some parents in acutely difficult circumstances, anxiety and depression might fuel tensions that flare up when they come to school to talk about their children. For these sorts of reasons, as well as differences such as social class and/or ethnicity between teachers and parents, partnerships might not be that easy to realize in practice (Roffey 2002).

Conclusion

The urban primary school is the setting where many of these tensions and contradictions are played out. As we saw in the two previous chapters, urban headteachers and urban teachers acknowledge the centrality of working effectively with their parents. But what this can mean in practice is often less certain. Teachers in difficult situations may well take up well-established 'deficit' discourses about parenting, perhaps as part of self-maintenance. As we saw also in the earlier chapters, teachers identified relationships with parents as one of the biggest challenges they faced in their urban primary schools. Parents may well feel that teachers 'blame' them and exclude them from decisions about their children. Teachers may feel undermined or unsupported, particularly if there are other pressures, such as shortages of staff, bearing down on their working lives. Teachers quite simply might just not have been adequately prepared to work with parents at all.

Some of the high-stakes interactions between parents and teachers, such as dealing with challenging behaviours or working with young children 'at risk' of exclusion from school, are far more likely to occur in urban settings. Building 'partnerships' is always going to be complex, particularly in settings where one person or group is seen to have more power and influence than the other. Building and sustaining relationships between urban teachers, who may be experiencing high levels of stress, and parents, who may also be experiencing high levels of tension in trying to cope with the pressures of daily life, is a demanding task.

While research into home–school relationships is not overly 'optimistic' (Crozier and Reay 2005: 160), 'each school will have a different set of circumstances and issues to deal with' and these will impinge on home–school relationships. The distinctiveness of urban primary schools may well generate more 'high-stake' interactions. In turn, these interactions could produce more forms of what Gewirtz calls 'active parenting' where black and white working-class parents could work together with their local schools to challenge some aspects of education policy that work against their interests.

Questions

1. To what extent do you think 'partnership' between parents and teachers is possible in the urban primary school? What gets in the way?
2. What more can be done in urban primary schools to promote better home–school relationships?
3. What can schools and teachers do to gain the support of parents from minority ethnic backgrounds?

6

SUPPORTING DIVERSITY

Social identities are forged out of complex interplays between a variety of factors such as age, 'race', ethnicity, class, gender, (dis)abilities, sexualities, faiths as well as the places in which we live. Some aspects of diversity, particularly those related to culture and ethnicity, are more likely to characterize inner city urban classrooms and these provide the focus for this chapter. In the chapter, we start with a discussion of inner city diversity and we explore some of the ways in which diversity and social identity have been conceptualized. We then examine research that illustrates the need to avoid over-generalizations and categorizations in relation to children and teachers in inner city schools. All schools need to respect and recognize the diverse social identities that are present in the school community and in society at large in order to provide a supportive and inclusive environment for learning.

Space, place and diversity

Before we focus directly on diversity, it is necessary to return to the role of space and place and the part these play in shaping patterns of social differentiation. Unlike the USA, where racialized locations characterize many of the major cities (Bashi and Hughes 1997), in the UK socio-spatial differentiation is regulated largely, but not wholly, by social class. In many ways, this is not surprising. Home ownership and other patterns of housing tenure decide settlement patterns in most European cities and housing is directly related to income distribution. But other factors are also implicated in where people live. For example, currently many new arrivals to the UK will settle in the southeast. This is due to the geography of where key airports and coastal ports are located as well as the desire to settle near friends or members of the family or communities who may already be in the UK. It is also due, in part, to the potential prospect of immediate employment in the large service sector. For these sorts of reasons, many refugees and asylum seekers settle in the London area, although recent policies of dispersal mean that this pattern is starting to change and families are being housed across the UK (Rutter 2003).

Historically, new arrivals to the UK have initially settled in major conurbations where housing and work were more readily available and where the communities established meeting centres, supplementary schools and places of worship. However, the settlement pattern in the UK in the late twentieth century has become more complex and diverse. While most communities initially settle in 'locales of concentration' (Byrne 2001: 124) many of these tend to disperse over time as middle-class families move out to the suburbs or into areas of gentrification. Other communities have tended to stay closer together rather than dispersing; for example, the Sylheti community in Tower Hamlets (Byrne 1998). These diverse patterns of settlement in areas that typically experience high levels of population mobility, generally in older working-class areas of the city, are reflected in the intake of many urbanized primary schools.

The intake of some urban primary schools may be characterized by the dominance of one community, for example the 'traditional white working class' of Newcastle and Manchester (Power and Mumford 1999) or the Bangladeshi community in Tower Hamlets. Other urban primary schools are characterized by high levels of heterogeneity. For example, Johnson (2003) has identified that children in London schools speak over 275 different languages, although it is important to recognize that many of the minority ethnic communities in urban locations are second and third-generation black British citizens. The key feature shared by all these urban primary schools is that they serve a predominantly working-class community. In the UK, as we have already argued, social class position frequently becomes conflated with housing provision. Typically, poorer families become housed alongside one another, frequently in poorer housing stock, often provided by local councils. These localized communities will send their children, in the main, to the local urban primary schools that serve their particular area.

We have already argued that in using the construction of 'urban' to signify the focus of this book, we want to ensure that we are including primary schools that serve the 'urban poor' (Grace 1994: 45), wherever they are situated. However, in much of this chapter we will be mainly referring to inner city primary schools – schools located in the cities. This is because, in this chapter, our focus is on cultural and ethnically constituted diversity. It is also because many groups thus designated mainly work and live in inner cities rather than elsewhere. In this chapter, we will also use the term 'minority ethnic', as this is currently the way in which racialized discourses related to immigrants and their descendants are reflected in policy texts and in much of the research in the area.

Diversity and social identity

Before we can start to consider the ways in which diversity can be positively supported in urban primary schools, we want to begin with a discussion of some of the conceptual issues involved in this area. Until recently, many educationalists have worked with what Mac An Ghaill (1999: 44) refers to as the 'older stable social categories, such as class and black identity'. Very often, researchers have focused on one structural attribute of diversity such as gender or 'race'/ethnicity. This approach has its uses. It has made it possible to chart the ways in which schools have been implicated in upholding and reproducing patterns and processes that exclude and oppress. For example, it has made it possible to document the fact that working-class males of African-Caribbean background have been over-represented in the numbers of children and students excluded from mainstream schools (Wright et al. 2000; Majors 2001). But, more recently, this unidimensional approach towards social identity has been called into question.

First, it has been argued that this approach contains within itself a tendency towards oversimplification and stereotyping. There could be, for example, a tendency to suggest that all black children underachieve at school (Gillborn and Mirza 2000). As research has demonstrated, the situation is frequently more complex than this essentializing and deterministic approach would suggest and other factors, such as class, gender and age, need to be considered simultaneously in relation to attainment (Gaine and George 1999). Second, a unidimensional approach lacks the theoretical capacity to explore the lived realities of complex social diversities (Shain 2003). For example, there may well be times when we are more aware of one aspect of our identities than another, for example our faith or our gender. Third, to focus on one categorization, such as 'African-Caribbean' for example, might not be precise or indeed accurate in terms of describing second and third-generation black British people who will inhabit a range of complex and hybrid identifications. Being born in Manchester and/or being gay may be equally, if not more, important to an individual who might also be described as 'African-Caribbean'. It is worth exploring this particular categorization in a little more depth, for frequently, in educational research and elsewhere, it is this group that is pathologized as 'failing'. For instance, concerns have consistently been expressed about the alleged underachievement of young working-class black males designated as African-Caribbean, although the evidence suggests that many white as well as black working-class males do less well in compulsory schooling than their middle-class peers (Gillborn and Mirza 2000). In a case like this, the continual focus on ethnicity can sometimes become interpreted as a 'reason' for underachievement in school. This 'understanding' might also distract attention away from considerations of what schools actually offer to working-class students and the part schools might unwittingly play in this process of 'underachievement' for children designated as minority ethnic (Sewell 1997).

Hall (1996: 2) has said that 'in common sense language, identification is constructed on the back of a recognition of some common origin or shared characteristics with another person or group, or with an ideal'. This perspective can be useful, as we have already stated. Demonstrating that some groups have been disproportionately excluded from decent state housing or from participating in higher education has created pressure for more socially just policies and practices (see Ginsburg 1992, for example). But there can be difficulties in assuming, on the basis of some apparent similarities, that a high degree of homogeneity exists. For example, in considering any differences in opportunities offered to females and males, we would need to explore the differences *within* these two groups as well as *between* them. Not all women have the same access to opportunities: 'race', class, sexualities and age all play a part as well.

Much of the contemporary approach towards social diversity concentrates on how claims about social categories become established and how they operate (Mac An Ghaill 1999). Social diversity is seen as 'a product of social and cultural experience' (Dillabough 2001: 21). So, rather than focusing on so-called differences between categories of children, the concern would be with what impact these categorizations might have for the children who are so identified. For example, if teachers are repeatedly exposed to claims about groups of boys who 'underachieve' in language and literacy and are exhorted to provide 'boy-friendly' support, they might not see that some of the girls in their class could benefit from this intervention (Mahony 1998). They might not recognize that some boys, in fact, do extremely well (Power et al. 2002). They might be less encouraged to recognize that the category of boys is itself differentiated by a range of factors such as class, age, ethnicity and faith. Additionally, if children themselves come to regard some identities as less/more desirable, or less or more prone to academic success, this may well have outcomes in terms of what they say, what they feel and how they behave towards one another.

Hall (1991) has recognized that social identities are complex. He claims that they are not fixed and stable; they shift over time and in different settings. They are constructed alongside and against other forms of identifications and what he calls 'otherness'. Hall uses the term 'identification' rather than identity. This is to signal that 'who you identify with, who you want to be and who you want to be with are key factors in thinking about "identities"' (Epstein et al. 2003: 121). So, for example, there will be times/places where aspects of gender will become more significant. Showing an interest in football or fashion may be important in terms of friendships and social acceptance in schools (Skelton and Francis 2003), but identification is also deeply implicated in 'who you wish to differentiate yourself from' (Epstein et al. 2003: 121). Schools are powerful places where children (and their parents and teachers) learn and are taught about identities, identifications and dis-identifications (Skeggs 1997); in other words, which identities 'count' and which do not. In these dis-identifications, some social identities may be rendered less visible, for example identifications of bilingual experience (Nieto 1999). Others are perhaps subject to forms of vilification; for example, some of the negative outcomes associated with being a refugee (Rutter 2003).

If we accept that social identifications are socially and culturally produced and that this production takes place in and through social encounters, then schools become powerful mediators of this process. In consequence, sensitivity is needed in supporting diversity and difference *within* as well as *between* various constituencies. As Gaine and George (1999: 121) argue: 'Groups often lumped together need examining separately, and even treating the subgroups identified as homogenous will be misleading and runs the risk of simply generating more sophisticated stereotypes.'

Schools need to be sensitized to the need for care in making attributions about children in relation to ways in which they are categorized. The example of boys of African-Caribbean background highlights the problems associated with this approach. However, at the same time schools and teachers do need to be able to recognize and support a wide range of diversities and differences between and among groups of children – a complex and demanding process, but one that is essential if schools are to help all children to benefit from their schooling. This is a requirement that has been endorsed in the National Curriculum (Education Act 2002).

National Curriculum and diversity

The National Curriculum now requires all teachers to take account of diversity in their work. For the first time in the UK, the National Curriculum now includes a statement on inclusion, 'which makes clear the principles schools must follow in their teaching right across the curriculum, to ensure that all pupils have the chance to succeed, whatever their individual needs and the potential barriers to their learning might be' (Education Act 2002: 3).

The National Curriculum document states that: 'Equality of opportunity is one of a broad set of common values and purposes which underpin the school curriculum and the work of schools' (Education Act 2002: 4). It adds that this principle of equality of opportunity includes valuing diversity in our society. The inclusion section of the National Curriculum documentation outlines three principles that all schools (primary and secondary) have to consider to ensure that a more inclusive curriculum is being offered. These are: setting suitable learning challenges, responding to pupils' diverse needs and overcoming potential barriers to learning and assessment.

More recently, these principles for inclusion have been considered by the Teacher Training Agency (TTA) (2000), which recommends that, in responding positively to children's diverse needs, teachers need to have an awareness of equal opportunity legislation. In relation to respect for and recognition of diversity, the TTA has stated that teachers need to plan for diversity, for example, by taking into account differences in religious and cultural beliefs. The advice suggests that teachers need to use materials that are free from stereotyping, that reflect cultural and social diversity and build on children's interests and cultural experiences. At the same time, the TTA makes it clear that teachers must positively value differences and challenge stereotyping, bullying and harassment. In what follows, we will explore some of the ways in which an appropriate pedagogy needs to be developed in order to support some aspects of diversity that typify inner city primary schools, particularly in the light of the TTA's strong and clear recommendations.

Valuing and reflecting diversity in the classroom

Socially just practice in the classroom is not always a matter of treating everyone the same. There are times when the recognition of difference is essential to good practice. This approach will benefit all children. For example, this approach would include the recognition of different faith perspectives as well as a no faith perspective, something that is frequently sidelined. One good example of the need for recognition and respect for difference, as well as the sorts of complexities involved, relates to the issue of diverse linguistic communities within the inner city urban primary school setting.

As we have already said, children in London use over 275 languages. Some children may well be fluent in two or more languages, as well as English. Others may just be starting to learn English. In all these cases, the role of the teacher in supporting language development is crucial, for languages are learned through interaction and through engagement in specific contexts such as classroom routines, turn taking and dialogue (Baker 2001). Classroom practices that rely on non-verbal and individualized routines such as filling in worksheets or answering multiple-choice questions might not offer speakers of other languages an optimum context for learning English. Furthermore, they might not offer a rich learning context for English-speaking children either. What is frequently recommended, however, to support language development is the provision of 'meaningful contexts for collaborative talk' (Datta 2000: 33). In all this, the teacher–child relationship is central in helping young children move positively and confidently into what might be their second or third language. Teachers need to recognize and celebrate the fact that the children in their class (and in the region, nation and world) speak many languages and use different scripts. As Datta (2000: 36) says: 'Language awareness activities endorse every child's identity, language and culture and help create a classroom community.'

The advantages of recognizing and including multilinguality in the primary classroom can be shared by all the children and their teachers and parents: 'Such sharing of experience energizes every child to develop a voice in culturally diverse classrooms, and motivation to learn is high' (Datta 2000: 238). Recognition can be achieved through the range of resources that are used, such as bilingual and multilingual texts and music, stories and poetry representing a wide range of cultural settings. Drawing on a wide range of cultural contexts to extend the curriculum can usefully expose all children in school to the diversity in society. However, schools also need to be sensitive to the wider social context where some languages are seen to have currency (and are included in the National Curriculum in the secondary school) while others are devalued and perhaps not even recognized, for example various Creoles or types of black English (Harris and Leung 2001). Inclusive language work is not just a matter of providing a range of resources, it involves supporting their inclusion and challenging any negative responses to this work.

At the same time, it is important not to make assumptions about language use on the basis of inferred and perhaps stereotyped perspectives related to ethnic origin. Children are also actively shaping new hybrid cultures for themselves – cultures that also need to be reflected in school (Pavlenko and

Blackledge 2004). They are 'at one and the same time aligned to both UK/English/British ethnic identities and those associated with other global locations' (Harris and Leung 2001: 211). In linguistic terms, this could, for example, involve drawing on the children's expertise and fluency in various types of black English or other local varieties of vernacular English. Harris (1999) argues that teachers need to appreciate that many children designated as speaking 'English as an additional language' (EAL) may be more comfortable with a local urban spoken vernacular than with a 'community' language more associated with their grandparents, for example. Some children might switch between their 'community' language and local vernacular Englishes, but as with some of their white British peers, might share some difficulties in writing. Other children, meanwhile, will have a high degree of spoken and written proficiency in a 'community' language as well as English. Harris (1999) warns of what he terms as 'romantic bilingualism' – where teachers may see their children as possessing 'expertise in and allegiance to any community languages with which they have some acquaintance' (Harris 1997: 14). What all these points highlight is the need for sensitivity as well as informed understandings of linguistic diversity in the urban classroom that start with a grounded appreciation of the children's experiences and perspectives. These points apply equally to diversity in religious and cultural beliefs.

Religious and cultural belief systems are complex aspects of human life and are areas that may also be susceptible to stereotyping, oversimplification and inaccurate representation. It is important to realize that, as with all aspects of diversity, there can be dangers of essentializing particular groups based on their faith, for example, displacing other dimensions of complexity, fluidity and hybridity. One strand of identification that illustrates these enactments of exclusion occurs around some of the current positionings associated with being a Muslim. In the light of current world affairs, being identified as Muslim can have consequences in terms of various exclusions and dis-identifications, regardless of complex historical formations and theological distinctions within Islam. For youths and adults, this may involve more 'stop and searches' on the streets (Alexander 2002). For children in the playground, this identification might elicit bullying and harassment (Archer 2003; Shain 2003). The school has a responsibility to accurately reflect and represent different perspectives, by drawing on experts other than teachers for support in this work if necessary, and through ensuring that materials used in the classroom are accurate and up to date in what they say. Valuing and reflecting diversity in the urban classroom is not just an issue of providing the 'right' resources or the 'correct' information, it is fundamentally concerned with respect for persons. This means that racism or racialized harassment and bullying must be challenged and dealt with promptly (Shain 2003).

Inequality and social identity in school

Social diversity, social identities and identifications are constructions. That is, they are shaped by and through the society in which they are situated and they are learned in social settings (Burr 1995). They shift and change over time and place. Schools may often become prime sites for the production of normalized identity constructions such as the 'good girl or boy' (Walkerdine et al. 2001). Although these identifications will be struggled with/against, the crucial element in their construction is that they are 'more the product of the marking of difference and exclusion, than they are the sign of an identical, naturally-constituted entity' (Hall 1996: 4). In terms of the production and maintenance of racialized and ethnicized identifications in schooling, many studies have identified the impact of racisms in schooling and the ways in which children identified as 'other' have been marginalized, bullied and excluded (Gaine and George 1999; Wright et al. 2000).

Phoenix (2001) argues that very few studies have concentrated on cases where racism (even if unintended) has impacted on very young children in the early years (but see Connolly 2003). She highlights a study in a nursery setting in Scotland (Ogilvy et al. 1992) that detailed how teachers responded more to white Scottish children's needs for attention than other children designated as 'Asian'. Phoenix also focused on the well-known work of Wright (1992) that found that teachers had categorized and stereotyped 'Asian' children as having language problems but as being hard-working and polite. Wright (1992) found that children of African-Caribbean heritage, boys in particular, were often seen by teachers as more likely to present challenging behaviours and were more likely to be reprimanded for behaviours that were also exhibited by white children in the class but not acknowledged by the teachers. These examples suggest that where the teacher holds some 'common sense' assumptions about racialized/ethnicized groups, these could lead to socially unjust practices in the classroom. We recognize that it could be argued that these studies are old and that practice has moved on. We would suggest, however, that it is worth exploring the work on the exclusion of black children from school in a little more depth because here we see evidence of inequality that has been consistent and has persisted over a long period of time.

Studies continue to reveal that black children, particularly boys, are disproportionately excluded from school (Majors 2001). One argument in the research suggests that, in some cases, boys have continued to be excluded from school because they have retaliated against racist harassment and racial bullying left unchallenged by the school (Ofsted 1993; Kinder et al. 1996). This 'oversight' on the part of some schools is deeply troubling. It suggests that some children in schools have been taunting and verbally abusing children who have been minoritized and categorized as 'other'. It also suggests that teachers might not always be even-handed in their responses towards children who are 'othered' in this way (Wright et al. 2000). Simultaneously, the statistics on black exclusions might also work to alert teachers to the 'fact' that children, boys especially, from particular groups, are more prone to challenging behaviour. In addition, what this might well do is sideline any concerns about girls and exclusion from schools (Osler and Vincent 2003). It might also sideline the evidence that shows it is mainly working-class children and children designated as having 'special educational needs' who are disproportionately excluded.

So, what we are suggesting is that schools need to ensure that any categorizations or 'marking out' of difference is not a lever for exclusion but a recognition and respect for specific needs. To put it even more powerfully, schools need to ensure that bullying and harassment, of all types, are challenged – in terms of immediate responses to incidents and by longer-term work in promoting respect for diversity (Siraj-Blatchford 1994; May 1999; Epstein et al. 2003).

Responding to diverse needs – children categorized as refugees

This need for recognition and respect can be powerfully illustrated in relation to the needs of refugees and asylum seekers. From what we already know, the majority of refugee children and their families are settled or awaiting settlement in urban locales. More than 65,000 refugee children live in the UK and about 80 per cent of these children live in London (Menter et al. 2000: 209). It is worth clarifying what is meant by the terms 'refugee' and 'asylum seeker'. "The term refugee means someone who has a 'well-founded fear of being persecuted for reasons of 'race', religion, nationality, membership in a particular social group and political opinion' and who cannot be protected in the country of their nationality" (1951 Geneva Convention). An asylum seeker is someone who has applied for refugee status and is awaiting a decision on their right to stay in the UK.

Schools need to recognize that 'refugee children' are diverse and have different experiences. The age of the children, their previous educational experiences, the languages they speak and their proficiency in English will influence their progression at school. In addition, schools will need to be aware that some of the children will be currently experiencing problems and anxieties around issues such as accommodation, safety of family members and racism from the wider community. Schools can do much to ensure that children are sensitively and carefully inducted into their new school. There is a need for sensitive and careful teaching that draws positively on the children's cultural and linguistic experiences in a non-stereotyped way. However, as with our earlier discussion of respect and support for diversity, the fundamental issue relates to an approach that is inclusive and based on an appreciation of human rights:

> The ways in which schools respond to refugee children are likely to be indicative of the way in which a school relates to all its pupils – treating them as individuals each with their own particular need and each with an enormous potential for contributing to the life of the school, its teachers and pupils. It is essential that the diverse cultural backgrounds are acknowledged and that the languages which refugee children bring into a school are treated as additional assets rather than as problems. (Menter et al. 2000: 227)

Teachers, diversity and social identity

So far in this chapter we have concentrated on some of the key reasons why all schools, but particularly urban schools, need to understand and respect diversity. Our approach has centred on the diversity that characterizes some of the children who attend inner city schools. Now we want to turn to consider teachers, diversity and social identity issues. One major concern relates to the under-representation of teachers from minority ethnic backgrounds in the UK and elsewhere (Gordon 2000). As early as 1985 in the UK, the Swann Report highlighted the under-representation of minority ethnic teachers as a matter of national concern. It was argued then, as now, that school staff profiles needed to reflect the diversity of a multi-ethnic/racial society (Siraj-Blatchford 1993). It was recognized that teachers of minority ethnic background are well placed in helping to promote tolerance and in supporting minority ethnic children, students and their families (Tomlinson 1990). Teachers from minority groups can enhance the development '(of white children) in a multi-cultural world' (Gordon 2000: 2). In the light of long-standing concerns about the educational performance of (some) minority ethnic children in the UK (Gillborn and Gipps 1996; Gillborn and Mirza 2000), it has frequently been suggested that the recruitment of more teachers of minority ethnic background is essential in raising the achievement of minority children and students. While this approach could be said to typify what we have called a one-dimensional approach towards identity, an approach that we have criticized earlier in this chapter, generally, policy-makers and schools have accepted the view that people from a minority ethnic heritage have a positive and affirming contribution to make to education provision (DfEE 1998b).

For some time it has been acknowledged that the interaction between white children and their parents with teachers of minority ethnic origin can help to eradicate racism (Tomlinson 1990). Further, the education system benefits from the multilingual expertise of some minority ethnic teachers, their understandings of racisms and their ability to act as advocates in school settings (Carrington and Skelton 2003). However, research conducted over time has consistently demonstrated that the numbers of minority ethnic recruits to teaching are lower than would be expected in relation to the demographics of the UK. Ross (2001) has estimated that, nationally, less than 5 per cent of teachers may be depicted as coming from minority ethnic backgrounds. In contrast, he notes that almost 13 per cent of the English school population can be described in this way. It is evident that under-representation in the teaching profession presents a challenge to policy-makers and for schools. Additionally, it might be the case that if there are few teachers of minority ethnic descent, and even fewer in senior positions (Osler 1997), this might also inhibit future minority recruitment. Teaching might not look as if it offers an inclusive occupation or career for people of minority ethnic descent.

In a range of empirical studies, minority ethnic trainee teachers have repeatedly reported that they believe themselves to be treated less favourably than their peers from the majority group (Jones et al. 1997; Roberts et al.

2002). Carrington et al. (2001) note that in their study of PGCE trainees, out of 149 trainees from minority ethnic backgrounds in their study, 41 per cent claimed that they had been 'anxious' about the reception they might receive from school staff during placement, in respect of their ethnicity. A similar proportion (36 per cent) agreed with the proposition that trainees from minority ethnic backgrounds experience problems during training that are different from those faced by white students and around one quarter reported that they had encountered incidents of racism in their placement schools. Some minority ethnic students report being caught up in a dilemma related to their social identifications in school; they can sometimes be regarded as 'experts' on all matters to do with 'race' or they are supposed to be 'better' at dealing with minority students (Jones et al. 1998). This is a complex issue that needs more interrogation than is possible here, but it can mean that some minority ethnic trainees face:

> [H]eavy responsibility and many black teachers find the burden great when they lose their individuality and become, consciously or unconsciously, seen as representatives for black people generally. White teachers retain a certain degree of individuality and their performance is perceived as being that of an individual with strengths and weaknesses.
> (Robbins 1995: 19)

Many trainee teachers now spend the majority of their training period in school and thus, the school experience frequently becomes the most important part of becoming a teacher. In these new 'partnerships' between schools and higher education institutions, sometimes 'scant' attention is paid to issues of equal opportunities and social justice (Blair and Bourdillon 1997). In many of the small-scale studies on minority ethnic trainee views of teacher education, it is the school placement that has caused the most concern (Robbins 1995; Jones et al. 1997; Jones et al. 1998). Some minority ethnic trainees have reported that some schools showed little sensitivity towards cultural difference or respect for religious diversity (Roberts et al. 2002). Other minority ethnic trainees have suggested that the placement locale itself has sometimes been problematic; sometimes they have been placed in complex and challenging multi-racial urban schools because they have been 'ethnically matched' even though their social class positions have not prepared them for these schools. Furthermore, placements in all-white schools with an all-white staff have sometimes meant that minority ethnic trainee teachers have felt isolated (Jones et al. 1998).

A Teacher Training Agency (TTA)-funded project that concentrated on the induction experiences of newly qualified teachers (NQTs) from minority ethnic groups (McNamara et al. 2002; Roberts et al. 2002) found that sometimes children who were not familiar with teachers other than those of their own ethnic group reacted to their presence in what the researchers called 'bemused' ways. The NQTs from minority ethnic backgrounds believed that they could act as role models and were in a position to challenge some of the stereotypes sometimes ascribed to people of minority ethnic heritage. Some trainees argued that their ethnicity afforded them an insight into social, cultural and religious issues. However, the biggest benefit of being a teacher from a minority ethnic group was thought to be the ability to communicate with minority ethnic parents in schools. Nevertheless, others believed that they faced disadvantages because of their ethnic background, notably the negative attitude of some colleagues and some parents (Roberts et al. 2002). Overall, what this study, and others in the area, point to is the need for sensitivity and care in relation to the social diversity and identities of all those who work in schools. To this we would want to add parents, carers and all those connected with the life of the school.

Conclusion

What we have tried to do in this chapter is to highlight some of the key attributes of diversity that make a distinctive contribution to working in the inner city primary classroom: 'Urban areas have a much higher concentration of low-income households ... urban areas are also far more culturally and ethnically diverse than the rest of England' (DfEE 2005: 7). At the same time, particularly through the example of linguistic diversity, we have tried to indicate some of the complex and sometimes contradictory issues involved in recognizing and supporting diversity in inner city primary classrooms. Many schools have taken their responsibilities seriously in this area and have worked hard to respect cultural and ethnic diversity and challenge racism. As Gillborn (2001: 24) recognizes, although national policies have never tackled racism and 'race' inequality directly, there have been pockets of good anti-racist practice'. However, in the current policy context, even though the National Curriculum talks of celebrating and supporting diversity, and the Teacher Training Agency makes it clear that teachers and schools must challenge and tackle racism, the competing demands of the need to raise attainment may sometimes marginalize this need. Some primary schools may feel pressured into focusing on literacy and numeracy without appreciating how respecting and including aspects related to diversity could sustain and extend this aspect of their work.

In this chapter, we have stressed that social and cultural diversities are constructions and identifications that are (re)produced in schools by teachers and also by the children. These identifications and attributions of identity will sometimes play a role in making decisions about resource allocations; which children get additional support or not; which children are regarded as 'gifted and talented' or not; which children are seen as more or less prone to 'acting out' behaviours. In recognizing the powerful outcomes of some forms of identifications and attributions, schools may be able to work more constructively towards a socially just pedagogy. The challenge of supporting diversity in urban classrooms and schools is as much to do with a sensitivity towards recognizing when a difference requires a focused response, for example, in the provision of texts in a community language or when a difference is being distorted into a stereotype that may result in exclusion or oppression (Hey et al. 1998; Brown 2004). By recognizing the distinction, schools might be better placed to challenge normalized identifications and interrupt and change some of the excluding practices and identifications that cause so much pain and harm in schools and in society.

Questions

1 What can be done in the white urban primary school to reflect diversity and difference found in the wider society?
2 How could teachers from minority ethnic backgrounds be better supported in training and in career progression?
3 What sort of tactics could schools employ to ensure that the playgrounds and other less supervised school spaces are free from bullying and harassment?

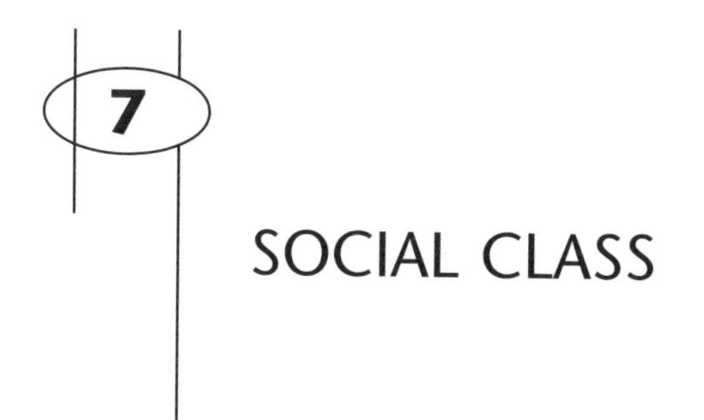

SOCIAL CLASS

In this chapter, we explore the ways in which educational provision has historically been constructed as a classed project. The chapter deals substantively with the consequences of different forms of choosing and the impact these choices have in relation to factors of social class in urban primary schools. We also consider the way in which some aspects of current policies aimed at urban schools may actually be reinforcing forms of internal differentiation and propping up class divisions rather than promoting the common good.

Introduction

In the first chapter of this book, we argued that the provision of state schooling was initially aimed at 'gentling' and 'civilizing' the urban working classes. The Victorian buildings that housed the first state-provided elementary schools, and which still stand in many of our inner cities, were designed to represent churches – churches in the city. These tall buildings dominated their local skylines with their distinctive church-like windows – too high for little children to look out of and become distracted from their work – and they stood as 'landmarks of working class education' (Hall 1977: 11). Their symbolic meaning was clear – they were bringing salvation (of a sort) but at a price: the subordination of one class culture and the celebration of another. These early elementary board schools and council schools were central to this 'civilizing' and classed project. Elementary schools were designed for working-class children who would not need anything more than some elementary schooling: basic skills of literacy and numeracy and some vocational provision (Williams 1961; Reeder 1977).

As the twentieth century unfolded, some primary schools remained the preserve of the working classes and never housed any middle-class children. In other areas, some primary schools became more class inclusive. However, fundamentally, the fears and dangers of 'contamination' of the 'gentler' middle-class child by 'rougher' working-class children continued to play a role in maintaining some separation. During the late nineteenth century and into the first half of the twentieth century, the final and formal 'act' of class separation was marked by the provision of non-compulsory secondary education that had to be paid for, unless a scholarship were obtained. Very few working-class children progressed beyond elementary school, for even if they passed the scholarship, uniforms, books and other essentials still had to be purchased.

The Education Act of 1944 finally legislated for free and compulsory secondary school for *all* children in the UK. This provision was differentiated to meet the needs of children with allegedly different 'abilities'. It was argued that academic children needed an academic curriculum as provided by the grammar school. Children who were good with their hands needed a practical education provided in the technical schools – few of which were ever built. The rest went to the secondary modern school and these were frequently housed in the old elementary schools and provided a curriculum based on a diluted grammar school programme. Most working-class children went to these schools. In this way, even though all children now had access to secondary schooling, the provision reflected 'the survival of a familiar kind of class thinking' (Williams 1961: 166). However, a small minority of working-class children passed the national selective examination, the 11 plus, and went to their local grammar schools (Weeks 1986). Middle-class children now attended state secondary schools but they were over-represented in the grammar schools that remained, in the main, their provenance.

In the 1960s, when the 1944 Education Act had been bedded down for some time, Jackson and Marsden conducted a study in Huddersfield, Yorkshire, in the north of England, that focused on two class-related issues. First, Jackson and Marsden (1966: 16) were interested in 'the colossal waste of talent in working-class children' who still tended to leave school as soon as possible and were (and still are) under-represented in institutes of higher education (see Archer et al. 2003). Second, they were concerned with the cultural trade-off between working-class origins and middle-class schooling, which, they believed, could occur when working-class children did attend their local grammar school:

> In the search for equality through education there is a peculiar blockage. Much has been gained – compulsory schooling, free schooling, secondary schooling for all. But was it altogether worth it? Did the child gain or lose in winning through to middle-class life and growing away from working-class origins? (Jackson and Marsden 1966: 16).

Their argument was that state education had not accepted 'the best qualities of working-class living' and this was not reflected in educational provision or in what Jackson and Marsden (1966: 246) called 'our central culture'. What had happened over the decades of the twentieth century was that by the 1960s, state schooling, which now included the majority of middle-class children, had expanded but was still a selective and elitist provision. It is worth quoting Jackson and Marsden at length because what they wrote, over

40 years ago, seems so relevant to the contemporary situation of classed choosing. Writing of what they found in Huddersfield, they said:

> The crudest economic barriers (school fees etc.) have now been removed, only to reveal subtler ones at work. It is now clearer to see the many small ways in which money and power in society prepare early for a competitive situation. In particular, we can note how the middle classes (supported by the primary schools) respond to, and prepare early for, the divisions of eleven plus at which their children do so conspicuously well . . . Middle-class families are in so many ways insured against failure by virtue of their class position; and any form of nominally academic selection will, in effect, be a form of social selection . . . It is a process that is at work all the time from the moment a child enters school to his final leaving: a gentle shaking of the sieve, with now and again one or two big jerks. (Jackson and Marsden 1966: 231)

State schooling in the UK has always been a classed project, overt and direct in the late nineteenth century when it was set up, and while perhaps less overt, was no less influential nearly 90 years later in the 1960s. This connection has persisted through the 'sorting and grading process, natural to a class society' (Williams 1961: 168) and continues to this day (Ball 2003b).

Before we proceed further, it is necessary to discuss the tensions involved in the way in which we will deploy the categories of middle class and working class in this chapter. By and large we will simply be contrasting middle-class with working-class experiences of the educational system and the urban primary school. Yet we recognize that this approach runs the risk of homogenizing and essentializing the complexity of class positions and classed values. The working classes and middle classes are internally differentiated: there is not one undifferentiated set of experiences, values and beliefs. Values and concerns sometimes overlap between and within classes. Not all middle-class families reject their local urban schools; not all working-class families choose locally either. The lived situation of social class is more complex than simple binaries might sometimes suggest. And yet, there are undeniable 'brute realities of social inequality' (Savage 2000: 159, cited in Ball 2003b: 5) that pattern the classed experiences and opportunities of life chances of many children and their families.

Urban theory, social consumption and education

We now want to return to some of the central themes in urban theory: space and consumption, which offer some explanation for how this class project 'works'. Briefly, the urban has sometimes been theorized as a spatial/density problem, that is, a city is defined by its population size and the physical space it takes up. A study of the urban has, in this perspective, simply been a study of and about cities. A broader political-economic approach to the 'urban' concentrates on the consequence of advanced capitalism and industrialization processes. This second approach tends to 'collapse' urban theory into a study of capitalism (Saunders 1981). To avoid this, urban theorists like

Saunders (1981) and, more recently, Byrne (2001) have argued that urban theory connects to spatial sociology and involves an exploration of the consumption of social goods and competition for these goods in localized struggles. So, while locality/locale is important, so are processes of competition and the places where competition is located as well as social patterns of consumption (who gets what).

When we come to examine education, it is evident that there is local competition and struggle over this provision – how to get into the 'good' or even 'best' local primary school, for example. Access to and consumption of education are critical to 'success' in post-industrial knowledge-based societies like the UK (Castells 1997). Failure to access a 'good' school or just the fear of not being able to access a 'good' school can induce great anxieties (Walkerdine et al. 2001; Swift 2003). Some time ago, Pahl (1968) talked about the distinction between 'proximity' and 'access' in urban settings. He suggested that some people live in proximity to negative environmental provisions – such as factories emitting harmful gases, or, for our purposes, less successful schools. Other people were better placed to 'access' social goods by virtue of where they lived or through their capacity to move to or travel to where they could access advantage (Harvey 1989). Thus, in locations that have become colonized by the middle classes as a consequence of gentrification, it is likely that the local schools, both primary and secondary, have become middle-class dominated in terms of their intake. Locale becomes crucial in any struggle over consumption. Where you live can dictate which hospital you are treated in, the doctor you get, what dentistry is available, as well as the sorts of schools you can actually attend. In newly gentrifying locales, where schools may be more 'mixed' in terms of their intake, and certainly in global cities like London, where different forms of housing stock exist side by side, schools (certainly primary schools) will be more heterogeneous in their intake. However, fuelled by league tables and an awareness of the role of 'good' schools in accessing additional life chances, local competition for access to the 'best' primary and secondary schools will frequently be characterized by social class differences in urban settings.

Class and schooling

The sociology of education has recently seen a return to interest in understanding class inequalities through exploring the ways in which the middle classes manoeuvre to bring off class advantage through accessing particular forms of educational provision and avoiding others (Power et al. 2002; Ball 2003b). Much of the earlier work on class and schooling, which started in the post-war period of the 1950s and early 1960s, was caught up in 'explaining' why it was that working-class children did not succeed in school and their middle-class peers did. Mostly this disparity was 'blamed' on factors to do with the family. Key publications of the period, such as Douglas (1964) and the Plowden Report (1967), alleged that working-class families were less able or willing to support their children's school careers and invest in their longer-term futures. They suggested that education was less valued in working-class families than in middle-class homes. One of the most damning episodes in this period was the allegation that working-class families and their children used a 'restricted linguistic code' and for this reason, were less able to access the benefits of schooling that were delivered in an 'elaborated' middle-class code.

This spurious claim rested on an incorrect appropriation of Bernstein's theory of elaborated and restricted linguistic codes. Bernstein had argued that, wherever there was a 'strong sense of shared identity' (Edwards 2002: 529), the group would produce a restricted linguistic code that maintained group coherence. Working-class communities were examples of groups that produced these restricted codes but so too were occupational networks and other groups with closeknit interests and concerns. Bernstein also argued that restricted codes could 'carry great expressive power' (Edwards 2002: 529). However, his work was widely misrepresented. The consequence was that it was argued that working-class children did not do well in school because they lacked 'the necessary verbal strategies' (Deutch 1967: 179, cited in Edwards 2002: 528). Even though this perspective was challenged, its appeal lay in providing a 'reason' for working-class 'failure' in schools and an excuse for some schools to do little to challenge classed outcomes. One dilemma was that the sociolinguistic debate that was spurred on by Bernstein's work took place in journals and lecture halls. Many teachers in training were simply exposed to a dichotomized version of elaborated and restricted codes as 'reasons' for different patterns of success in primary schools. What happened was that working-class families, and their children, became socially pathologized and were seen as 'deficient' (Walkerdine et al. 2001). Working-class families were to 'blame' for their lack of success in the educational system. Perhaps even at this point in time, working-class children were seen as needing to avoid success if success were to be achieved by the middle classes in the school system.

A key ratcheting up of the classed project of schooling occurred as a result of the changes that were put into place through the Education Reform Act (ERA) 1988. The insertion of market forces into education provision and the complementary strategies of parental choice and market competition positioned education as a commodity, another asset to be acquired. Gewirtz et al. (1995: 2) suggest that this process of acquisition is 'driven by self interest ... the self-interest of parents, as consumers, choosing schools that will provide maximum advantage to their children'. In this classless discourse, it is the individual family and individual parent who are positioned as having choices. This means that 'good' parents need to put 'the family first' (Jordan et al. 1994). In these new times, it is the task of the 'good' parent to be vigilant to ensure that they access the best advantage for their own child – and this may well be at the expense of someone else's child. As Bourdieu and Boltanski (2000: 917) have argued, in the contemporary setting 'the education market has become one of the most important loci of class struggle'.

In consequence, interest has turned once more to issues of social class and schooling. However, that interest now lies mainly with the strategies and tactics that the middle classes deploy to ensure that they choose and get the best available in order to secure longer-term advantage for their children in a competitive and risky social world (Beck 1992). As Bynner (2003) has demonstrated, the UK is a stratified society in which the middle classes 'elbow' their way into any advantages that are offered. One way in which this elbowing is evidenced is in the classed manoeuvrings associated with primary-secondary transfer, although it is important to appreciate, as Lynch and Lodge (2002: 3) remind us, that 'social class inequality ... begins at the pre-school market stage when income and wealth are stratified' (see also Vincent et al. 2004).

Choice and class in primary/secondary transition

A great deal of research has concentrated particularly on the transition from primary to secondary school in the UK (Adler et al. 1989; Echols and Wilms 1990; Gewirtz et al. 1995). The study conducted by Gewirtz et al. (1995) drew on in-depth interviews with 137 parents from across all social classes who lived in four different local education authorities. The middle-class families interviewed for the study were concerned about many factors in coming to make their choice of secondary school for their children. As Gewirtz et al. point out, the families worked to find a school that 'matched' their children's needs and personality. However, in choosing schools for some positive factors, simultaneously they chose to avoid other less desirable factors:

> The main reason we want Max to go to Suchard (school) is because he tends to gravitate towards the rougher children in the (primary) school and they're nice enough kids but they're not very motivated, they're not very bright, and he tends to work at the level of the children he's working with. (interview with a mother, cited in Gewirtz et al. 1995: 35)

Class choosing is rarely direct and unambiguous (Gewirtz et al. 1995). It is part of a wider set of concerns. Nevertheless, in expressions like 'the rougher children', it is possible to see a desire to avoid a social mix that might jeopardize Max's progression. And indeed, many other studies into primary/secondary transfer reveal a range of tactics that middle-class parents sometimes deploy to ensure that their child avoids the 'rougher children' and gets placed in a 'good' school – attended by enough other middle-class children (David et al. 1994; Woods et al. 1998). These tactics may include attending a particular church to ensure acceptance at a popular denominational secondary school; moving house to be in the right catchment area for a more desirable school; using a friend's address for the same reason. In some cases, parents may transfer their children out of local urban primary schools, after good early years' provision but before formal schooling starts, into local denominational primary schools that 'feed' popular and oversubscribed denominational secondary schools but which do not have good nursery classes (Maguire 1999). Overall, the ethics and the politics of choosing schools are classed, complex and highly contradictory (Swift 2003).

One issue that has not been as fully researched as the primary/secondary transition is the need to get into a 'good' primary school right at the start. In some cases, this can increase the prospect of later access to a 'good' secondary school for which the primary school is a recognized 'feeder'. Therefore, particularly in urban contexts, where there is much more choice and greater capacity to transcend the limits of space (driving children to schools in different areas), some primary schools become oversubscribed, housing prices rise in the immediate vicinity and the process of class choosing/class segregation is initiated in the early years and primary sector.

Obviously, families who cannot buy and sell property and who cannot move into the 'right' area are sometimes excluded from access to particular primary schools. It is not that they are not 'good' choosers; rather, they have little to choose from and between. Housing thus becomes a powerful factor that shapes the intake of the local primary (and many secondary) schools. The capacity to transcend space gives advantage to those best placed to do this.

There is another factor implicated in choosing and getting into a 'good' primary school: the factor of religion. Many parents continue to regard denominational schools as 'good'. In some cases, denominational schools are seen as providing 'a selective education by any other name' (Cohen 2005: 29). Parents frequently claim that church schools are able to engender an ethos that is conducive to hard work, high standards and school 'success'. For this reason, parents may well be positively disposed to select denominational primary schools, regardless of their own faith perspectives – that then offer the additional 'bonus' of feeding generally better regarded denominational secondary schools. As denomination Christian schools are grouped in dioceses that extend over a larger geographical area than the local educational authority, these schools offer additional choices to some parents (Whitty 2002). Depending on their selection criteria, these schools may find it easier to reject some groups; other people may find it easier to meet the entrance criteria through starting to attend their local churches.

As a consequence of the competition between schools, bolstered by the publication of league tables, schools become set in local hierarchies. 'Good' schools become popular, other schools are seen as 'acceptable', while yet other schools are demonized – and more frequently these are the urban schools, the schools for the working classes. Some families have enough assets to overcome this problem and are better able to get what they want. Other families have to take what they get (Reay and Ball 1997). And this applies to primary as well as secondary schooling.

Again, it is useful to look back to the 1960s and see what Jackson and Marsden had to say then about choosing a primary school as there are parallels with the contemporary policy context. They wrote of that first move from the home into the primary school for the working-class families in their study: 'Nevertheless, when the moment came for schooling to begin, many of the parents were less sure of their choice and guidance. This was the point of entry to unfamiliar worlds' (Jackson and Marsden 1966: 99). The Huddersfield middle-class parents were far more aware that 'all kinds of advantages may flow in from choosing the best school for results, rather than accepting the school which is simply the nearest' (Jackson and Marsden 1966: 99), a factor that few of their working-class families seemed to realize. As Jackson and Marsden (1966: 100) found, '*early* success in the primary school was a prerequisite to any further achievement' so unfamiliarity with the system could penalize some working-class children.

In their study, Jackson and Marsden recognized that different fractions of the working class had access to different forms of knowledge and social networks. They talked of working-class families with 'blood relatives in the professional classes, or with middle class links through church or club' (Jackson and Marsden 1966: 99) who found out about the reputations of different primary schools and who took advice as to which school would be best for their child's future progress. Then, as now, the working class was internally differentiated and this could increase or limit their capacity to choose. Overall, however, in the Huddersfield study (and in studies such as Gewirtz et al. 1995) many of the working-class families 'chose' very differently from the middle-class families:

> Middle-class parents . . . know that all kinds of advantages may flow from choosing the best school for results, rather than accepting the school which is simply nearest. Consequently they use the system's elasticity, and by doing so, reinforce differences in standard, tone and expectation. Few working-class parents realized that. Apart from those with middle-class connections, they accepted the local school in a natural 'neighbourhood' spirit. (Jackson and Marsden 1966: 99)

Children and choice in urban locales

While Jackson and Marsden's work has a strong contemporary 'feel' about it, one consequence of the insertion of choice and competition (market forces) has been the upsurge of research into parental choice (David et al. 1994; Gewirtz et al. 1995). What has sometimes been sidelined in all this is the voice of the children themselves and their participation in choice of secondary schools. Although many of the best-known studies recognize that the children themselves do have a part to play in choosing their secondary schools, the way in which middle-class children's capacity to choose is 'managed' within the family is worth considering here. Many middle-class families start preparing their children for secondary transfer at an early stage in their primary schooling. Sometimes this involves extra tuition to help the child do well in competitive entry examinations. While the children will be consulted about where they would like to go, from family discussions that take place over time, the children will have absorbed messages about which secondary schools are appropriate/inappropriate for people like themselves (David et al. 1994). These discussions will continue in primary schools within the children's peer groupings. A reservoir of information about 'good' schools and 'bad' schools will be constructed throughout the primary phase. Middle-class choosing becomes a process of manoeuvring through options from a subsection of the better/good schools. Other schools, the 'rougher' schools perhaps, will already have been rejected (Gewirtz et al. 1995).

In contrast, some cohorts of working-class children will be more directly involved in choosing their secondary school by themselves. Reay and Lucey

(2000a: 86) found with the primary school children they interviewed 'locality is important and is integrally linked to feelings of security, belonging and connection'. Working-class children were more likely to want to stay in 'their' own area with people like themselves even if these schools were not always 'academic' or high status. As Massey (1995) argues, where we live and grow up influences us and helps shape our identities. Who we are is connected to where we live and how we identify ourselves. Moving away from familiar settings can be emotionally costly.

One of the first urban-based investigations conducted after the ERA (1988) had introduced market forces, competition and 'choice' into education was carried out by Thomas and Dennison (1991). They were concerned that 'previous studies on choice of secondary school have not gathered data from primary school pupils themselves' (1991: 247). They gave all the Year Six children in one inner city northern England primary school a questionnaire in order to find out more about who actually did the choosing of the secondary school. In this locality, there were two secondary schools available to choose between. They also interviewed a random sample of parents and a core of primary and secondary teachers. Thomas and Dennison discussed the powerful and pervading influence of local networks that passed on 'bad messages' about less desirable schools – even where these messages were unfounded. These messages were about fighting, bullying and 'trouble'. The study concluded that 61 per cent of the children were the main choosers of their own secondary school. Much of this choosing was about 'avoiding' the sorts of difficulty outlined earlier rather than choosing 'for' a particular reason.

In a study conducted by Wooldridge (1997) a cohort of children from an inner city primary school were interviewed frequently over the course of their last year of primary school in order to tease out the processes involved in choosing a secondary school in more detail. Wooldridge was a teacher in the school and had taught all of the participants. He talked to the children at opportune moments, conducted a series of focus group interviews and short one-off interviews at key moments such as before and after visits to prospective schools. He found that the children relied on local sources of information, mainly older siblings and friends already at the available secondary schools, to inform their choice making. In their immediate location, there were six secondary schools. None of these schools enjoyed a strong academic reputation. Other schools in the locality were generally considered to be too far away to be actively considered. As Wooldridge (1997: 37) suggests from his work with the children:

> Fighting, bullying, smoking, school uniform, the school buildings and finally the existence of after-school clubs appear to be the most important indicators of 'good' and 'bad' schools. Rumour and hearsay had spread about these factors in school life, issues that are important but away from the classroom and not directly associated with education.

The children viewed 'good' schools as those they described as 'easy' – schools where there was no trouble. Issues of race and gender were 'a means by which the girls, in particular, distinguished between schools' (Wooldridge 1997: 38):

> I don't want to be bad but some people don't want to go to a school because they're all one race and people are like typical racists. You know Ryan's Mum? She took the boy out because the school was full of Muslims, Bengalis. That's really bad. (Sophie, a white working-class girl)

Wooldridge discovered that social class and ethnicity had a considerable impact on children's choice of secondary schools. His study was conducted in one inner urban primary school in a deprived locale. The primary school intake was made up largely of children whose parents had come from Bangladesh. Many of these parents would have some difficulty in accessing information about schools out of the borough and schools too far away from home would have not been desirable for families concerned about racism and the safety of their children. Wooldridge argued that, in this case, the specificity of locale and issues of ethnicity had shaped choice patterns and access to secondary school. What happened was that most of the children went to the nearest school – the main issues arose in relation to a perceived need for single-sex provision. In relation to this setting, Wooldridge (1997: 55) found that: 'Many parents do not engage with the market at all.' The children did what 'choosing' there was to do. His final conclusions are worth reproducing here:

> For these children, the process of choosing a school has been difficult and confusing. The messages they hear are contradictory, deeply rooted in myth and riddled with exaggeration. Choice has not empowered children, instead it has given them one more thing to worry about in their final year of primary school. (Wooldridge 1997: 56)

Reay and Lucey (2003) conducted a large study with over 400 inner city primary school children where their attitudes, perspectives and processes of choosing were explored before and after transfer. One finding was that the reputations of schools shifted according to location – a secondary school could be regarded as 'good' by children in one school while simultaneously being seen as 'bad' by children from a different primary school. Reputations were shifting and complex. However, the same sorts of key choosing issue that had been identified in earlier studies were also found by Reay and Lucey: the need to avoid 'trouble' rather than choose positively; the powerful role of housing location; choosing locally and 'not too posh': 'Primary to secondary transition is one of those regular stages at which the educational system filters out those whose cultural capital it is not designed to recognize' (Reay and Lucey 2003: 139); a finding that replicates the 'gentle shaking of the sieve, with now and again one or two big jerks' described by Jackson and Marsden (1968: 231).

Reay and Lucey (2003: 139) found that: '"Choice" operates in the inner city as a process of differentiating schools and concentrating problems' (Reay and Lucey 2003: 139). Like Wooldridge, they found that working-class boys (black and white) and their parents were more likely to choose single-sex schools with reputations for a 'firm' approach towards discipline. Like all the studies on working-class choosing, they found that most children were choosing on the basis of 'a sense of one's place'. As Reay and Lucey undertook qualitative work with a large number of children, they were also able to tease out subtle issues that gradually became apparent. For example, children in their study who 'knew' that some schools were out of their reach and who chose less high-status but more accessible schools, demonstrated a keen awareness of stratification and what was going to be possible. They had a limited choice from a range of second-tier schools and as they knew they did not have a real choice, they were making the best of what was on offer to them.

One interesting issue raised by Reay and Lucey concerned the small number of working-class children in one of their socially mixed primary schools who were keenly aware of the different academic reputations of local secondary schools as well as which schools were more desired by their middle-class peers. Some of these children applied for and gained places in the higher-status secondary schools although they reported difficulties post-transfer. In any discussions about class and transfer it is important not to forget this part of the cohort. Walkerdine et al. (2001: 162) have argued, in relation to girls who make and get this sort of choice:

> [W]hy some girls long for something different and have the strength to make this happen through what is an emotionally and socially terrifying shift while others feel safer staying within the well understood and maintained practices of school failure is a question that demands to be asked, but is not usually addressed by the educational literature.

This is an important issue that needs more research – in respect of girls, and boys as well.

The process of choosing is a classed process. It circumscribes the 'feeding' roles of primary schools – some are more likely to feed 'good' schools, others are more likely to feed local schools that may be under-subscribed and more likely to serve their local communities. The location of the primary school, the secondary school(s) it feeds and the culture of the local primary school will shape, to a degree, what is possible, desirable and available. For working-class children, the choice is likely to be localized and randomized; getting to a 'good' school will be a matter of luck. For the middle-class child, it will be the result of a long sequence of careful selection, of processes of inclusion, exclusion and familiarity with the system, a process that starts even before compulsory schooling itself.

Choosing/avoiding: the consequence for urban schools

One reading of this chapter might seem to be suggesting that working-class children make a school 'bad' and that 'good' schools are those that attract middle-class children. While the evidence does suggest that so-called successful schools are generally characterized by a more middle-class intake (Thrupp 1998), the situation is more complicated. Sometimes schools that have good (relative) success with specific constituencies are still rejected by middle-class families:

> Parents choose on the basis of social mix. Beatrice Webb [a secondary school] was unlikely ever to be popular with its reputation for violence (because of a tiny minority of violent students) and its intake of mainly working-class students, refugees and bilingual speakers. Local primary headteachers had told the teacher responsible for primary liaison, that some parents rejected the school because of 'its very good reputation for being welcoming and helping all sorts of refugee kids'. (Gewirtz 2002: 114)

Put another way, the social costs of choosing have different outcomes for the schools of the working-class child and the middle-class child. Pahl's (1968) notion of 'proximity' might mean closeness to a less successful school in an area where the more successful schools are two bus journeys away for parents without their own transport or the time to take children to a more distant school. The outcome of class choosing – a polarized provision in some cases but a clear pecking order in others – will reinforce the 'colonization' of some primary schools by the middle classes, who will sell up and move in order to access 'good' schools or at the very least 'avoid' those which they see as threatening to their children's development (Butler and Savage 1995).

The consequences of this strategy can work to further demonize some schools and certainly make it harder for these schools to survive. For example, in a particular locale, the least popular school may well have the lowest number of children on its roll. It will be compelled to accept some 'harder to teach' children who may have been excluded from other schools (Maguire et al. 2003). In turn, this may have consequences for the schools' capacity to recruit and retain staff. Higher staff turnover, too many supply teachers and higher numbers of transient children who move from school to school can make it much harder to provide stability and continuity (Power et al. 2002). The stress and emotional pressures of working in schools in these sorts of circumstance can make excessive demands on teachers. It is much harder to meet targets with a transient school population and an ever-changing staff. Higher levels of staff ill-health, caused by these greater pressures, can mean the budget is overstretched on staffing costs, which will result in less money for other resources. Finally, schools in disadvantaged locales will be less able to make up any budget deficiencies through the sorts of fundraising activities that are available in more prosperous areas. In many ways, the schools that serve the more disadvantaged fraction of the working classes will be 'punished' for their work. This applies equally to primary and secondary urban schools.

Supporting and sustaining urban schools in a 'choosing' environment

When New Labour came into power in 1997, education became its top priority. However, in its concern with 'raising standards' it showed more continuity with the previous Conservative administrations than with a more radical approach towards schooling (Demaine 1999). New Labour took on the damaging rhetoric of previous administrations and made it their own. If anything, it became tougher and more aggressive about challenging alleged low standards, particularly in urban schools and needing to increase performance management in schools and elsewhere in the public sector. However, New Labour inherited a country in which levels of poverty had risen considerably and recognized a need to challenge this situation (Whitty 2002).

As Tomlinson (2001) has stated, during the 1980s and 1990s, it was repeatedly argued that 'poverty was no excuse' and that schools were responsible for their own success or failure. Social and economic disadvantage was not recognized and schools 'succeeding despite the odds' were used to berate those who failed to meet their targets. In some ways, it might be argued that at least and at last schools were being asked to ensure that working-class children were succeeding in school. But, at the same time:

> By the 1990s, there was an important section of the middle class, educated in private or good state schools and 'good' universities, dominating the communications, information and propaganda industries, and the political arena, who were easily able to resist egalitarian and social democratic school organization. These and other knowledgeable groups were determined that their children would have similar access to privileged education. (Tomlinson 2001: 133)

These groups and other aspiring middle-class cohorts recognized the need to 'avoid their children being educated with the poor, to ensure their children attended well-resourced schools and avoided stigmatized forms of education' (Tomlinson 2001: 139). The outcome was that schooling became more socially polarized and this impacted on school performance (Gibson and Asthana 1999). In response to these sorts of pressures and also in an attempt to 'benefit the many, not the few' (DfEE 1997: 11), New Labour implemented a set of policies to deal with schools where attainment was below the national average. Education action zones (and to start with, these were mainly urban), Excellence in Cities (initially in six large conurbations and their adjoining areas – inner London, Birmingham, Leeds/Bradford, Liverpool/Knowsley, Manchester/Salford and Sheffield/Rotherham) and Fresh Start, which would close and reopen 'failing schools', were all set up to 'rescue' urban schools.

It is not possible to do justice in this chapter to these policies; however, they did pump in some additional resources to urban schools. Particularly through Excellence in Cities, schools could now employ learning mentors to give additional support to children who were experiencing difficulties in their learning. Schools could also set up 'fast-track' schemes and additional support for 'gifted and talented' children. There was to be an expansion of specialist schools in the inner city that would 'cater for ambitious and high achieving pupils' DfEE (1999c: 1). As Maden (2001: 336) argues, it is important for schools' success that they are able to attract and retain a 'critical mass' of children who are 'pro-school'. However, while these sorts of policies might have given succour to some middle-class/middle-class aspirant families and might have worked to retain their children in (some) urban schools, these policies have simultaneously promoted internal differentiation and segregation within schools. As Lynch and Lodge (2002: 40) have found in similar projects in Ireland, there is mounting evidence 'that schools feel pressurized to provide "fast tracks" which mainly serve middle-class children and this is a tactic to maintain middle-class enrolment'. Without any commitment to challenging structural inequalities such as unemployment and poverty, the focus on 'standards' has seemed strangely inappropriate at best and has worked to ensure that, in the main, middle-class children are educated 'apart from the poor' (Tomlinson 2001: 140). Recently, the emphasis on standards has led to an increase in 'ability setting' in primary schools, particularly for numeracy and literacy work (Hallam et al. 2004a: 531). While some of the literature that focuses on children's attitudes towards grouping practices reveals that 'the nature of language adopted, such as 'thick' or 'dumb', with its negative connotations, stigmatizes those of lower ability', one key question remains: which social class of children are more likely to be allocated to the 'lower ability' groups? (Willig 1963; Boaler 1997). The reality is a society that is still divided along class lines where education works to support and maintain division and the privilege of some rather than the common good of all (Tomlinson 2001).

Social capital and urban education

Whitty (2002: 120) claims that New Labour is developing social policies that have started to 'look beyond the failures of the school for the causes of underachievement'. He argues that New Labour has turned its attention to the 'social capital thesis' and that this approach has influenced policies set up to challenge exclusion, such as Sure Start and family literacy. The social capital thesis argues that 'relationships matter' (Field 2003: 1), that the capacity to gain support from networks and relationships can help (and sometimes hinder) in accessing wider resources. The implication is that policy needs to facilitate relationships and connections. Halpern (2005: 142), a keen advocate of policies to enhance social capital and who works in the Prime Minister's Strategy Unit, has produced a review of international research that suggests that 'deficits in social capital can lead to negative outcomes'. Parents' social capital can positively affect educational outcomes and 'differences in family social capital help to explain differences in educational achievements' (Halpern 2005: 167). One example of the positive effects of social capital are Catholic schools in the USA where working-class children perform much better than children from similar backgrounds attending non-denominational schools. Halpern believes that shared aspirations, similar values and strong ties between parents and the school help to make this difference. He recognizes that enhancing social capital 'is not a simple or single magic bullet for solving all policy problems' but claims that it is a 'useful source of insight into new policy levers'.

Recent policies in England (and elsewhere) have started to concentrate on enhancing social capital. Some schemes have focused on supporting parents of young pre-school children through extending provision, other schemes have offered parents free bags of books to promote reading and literacy in three age groups: up to 1 year old, from 12 to 24 months, and up to 4 years of age (Hill 2005: 10). School-based projects such as mentoring have been developed to raise aspirations and build social and educational capital both in primary and secondary schools. At a community level, Tony Blair has controversially sought to provide more church schools in a partial attempt to enhance social capital. Community-level efforts at enhancing social capital have been attempted through volunteer schemes, promoted in schools by citizenship education. While it is evident that these schemes can offer support to parents and bring some additional resources with them, we would want to echo Whitty's criticism (2002: 123) that 'policies that are about building social capital are also important, but they are a necessary complement to rather than a substitute for policies that attack material poverty'. In concentrating on enhancing social capital, wider structural and economic concerns might become marginalized or even become displaced.

Conclusion

In this chapter, we have considered what happens in urban settings as a consequence of the differential capacity to exercise choice and transcend space. We have explored the ways in which location plays a critical part in the allocation of school places. In particular, we have examined research into the 'choice making' of parents and children that works, in effect, to maintain a society divided on class lines. We have also briefly examined some of the urban policies that, while seeking to ameliorate some of the financial disadvantages that inner city schools experience, can work to set up processes of internal differentiation in urban schools themselves. In the past, working-class families were 'blamed' for poor parenting that held their children back – now they can be 'blamed' for 'poor' choosing or even for having the 'wrong' sort of social capital or none at all.

Williams (1961: 12) wrote of what he called the 'long revolution'. He saw this as a process involving struggles for democracy, changes in production and industry and the need to extend communications that would result in 'deep social and personal changes'. In terms of education, Williams (1961: 168) saw the 'long revolution' as needing to move beyond the 'sorting and grading process, natural to a class society'. Williams (1961: 176) warned that there was a choice between persisting 'in social and educational patterns based on a limited ruling class, a middle professional class, a large operative class, cemented by forces that cannot be challenged and will not be changed' or moving towards 'a public education designed to express and create the values of an educated democracy and a common culture'. We are still, it seems, caught between these choices.

Questions

1. In what sorts of ways does social class impact in the urban primary classroom?
2. To what degree do you think that 'educational destinies are tied to geography' (Reay and Lucey 2003: 123)?
3. To what extent is it productive for policymakers to try to enhance the social capital of urban children and families?

8

LEARNING IN THE CITY

Urban schools have often been viewed by policymakers as in need of compensatory action to overcome their deficiencies or 'problems'. In this chapter, we argue that there is also a need to positively value urban experiences. Valuing cultural differences and working to support participatory and localized policymaking have an important part to play in promoting learning in the urban school. The urban locale can and should be seen as a positive site for promoting and sustaining learning. We start by reviewing some dominant policy approaches towards urban schools. We then explore research into children's experiences of the city and consider the potential of the city in the curriculum. Finally, we examine some of the contemporary strategies to raise attainment and raise standards in urban schools and we argue that policy needs to employ a more consultative and critical approach towards what counts as knowledge in urban primary schools.

Policy approaches towards learning in urban schools

The 'stark differences in the lives of pupils with different family backgrounds have not gone away, nor has the problem of knowing how to deal with them' (Mortimore and Whitty 1997: 1). Much of the earliest policy work in the area of urban schooling originated in the United States and was driven by these 'stark differences'. As Cicirelli (1972: 31) explained:

> For many years in the United States, most children of the urban poor have been inferior in academic achievement to middle-class children and have suffered the consequences of being rejected by teachers, becoming school dropouts without jobs, and contributing excessively to welfare rolls and incidence of crime, drug addition, and mental illness. The cost for the individual and society has been staggering.

Over time there has been a degree of continuity in the policy responses towards urban schooling in the USA and in the UK. During the early 1960s in the USA, and in the later 1960s and early 1970s in the UK, urban education dominated the policy agenda as a focus of concern. In the USA, there was an upsurge in 'awareness of and concern for the urban poor' (Cicirelli 1972: 31), which was later mirrored in the UK. Cicirelli identified three major approaches in policy attempts that, at this time, tried to reduce the differences in school achievement between middle-class and urban poor American schoolchildren. These approaches, which are discussed below, still continue to influence contemporary urban education policy and thus it is worth considering the forms they take.

Cicirelli suggested that one major set of approaches was based on assumptions of 'deficit' where it was suggested that urban children 'lacked' some key essential ingredient to success that prevented their achievement in education. For example, living in a run-down environment or experiencing reduced support from within the family at an early stage in development could, it was argued, compound later underachievement in education. A 'strong' version of this approach could be seen as pointing to structural disadvantages that could only be tackled by a politics involving redistribution, perhaps through taxation reforms or additional state welfare. A 'weaker' interpretation, which located the 'deficit' in a culture/community, might only lead to policies based on supplementing so-called cultural deficits rather than tackling structural inequalities; policies based on compensating children for these 'lacks'. Corson (1998: 124) believes that one consequence of the 'weaker' policy approach that was developed in the 1960s was that it signalled that urban working-class families and communities needed the help of professionals in order to manage their problems.

A second policy approach that Cicirelli identified focused on arguments around school disparity: some schools were 'better' than others at working with the child in the city. Some successful schools, which allegedly shared similar intakes to less successful schools, were helping their children to achieve more in education. This approach could be seen, at the very least, as indirectly 'blaming' the less successful school. It could also mean that any politics of redistribution would be less likely to be advocated. If some schools were doing well without any additional financial support, then all schools should be able to cope. More recently, this approach has characterized some of the mainstream schools improvement discourse in the UK. If some schools were able to 'succeed' then other similar schools would either need to be helped, changed or perhaps even closed down.

Cicirelli identified a third major policy approach that was based on the need to help urban children develop their self-esteem in order to fulfil their potential. In this third policy approach, the emphasis was on helping students to overcome disadvantage through generating positive views about themselves and their capacity to do well in school. It was argued that interventions that helped young learners enhance their self-esteem, raise their aspirations and their attainment were needed. However, it could also be argued that in this approach, the 'blame' for underachievement rested with the individual child and their family. It could also be argued that this perspective still disregarded the impact of poverty, poor health and poor housing on learning attainment (Grace 1995b).

In the USA, these three dominant approaches underpinned various strategies that were put into place in order to reduce the so-called 'achievement gap' for urban children. These approaches were characterized by attempts to 'compensate' urban children for the forms of social disadvantage they experienced. The policies took two main forms: compensation and intervention; many policies incorporated both of these strands. For example, in the USA in the 1960s, one of the best-known compensatory-interventionist strategies was the Headstart programme that was based on early interventions for very young children such as breakfast clubs and extra support for learning. This programme was an attempt to compensate for a less advantaged start to life. Longer-term interventions into the schooling process, such as High Scope, promoted child-centred active learning (see Herman and Stringfield 1995). In other urbanized nation states, similar concerns about the educational achievements of the urban poor were expressed and policies of early intervention were initiated. One notable intervention was the Reading Recovery programme set up in New Zealand by Marie Clay and later imported into the UK and elsewhere (Rowe 1995) to assist 'disadvantaged' children overcome early literacy difficulties (Clay 1982).

In the UK, in the mid-1960s, the educational priority area (EPA) schemes put more money into designated schools that served 'deprived' areas to compensate for a less advantaged start to life (Halsey 1972). This was a policy that attempted to compensate as well as intervene into provision. One problem with this particular policy was that while it did signal government concern with social inequality and social disadvantage, the money paid to schools and the small additional sums paid to encourage teachers to work in those inner city schools deemed to be in an EPA, were little more than 'drops in the ocean'. This was a policy where rhetoric disguised the underlying complexities and displaced the fact that very little money actually fed into the schools concerned. A case perhaps of treating the symptoms rather than the cause? As Tomlinson (2001: 18) has argued, this was undertaken without any debate about the 'macro-economic conditions that create poverty or the political failures over redistributive social justice'.

While the study of urban education was popular for some time in teacher education in the UK in the late 1960s and early 1970s, its political edge (asking hard questions about the causes of poverty and inequalities in society) meant that when education policy shifted towards neo-liberal and individualistic perspectives with a weakening of principles of concern for the 'common good', its use was displaced (Dyson 2003). During the mid- to late 1970s, more radical concerns about the need to combat poverty and inequality in education were gradually replaced (in policy terms at least) by a market discourse that privileged choice, competition and standards; 'a thin cover for the old stratification of schools and curricula' (Bernstein 1990: 87). In this new policy setting, the focus shifted to individual competition and testing. However, social inequalities did not go away (Walker and Walker 1997).

What is currently apparent, in the UK and elsewhere, are the same concerns about social unrest, social upheaval and the individual 'waste' as a consequence of low educational attainment in urban schools, which were expressed by Cicirelli (Ravitch 1997; Bell 2003). Thus, in the UK when New Labour came to power in 1997 it set up the Social Exclusion Unit expressly to combat poverty, promote inclusion and reduce youth disaffection and youth crime rates through increasing participation rates in educational provision. Urban schooling was back on the policy agenda:

> The long association of inner city schools with disadvantage, disaffected and disruptive pupils continued to be regarded as a major public policy challenge by New Labour. Dealing with the children of those whom the Victorians had called the 'feckless poor', now known as 'disrupted families', who constituted a major reason why aspirant parents wished to move their children away from inner city schools, took priority. (Tomlinson 2001: 103)

New Labour has taken up many of the policy approaches of Cicirelli summarized earlier. They have intervened in early childhood provision in order to reduce the achievement gap. Projects like Sure Start and family literacy are attempting to support parents before the start of compulsory schooling. At the same time, there have been tax breaks and increased benefit payments to some of the poorest families in the UK. Through the standards 'crusade', New Labour has also taken the approach that some schools are more successful than others and need to be emulated; through, for example, the Beacon Schools Programme and highlighting primary schools that exhibit 'leading practice' (DfES 2003). It has to be said, however, that the 'better' or more effective schools have nearly always not been in urban locations (but see Maden 2001 who offers some cases where urban schools have 'succeeded against the odds' in terms of effectiveness and improvement). New Labour has also taken up some of the ideas of raising self-esteem and aspirations through extending social capital, particularly in the swathe of mentoring approaches that it has adopted 'as an intervention with disadvantaged young people' (Colley 2003: 1). In spite of all this, as Whitty (2002) has argued, the children of the poor still achieve less than their middle-class peers.

There has been some continuity over time in policy approaches to the 'problem' of the urban as 'deficit', the urban learner as a 'low' achiever and the urban poor as needing professional intervention, advice and support. There have also been some changes, particularly under New Labour, that recognizing the 'local' knowledge that parents have of their own children needs to be complemented by, rather than being replaced by, professional expertise. However, this shift may sometimes be more apparent in rhetoric than in practice or be more evident in particular settings such as pre-school provision, where this approach has always had more salience (Sylva and MacPherson 2002).

What we want to do now in this chapter is make a case for a different policy approach towards the urban school. There has sometimes been a tendency in the past, and continuing to the present day, that sees the urban experience as a set of binaries. That is, the urban is 'good' in that it offers access to cultural enrichment and diversity and it is 'bad' in that it stands for dereliction, poverty and crime. These sets of contradictory, and sometimes stereotyped, approaches to the urban world have influenced urban policy. For example, primary school teachers are exhorted to 'exploit' the cultural resources of the city (DfEE 2005: 25), although there is, simultaneously, a need to 'develop the aspirations of those who live in our inner city areas and outer estates' (DfEE 1999c).

Rather than starting from the cultural 'wealth' or the 'problems' of the urban approach, we want to suggest that another useful approach would be to explore some alternative understandings of the ways in which 'children's lives and experiences outside school shape and affect their activities and performances inside school' (Corson 1998: 25). For understandable reasons, New Labour has concentrated on boosting attainment in numeracy and literacy in urban primary schools. What we suggest in this chapter is that this work be extended to make the curriculum and pedagogy of primary schooling more 'relevant to the lived experiences of children from diverse backgrounds' (Corson 1998: 25). What is also required is a greater degree of active participatory decision making for local communities in this education project.

Children's experiences of the city

In this section, we explore the complex ways in which children themselves construct the places in which they live, their homes, their communities and their localities. We want to argue that urban children learn from their contextualized setting – but might be learning things that do not 'count' as learning in terms of the National Curriculum and its assessments. For example, children may be learning about inequality, injustice and disadvantage.

We will start by looking back at some earlier contributions to urban theory that are helpful in this process. In particular, we want to start with considering the twin concepts of access and proximity as used in the early work of Pahl (1970). Pahl argued that social space played a powerful part in shaping who got what in cities. 'Access' to the advantages that existed in cities was going to be more available to more mobile middle-class families. Poorer families would be less able to reduce their 'proximity' to 'negative' features of social life. As Harvey (1973: 82) has claimed, those with the capacity to 'transcend space . . . command it as a resource. Those who lack such a skill are likely to be trapped by space.' While we can see some usefulness in understanding the way in which urban space patterns and shapes access to advantage and proximity to negative variables, we would want to ask a different question altogether. Is 'proximity' always negative and is the world not more complex than these sorts of binary might imply?

This is not to argue that living in 'proximity' to environmental hazards is positive. Rather, it is to suggest that children who live on council estates or in settings that have been demonized as undesirable or 'no-go areas', for example, might not actually always share these negative perceptions about where they live. Pons (1975: 9) argued that 'our cities are "real" for their inhabitants'. He added: 'One way of approaching them (cities) in all their complexity is to examine ever more closely how their inhabitants define them, how they define their own situations in them, and how they make sense of the complexity which surrounds them.'

Reay and Lucey (2000b) conducted research with a group of young inner city primary school children about their views of living in a council estate. These researchers were interested in how the children spoke and felt about living in a particular social-spatial setting which had often been 'demonized' in the local papers. Reay and Lucey (2000b: 412) argued that 'the places we grow up in shape the people we become', although they recognized that the same place can be differently experienced. For example, middle-class children cutting through a council estate saw it differently from the children who lived on the estate. Furthermore, Reay and Lucey's study, which focused on 'life on large estates', did point to some dilemmas of 'proximity' (Pahl 1970). They found that 'children living on these urban estates map out a risky, often child hostile, geographical landscape' (Reay and Lucey 2000b: 418).

It was evident that the children were aware of violence, family difficulties, low-level crime and 'trouble' on their estates. Reay and Lucey also highlighted the children's direct experiences of racism. They commented, 'we cannot afford to underestimate the effect on the emotional development of children who witness the daily humiliation of their parents and other parental figures' (Reay and Lucey 2000b: 421). For example, in their paper they cite the experiences of Kelly (white working class):

> The grown ups will shout out their window, sort of 'Stop speaking like that and go back to your own country' ... The Asian kids were saying, 'Leave my Mum alone' and things like that. And then the kids say, 'No we won't leave your Mum alone, just go back to your own country'. (Reay and Lucey 2000b: 420)

The children were aware of injustices, stereotyping, sometimes a lack of resources as well as the strength and familiarity of being embedded in their locale – not a set of knowledge that invades the contemporary primary classroom very often, if at all.

In Reay and Lucey's research, it seemed that although the working-class children in their study were 'out and about' on their estates, they did have clear and localized boundaries. They played in front of their block, in sight of their balconies where their parents could easily check their presence. The children did not talk about travelling great distances on their own to play in parks. Their estate was their playground – although it may well be the case that older primary-aged children have also become 'new homestayers' – in the home on their own while the adult carer is at work (Solberg 1997). As one girl reported: 'Nothing will happen to me because it is so safe around my flats for me. Even though they take drugs and that, it is really safe cos they all know me so they wouldn't do anything' (Sarah, in Reay and Lucey 2000b: 422).

One further finding from the Reay and Lucey study was that while the working-class children experienced a confined and highly localized world, the middle-class children in their study were encouraged and supported in moving out of the local area and into the wider city space of London. Part of their 'growing up' was marked by their capacity to travel independently.

Conversely, Lucey and Reay (2000) found that very few working-class children were allowed to travel alone while all the middle-class children in their sample were allowed to travel independently on buses (on selected routes). While this may be an unexpected finding in terms of parental fears for young children's safety (McNeish and Roberts 1995), the significant issue relates to the capacity of the middle-class children to 'transcend space' (Harvey 1973: 82). In contrast with their middle-class peers, the working-class children identified strongly with a small localized area. The middle-class children, in Reay and Lucey's study, were growing up with a sense of empowerment in spatial terms and a capacity to extract all that the city had to offer.

However, there is another aspect to all this: 'Places form a reservoir of meanings which people can draw upon to tell stories about and therefore define themselves' (Thrift 1997: 160). First of all, children who are 'born and bred' in particular locales/estates reported feeling safe in their areas – things wouldn't go wrong for them as people on the estate knew who they were (Lucey and Reay 2000). Living on their estates is where the children want to be, although they may well have reduced access to a wider locale. Their families and friends are all close to hand and they develop tactics to manage some of the stresses and potential difficulties of urban life. Many of the children spoke of their mixed feelings; they knew about the downside but really, as they explained, they would not want to live anywhere else. Overall, the working-class children in Reay and Lucey's study demonstrated a powerful sense of being 'embedded' in their local community and their horizons were characterized by locality and familiarity. At the same time, as Reay and Lucey (2000b: 424) recognize, 'when the places where they live clearly do not come anywhere near popular representations of "desirable residences" and are subject to the most negative and damning descriptions by others' it must sometimes be hard to hold onto a positive feeling about their homes. A key question here, therefore, is to what extent do schools sometimes contribute towards a negative perspective, in terms of the hidden as well as overt curriculum?

Urban children experience their city/their locale as a complex, rich and sometimes conflicting place in which to live. At the same time, we recognize that being tied to a more immediate locale – not being comfortable with travelling far beyond the immediate neighbourhood – might 'limit' or reduce access and opportunity. Some useful questions for educationalists might include: to what extent is the social world of the children outside school seen as a restriction or as a source for learning and empowerment by their teachers? What sort of learning is involved in living in urban settings that goes unacknowledged in and by schools? And finally, would recognizing and including this informal knowledge make school learning more accessible for more children?

Potential of the city in the curriculum

One of the concerns of earlier work on curriculum provision for inner city schools was the attempt to bring the everyday lived experiences of the children, some of which we have outlined already, into the world of the schoolroom. By the 1960s it was being argued that children's needs and interests needed to shape the content and pedagogy of primary education (Plowden Report 1967). Starting from where the children were, with what they knew and recognized, was seen as crucial to engaging their interest and sustaining their motivation. Some educationalists argued for a stronger, community-based approach. For example, Midwinter (1972: 116–17) argued:

> We must prepare children not only for the life that they would like to lead but for the life that they are likely to lead. Thousands of children will continue to live in these kinds of urban conditions; soon they will be citizens and parents in these areas. Will they have been any better equipped than their parents to handle the day-to-day pressures of the life-issues that inevitably face them?

In many ways, reflecting on the comments of the children interviewed by Reay and Lucey, it is evident that urban children are exposed to the 'day-to-day pressures of life'. What might be less apparent is the capacity of the National Curriculum, as it is currently expressed, to help them handle these and other pressures. (It is useful to note here that there have been attempts to contest, subvert and reclaim space in the curriculum for more radical work e.g. White 2004.) At this point, it is useful to return to some of the earlier curriculum critiques that argued for a need to engage directly with children's wider experiences.

In 1972, Midwinter argued that urban children needed to do more than learn their place in a sometimes hostile world, they needed to learn how to change it. With great prescience, in view of current policies, he argued for community education that drew on 'the potential and the experiences of the city child in his [sic] own right' (Midwinter 1972, in Connor with Lofthouse 1990: 120). He argued for a critical education which would inspire self-renewal and community revitalization:

> The community educationist is, at once more long-sighted and more pessimistic than the compensatory educationist. He looks far beyond the short-term blandishments of an improved reading age to the sunny vision of a highly skilled citizenry recreating high quality civic life in our cities. In doing so he notes, at base, that education cannot go it alone – he is not, then, optimistic about the school as a kind of Lone Ranger solving all educational and thereby social problems, with the silver bullets of language programmes and literacy drives. (Midwinter 1972, in Connor with Lofthouse 1990: 121)

Midwinter argued that a real and relevant curriculum for urban children would be one that worked with them and their families to produce 'social criticism and action'. This did not mean that core skills would not be learned, rather that they would be 'rooted' in what the children knew and understood. He suggested that this approach might even boost attainment. Midwinter was arguing (although not in these terms) that the cultural capital of urban working-class communities was often regarded by educationalists as 'deficit' in relation to that of the middle classes. As Dyson and Gains (1993: 8) have argued, while schools have improved in terms of recognizing some 'cultural mismatches and misunderstandings that can occur, and of the efforts that institutions need to make to value and build on learner's cultures' this has not always occurred in respect of working-class families. Friere (1972) claimed that no curriculum was ever neutral. In order to empower the learner, he claimed that teachers needed to use themes or topics that were familiar to their students. In this pedagogy, students' motivation would increase and they would become more empowered through a relevant curriculum (Friere 1972).

Corson (1998: 111) has claimed that attempts to 'change the education of the urban poor' must start from a perspective that recognizes that urban settings have distinctive cultures and values. He adds: 'These urban neighbourhood cultures can be just as systematic and regular in their practices as any culture, and they deserve the respect that any culture should receive.' Corson argues that teachers should value the homes and community cultures that children bring to school with them. Even more strongly, he believes that the children's out-of-school cultures should be reflected in the curriculum of their schools in order to help the children improve their life chances. Echoing Midwinter's work, Corson (1998: 126) writes: 'Instead of changing children from diverse backgrounds in some way, to suit the school, I prefer to think more about changing the forms of education that undervalue the things that many children bring to school with them.'

As an example, Corson (1998) cites the work of Nieto (1999) undertaken with Cambodian refugee children in cities within the United States. These children believed that their culture was not valued in school. So they tried to behave like their US peers and their emotional adjustment decreased the more they attempted this behaviour change. 'Valuing children's culture in engaged ways and in sensitive settings, enhances the educational opportunities of inner city children' (Corson 1998: 130). The same will hold true for all children.

Curriculum and pedagogy in urban primary schools

Ladson-Billings (1995) has called for a 'culturally relevant curriculum' in urban schools. While she is writing about the ways in which the experiences and cultures of African-American children are not reflected in their schools' curriculum in the USA, what she said has resonance for the UK setting. In many ways, what she says reflects the work of Friere. For example, she believes that schools must ensure that children experience academic success. They must maintain and extend children's cultural competences. Schools must also support children in developing a critical perspective through which they can challenge the status quo.

Corson (1998) has highlighted two main ways in which the curriculum and pedagogy in urban schools can become more sensitive and responsive to children's backgrounds and experiences. First, he suggests that schools need to show that they value and respect socio-cultural differences. They need to do this by 'allowing those cultures and meaning systems to enter the school in formal and informal ways' (Corson 1998: 129). In addition, teachers who hold high expectations and speak 'openly about issues of race and discrimination' can start to eradicate bias and promote respect for difference. They can support this work by using culturally appropriate ranges of books and resources and by providing a curriculum that contains 'fully integrated minority culture history and studies' (Corson 1998: 136). Second, urban schools need to ensure that children are given access to high-status 'academic meaning systems' (Corson 1998: 141). In many ways, the literacy and numeracy strategies are attempts to do just this in the English context. A difficulty lies in concentrating on this goal (Midwinter's silver bullets) at the expense of a wider, more enriching curriculum or through using texts or materials that are perhaps not always accessible to the children, or even through using a skills-based approach that can interrupt meaning-making processes.

New Labour has talked of a 'renaissance in our urban centres' (DfEE 2005: 1) and has recognized that 'urban schools often have a negative reputation they do not deserve' (DfEE 2005: 2). They have celebrated the progress recorded in Key Stage 2 results in primary schools. In terms of building on the gains that have been made, New Labour has recognized the need to support schools 'to develop a curriculum that draws on the rich resources' of urban areas (DfEE 2005: 24). However, other than extolling the virtues of visiting museums and art galleries and after-school activities much of its approach relies on strategies such as Building Schools for the Future and delivering the National Curriculum more effectively. While there is a focus on Corson's 'academic meaning systems', there is no recognition of sensitivity and respect for localized cultural differences. Other than a recognition of the need to have a 'clear approach to racism' (DfES 2003: 43), there is no discussion of active ways to reduce bias and promote the critical pedagogy identified by Ladson-Billings (1995) or Corson (1998).

Mortimore and Whitty (1997: 8) recognize that what currently counts as knowledge in schools might have marginalized some groups. They add that children can attain similar goals by experiencing different 'routes' that take sensitive account of their backgrounds. However, they, like Midwinter, are concerned that schools on their own cannot counter disadvantage. They argue that what would make a difference would be policies that tackled poverty and disadvantage head on. If children go to school in old buildings that might not be attractive, if they experience a series of short-stay teachers who find them 'hard' to teach and quickly leave, if they are exposed to discourses that might not make 'sense' in their worlds, then the hidden curriculum of schooling is an excluding curriculum.

If the overt curriculum positions some children's lives as 'other' or 'deficit', or simply does not reflect their social worlds at all, then it will be harder to come to care about that content. If urban children consistently 'fail' at a learning that privileges another culture without building bridges between these cultures, then schooling may be seen as less relevant to their lives (Balfanz 2000). As Dyson (2003: 8) has asked, 'have we simply failed to understand the richness and complexity' which inner city children experience and have we failed to capitalize on this and the creativity and tenacity of some inner city children to sustain and extend their learning?

Excellence in Cities

Since New Labour came to power in 1997 many initiatives have been developed that have targeted aspects of social deprivation. There has been an attempt to ameliorate some of the debilitating effects of child poverty through policies of redistribution of taxation such as family credit and also through pre-school interventions such as Sure Start (Wilkinson 1997; Ennals 2003). New Labour was also serious about tackling the challenge of urban schooling:

> Successive governments have failed to resolve the educational problems of the major cities. Standards have been too low for too long. Raising standards in order to lift opportunities for our children is the key priority for the Government. It is clear that schools in our inner cities demand urgent attention. (Blair and Blunkett, in the Foreword to Excellence in Cities (EiC), DfEE 1999c: 1)

Excellence in Cities (DfEE 1999c) was its flagship policy designed to tackle this 'key priority'. The policy document argued that low standards and low aspirations had to be changed (Tomlinson 2001: 104). EiC was going to set up more beacon schools and specialist schools in urban areas to lead the way. There were going to be more opportunities for 'gifted and talented' children – the top 5–10 per cent in every school would be given additional support and enrichment – and there would be greater support for disruptive children. Learning mentors would work in schools alongside children who could benefit from the support of engaged adults who were not teachers and this would help raise their aspirations, increase their confidence and lead to higher levels of achievement.

The main thrust was on raising standards through raising performance and achieving excellence. EiC was linked to the standards agenda and not the amelioration of social and material injustice – although the document did recognize that 'unemployment, poverty of both expectation and income, poor health and a low quality environment all make a difference' (DfEE 1999c: 4). These 'problems' were being tackled through other programmes and 'social inclusion policies' (DfEE 1999c: 4). EiC was initially set up to work in secondary schools. In 2000 this was extended to include primary schools and focused on three key aspects: the learning mentor, primary learning support units and the gifted and talented strand.

It could be argued that in policy terms, EiC draws to some extent on a version of the 'deficit' approach outlined by Cicirelli (1972). It also partly works, albeit indirectly, to further demonize urban schooling by reporting and reproducing a picture of failure and underachievement, rather than a more complex and nuanced understanding of schools that work with disadvantaged constituencies and may well be extremely successful in this work. It also picks up the other policy approaches identified some time ago by Cicirelli; the compensatory approach and the self-actualization model too. It has brought additional resources into some urban primary schools that have been welcomed. At the same time, the ways in which this policy imperative is justified or seen as necessary might be counterproductive and work to amplify concerns about urban schooling rather than celebrating their successes. Perhaps one of the most invidious elements of EiC is that some urban schools are funded while others are not. In the EiC schools themselves, some children get more support than others – those designated as gifted and/or talented as well as those with learning difficulties.

There are many questions to do with the EiC policy. First, even if 'standards' do rise in EiC schools, there will still be a hierarchy of attainment overall and it is likely that middle-class children will continue to outperform working-class children, regardless of policy initiatives (Mortimore and Whitty 1997). It could be argued that at least urban children are getting a foot on the ladder of achievement, even if they are not as high up as their middle-class peers. Second, there have to be questions about the context in which attainment is performed and measured. Whose cultural capital is valued in the educational system? Whose view of learning and knowledge is valued (Ladson-Billings 1995)? Third, is there any evidence to suggest that a competitive system that may well be rationed in favour of some groups more than others (Gillborn and Youdell 1999) is systemically able to enhance the attainment of historically excluded constituencies? Can schools really repair the damage done in the wider social setting?

Conclusion

In this chapter, we have suggested that at specific moments, the attention of policymakers turns towards the children of the inner city and their 'lack' of attainment in learning. Currently, in the UK, concerns are once more being expressed about urban schools and a plethora of projects have been set up to 'include' these children and ameliorate aspects of their exclusion. The focus has been on 'raising' their attainments and raising standards as measured in relation to the National Curriculum.

These policies have not started from a position that necessarily respects what the children and their families already know. They have not appreciated that a good education might involve 'a more nourishing diet than the rather thin gruel of the standards agenda' (Dyson 2003: 9). And while these policies have focused on 'raising standards' and removing 'barriers to learning', which are laudable, few if any of these projects and policies have at their core 'concurrent strategies to tackle poverty and disadvantage at their roots' (Mortimore and Whitty 1997: 12). In terms of learning in the city, as Black concludes (2000: 349–50):

> We often overlook the obvious – the spaces outside our doorstep. Yet our communities, towns, cities are 'living' curricula that teach us lessons about cultural diversity and difference, racism and anti-racism. As such, they are also a powerful and rich resource for students' cultural experiences and understandings.

Questions

1. What do children learn in urban settings that could be used to enhance their learning in school?
2. In what ways could the National Curriculum be extended to take account of the urban as a resource for learning in the urban primary school?
3. To what extent do you think that EiC (or any other policy) 'can succeed where other urban education initiatives have, on the whole, failed' (NFER 2004b)?

SOCIAL JUSTICE

This chapter is concerned with the 'practical difficulties teachers have to face in trying to implement socially just practices' (Cribb and Gewirtz 2003: 16) in the urban primary school. In the first part of this chapter, we explore some of the different ways in which the concept of social justice has been understood and some criteria that can be used to work towards socially just decision making. In the second part of the chapter, we draw on a number of situated 'test cases' for social justice decision making in urban primary schools, to illustrate the contradictions that exist between different dimensions of social justice.

Understanding social justice

Harvey (1973: 97) has argued that 'justice is essentially to be thought of as a principle (or set of principles) for resolving conflicting claims'. However, as Vincent (2003: 1) has pointed out, social justice has more frequently concentrated on questions to do with economic distribution. This approach, usually referred to as *distributive justice*, refers to 'the division of benefits and the allocation of burdens arising out of the process of undertaking joint labour' (Harvey 1973: 97) and is generally associated with the work of Rawls. Rawls (1972: 7) maintained that, in society, the major institutions should 'distribute fundamental rights and duties and determine the distribution of advantages from social co-operation'. According to Rawls (1972) the essence of justice, and the overriding principle on which it is based, relates to the principle of fairness in distribution. In order to determine whether something is fair, Rawls asks us to perform mental acrobatics each time we make a decision. We should ask ourselves from behind a 'veil of ignorance' whether, as rational persons, we would accept any position in the social system that may arise out of any given decision. In other words, if we were not prepared to accept any of the possible outcomes ourselves, then the decision would not be socially just.

Conflicts may arise when it is not straightforward to arrive at a decision or when the decision makers are unable to reach a conclusion that will satisfy every group or constituency in society. Runciman (1969) argued that three criteria needed to be applied in attempting to arrive at a socially just decision. The first criterion was 'need'. The second criterion related to whether the distribution being considered contributed to the common good and the third was 'merit'.

The major question that arises out of the first criterion is how to determine where the greatest need exists. One method is to establish where there is a large demand for facilities and amenities, as then it can be argued that there is a need for resources in these areas. For example, where there are large numbers of homeless people there is a greater need for housing provision than where there are few homeless people. An addition that Runciman (1969) proposed was that a need existed where there was 'relative deprivation'. For example, if one type of school was provided in a particular locale and not in another then this could be seen as socially unjust. A further proposal for determining the greatest need was to rely on the assessments of experts in evaluating the relative needs of potentially disadvantaged groups. For instance, where there are school buildings in a poor state of repair, the designated experts will be able to recommend the allocation of additional resources to improve the conditions of these buildings. A key dilemma in a needs-based approach towards distributive justice was highlighted by Harvey (1973: 105), who pointed out that 'defining social justice in terms of need thrusts onto us the whole uncomfortable question of what is meant by need and how it should be measured'.

Runciman's second criterion related to the contribution to the common good. This is not an easy criterion to apply in practice either as it depends on how the 'common good' is interpreted. For example, does the 'common good' refer to the global population, the national population or to more localized communities? It could be argued that allocating resources to areas of need – for example to urban regions, might do little to add to the benefits that may be accrued to the nation as a whole and could potentially draw resources away from areas where substantial progress is being made. Harvey (1973) argued that in the search for a socially just distribution, the contribution to the common good should take second place to providing for the needs of localized communities. He justified this claim on the basis that the damage to a community by not having its concerns addressed would be larger than any overall negative impact on the population as a whole. However, in his discussion of distributional justice, Harvey was writing about geographical and spatial organization and investment, not educational justice.

In terms of the criterion for socially just distributions allocated on the basis of 'merit', Harvey claimed that 'merit' related to the degree of difficulty that was experienced through living in a certain area. This would not necessarily mean that someone who lived in a 'deprived' area would automatically receive additional support. Rather, if it could be shown that they had been forced to inhabit an area because circumstances prevented them from living elsewhere, then they would be worthy candidates for assistance. 'Merit can therefore be translated in a geographical context as an allocation of extra resources to compensate for the degree of social and natural environmental difficulty' (Harvey 1973: 107). Need and merit are overlapping criteria in determining a socially just distribution of social goods.

More recent work on social justice has argued that social justice is conceptually complex, more 'plural' and goes beyond its distributional form (Griffiths 1998; Cribb and Gewirtz 2003): 'It [social justice] is viewed as simultaneously concerning the distribution of goods and resources on the one hand and the valorisation of a range of social collectivities and cultural identities on the other' (Cribb and Gewirtz 2003: 15). This second strand of social justice is what Fraser (1997) and Young (1990) have called *cultural justice*. This category of justice concerns the need to recognize and respect the cultural differences that exist in society.

Sometimes, competing claims and 'tensions' between these different forms of social justice may arise (Cribb and Gewirtz 2003). Fraser (1997) has argued that the politics of redistribution and the politics of recognition often have contradictory intentions and outcomes. For example, in schools, we might want to claim that one group (cultural justice) needs to be treated differently (distributional justice) in order to achieve a socially just outcome. Any distribution made on the basis of the politics of recognition might exclude those not identified as part of the group.

A third form of social justice is *associational justice*. If social justice is to be realized then it will be 'necessary for previously subordinated groups to participate fully in decisions about how the principles of distribution and recognition should be defined and implemented' (Cribb and Gewirtz 2003: 19). However, as Cribb and Gewirtz (2003: 19) also note, groups that have been subordinated through distributional and cultural injustice, are less well placed to 'become involved in decision making, even when the opportunities are there'.

So far, we have argued that social justice is a complex and multifaceted concept. Issues of distribution, recognition and association need to be identified and interrogated in arriving at decisions about what to do in practice. Decision making needs to consider criteria such as need, the common good and merit. However, there is another key point that needs to be foregrounded in this discussion of social justice and its meanings. Griffiths (1998) and Seddon (2003) have argued that dominant constructions of social justice shift over time and are interpreted differently in different contexts. As Vincent (2003: 2) puts it: 'What is considered as just at one juncture in history, or in one place, or amongst one social group, is not necessarily considered so in another.'

Social justice and education policy approaches

In terms of social justice and education provision, changes have occurred in policy and practice as a consequence of differences in interpretations and, sometimes, more responsive concerns for enacting social justice.

Gamarnikow and Green (2003) argue, for example, that the post-Second World War setting marked a key shift in public policy constructions of social justice. The setting up of the welfare state in the UK challenged some of the rigid classical economic doctrines of the free market. The social justice focus was dominated by attempts at more socially just distribution, particularly the distribution of health, education and housing.

After the Second World War and continuing into the 1960s, there was an effort to create a more egalitarian society. Through the creation of the welfare state, the national health service and the widespread changes in education policy, Britain set up a number of provisions to ameliorate poverty and ill-health and support for egalitarian reform was widespread. These egalitarian beliefs, 'posed a challenge to institutions, administrative systems and ideologies which had been created by old elites, in the interests of dominant classes. But in practice, these radical impulses did not prevail' (Jones 2003: 13).

In the late 1960s and early 1970s, against the backdrop of economic recession and mass unemployment, it was argued that educational standards were too low and that schools were failing in their task (CCCS 1981). In relation to the contestations of social justice initiatives that were produced, Tomlinson suggested that:

> Underlying these charges was a concern voiced by those on the political right, that social democracy itself, by encouraging groups, hitherto destined for lower status jobs and lower levels of education to claim equal treatment, was undermining the authority of the state. (2001: 22)

However, social-democratic critiques of educational provision were also being produced at this time. For instance, Lawton (1977: 10) maintained that the post-war settlement had (eventually) given all children a 'right' to 11 years of continuing schooling but he argued that access on its own did not guarantee equality or social justice. To attend a school for a fixed period of time was simply not enough. Lawton argued that what was needed was a 'legal minimum' of shared curriculum content. Some schools provided access to a rich and varied curriculum while others did not:

> Social justice in education does not mean equality in the sense of giving all children the same education. But it does mean that all children should have the right to real education, not an inferior kind of instruction and socialisation. It will not be possible to achieve this kind of social justice without being more specific about a common core curriculum. Social justice in education must mean that all ... children have access to worthwhile knowledge and experiences. (Lawton 1977: 187)

The complex and contested question of what counts as knowledge in terms of curriculum content and social justice issues still poses many dilemmas. Social justice questions surround curriculum policymaking such as: the need for a common curriculum set against the need to recognize and respect difference; and the need to provide a culturally and practically relevant curriculum alongside the need to ensure that all citizens have access to the core skills of numeracy and literacy as well as a worthwhile enriching and critical curriculum.

When Margaret Thatcher's Conservative government was elected to power in 1979, education was not initially a key concern of government. However, during the Conservatives' second term in power, education moved into a central position. The Conservatives focused on individual rights rather than any notions of the common good. It was argued that individuals would 'choose' good schools, which would pressure 'bad' schools to improve or close. Diversity and competition between schools would ensure that parental choice worked as a lever for raising standards. The issue of poverty, or indeed inequality, or issues of the common good of society as a whole were simply not addressed.

Many commentators have suggested that Conservative educational policy, by enhancing individual choice, sidelined the needs of groups who were less able to exercise 'choice' and privileged those better placed to bring off social advantage, namely the enlarged middle classes (Ball 2003a; Vincent 2003). However, in 1997 New Labour were elected to government and placed 'education, education, education' at the centre of their policymaking. In practice, many of the educational policy interventions launched by New Labour seemed and still seem to be 'closer to that of the Conservative agenda than to Labour's traditional approach' in terms of social justice (Whitty 2002: 127). The policy imperative was social inclusion in a context where competition and choice still held sway. The thrust of education policy was still with raising standards through the policy intervention of curriculum tactics such as the literacy and numeracy strategies. For New Labour, as with the Conservative governments, the underlying cause of educational inequalities – poverty – was often less important than in-school actions. Robinson's suggestion (1997) that 'attacking' poverty would do more to reduce inequality than in-school reforms was dismissed as 'claptrap' by David Blunkett, the then Secretary of State for Education (Pyke 1997).

Under New Labour, Gamarnikow and Green (2003) claim that education policymaking is related to distributive forms of social justice. The overt concern with social disadvantage and the moves towards social inclusion demonstrate this approach. Gamarnikow and Green (2003: 217) argue that while Old Labour focused on a discourse of human rights and 'comprehensive social mixing to bring beneficial effects for all' (the common good), New Labour has a 'mixed' and 'confused' approach to social justice. New Labour is, they claim, concerned about social exclusion and its detrimental effects on human capital and economic prosperity. While some policy initiatives have addressed these concerns, other policies seem to be destined to exacerbate these issues. For example, Gamarnikow and Green cite the extension of educational hierarchies that have been reinserted under New Labour:

> It is difficult to envisage how such a system of stratified schools, located in education markets and articulated with the wider processes of power, can produce anything but unequal outcomes, disguised as organic diversity and specialisation, while in reality consolidating further the

> already existing social class and education hierarchy. (Gamarnikow and Green 2003: 220)

Policymaking involves more than just the enactment of legislation. One dilemma is that combinations of different policy changes, often introduced over several years, may work together to manufacture unintended changes. Another dilemma is that policy enactments take place in situated contexts on the basis of localized judgements. However complex social justice issues are, and however contradictory or muddled different aspects of the policy agenda appear to be, teachers in schools have a more practical problem. They have to 'find the best available means of managing the tensions' (Cribb and Gewirtz 2003: 28). In this process, therefore, what they understand by social justice and the criteria that they deploy in coming to any decisions will influence outcomes in practice.

Practical social justice decision making in urban primary schools

In this section of the chapter, we explore some dilemmas involved in enacting social justice in urban primary schools where decisions have to be made about pedagogy and practice. We focus on decisions related to selection and rationing, tensions between meeting individual needs and the common good, and potential conflicts between issues of fairness and recognition in centralized educational systems. These decisions have to be made at a macro level, across and between education authorities, as well as at a micro level, within schools themselves.

In what follows, we will explore a number of situated 'test cases' of social justice in urban primary schools through school-based vignettes that illustrate the tensions that exist. The vignettes that we deploy are drawn from events that arose in discussions with those teachers and headteachers whom we interviewed for this book. We are using a fictitious school, which we are calling Curtis Primary School, to ground our discussions. Curtis is an urban primary school, built in the 1880s and set within an estate that is largely made up of local authority housing. The intake of the school is predominantly working class and culturally and linguistically diverse. There are a very small number of middle-class families in the area whose children attend the school. Mrs Ali has been the headteacher at Curtis Primary School for some time. The school has a number of experienced teachers but often has to rely on newly qualified teachers (NQTs) and supply teachers to maintain adequate levels of staffing. The LEA sees Curtis as a school that is managing well, despite higher than average numbers of children who qualify for free school dinners.

We do not claim that the tensions we explore only exist in urban primary schools, but it is likely that the impact of decisions-in-practice will have more consequences for social justice outcomes in these schools. Schools and families in more advantaged settings will have a wider range of economic and social support systems through which to augment, extend and repair the work of the school.

Selection and rationing

Our first social justice policy issue relates to selection and rationing in education. Selection has always been a social justice issue in state education, although the intensity of its effects has been differently experienced at different historical moments in time. Lawton (1994: 96) raised one of the central dilemmas in any discussion about forms of selection: 'In a democracy is it fair to give less education to those who need it most ... is it efficient that a majority could be grossly undereducated?' In the case where 'selection' has historically involved providing one group (usually middle-class high performers) with a more academic education and others (usually working-class low performers) with a more vocationally oriented schooling of shorter duration, then the question of 'fairness' needs to be asked. It could be argued that processes of selection recognize and respect differences between children's attainment. It could be suggested that children's learning needs, for different pacing perhaps, might be better met through some forms of selection or, more positively, through sensitive grouping. However, if selection meant that we had to accept the less popular social good on offer, would we be happy with this outcome?

One current example of where selection occurs in primary schools is in the 'gifted and talented' schemes that operate under the umbrella of the larger Excellence in Cities projects (DfEE 1999c). Academically 'gifted' children or those who are perceived to have talents in a certain area are identified and then extra lessons, activities or after-schools clubs are set up and specifically targeted to meet the needs of these children. The justification for the scheme rests, in part, on the assumption that there is a failure on the part of the school to fully meet the needs of the 'most able' children during the normal course of the school day. However, questions of fairness arise. To illustrate this point let us use a contextualized exemplar.

> In Curtis Primary School, the Excellence in Cities project means that some children who are categorized as 'gifted and talented' are eligible for extra support. The children who qualify are, in the main, white and include the small number of children from middle-class families who attend the school. The staff are concerned that the extra resources available to the school are not being distributed in a socially just manner. Those children and families who are already relatively advantaged will receive more assistance. How can the school manage their resources in a way that is fair and equitable?

Currently, the New Labour government has a commitment towards raising standards in schools. In the New Labour policy lexicon, standards are measured through the test scores achieved by children in the end of Key Stage tests. For a variety of reasons, such as raising standards for individual children and individual schools, as well as ensuring that the government meets its own published standard assessment tasks (SATs) targets, schools have been supported in targeting children who are just short of the necessary levels. While what follows is another example of selection, it is also an example of a form of rationing of education provision. Gillborn and Youdell (1999) have argued that the way in which some secondary schools have concentrated on students on the C/D border in their GCSEs, rather than any other group, amounts to a form of education rationing. (Any improvements in the C/D cohort will give a measurable boost to the league tables that only record performance in the A through to C category as a whole.) It could be argued that booster classes are another form of rationing educational resources and, as such, issues of fairness and justice are intimately involved in deciding who will or will not be in the advantaged group.

Curtis Primary School has received funding to run booster classes after school for children in Year 6 who are about to take their end of Key Stage tests. The funding is only for children working at National Curriculum Level 3, just below the national target of Level 4. The teachers in Curtis Primary School are concerned that this policy is designed to ensure that national targets are met rather than help children's learning. What can the school do to ensure the management of additional funding is used in the best interests of the majority of children in the school?

Is this sort of funding fair and equitable in terms of Rawls' test of fairness? If it is not, what could the school do to divert the money to more of the children? How can the teachers select children for booster classes in a fair and egalitarian way? Perhaps the key question here is: should the requirement to work in a socially just manner preclude funding one group to the exclusion of all others? In cases such as this example, it is evident that 'need' as a criterion for distributive justice is being interpreted in a way that excludes 'merit' (Runciman 1969).

Forms of selection occur on a daily basis within all primary schools in often quite subtle and complex ways. For example, the literacy and numeracy strategies have meant that many more primary schools are using ability groupings in these curriculum areas (Hallam et al. 2004b). Are schools making decisions in the best interest of all the children or is it in the interest of the school that is trying to maximize its performance data? How can the school manage grouping in an equitable and fair way? What opportunities are missed through not teaching in mixed ability groups, for children who have EAL for instance? Are the pedagogical arguments in favour of setting children justified?

In the micro setting of the urban primary school, decisions about distributive justice take on a personal dimension. In schools where there may well be some concern to hold onto a 'social mix' in intake (Thrupp 1999; Whitty 2002) this may become distorted by questions of distributive justice.

Ms Johnson is a middle-class mother of three children who attend Curtis Primary School. She regularly talks to teachers in the school to find out what they are doing to support her oldest child, James. When the school decides to group according to 'ability' for maths and English (a social justice dilemma) the teachers know that she will be upset if her son is not put in the 'top' sets. The teachers are also aware that he will need to be given extra help to enable him to cope alongside the 'more able' children.

> Ms Johnson has hinted that she might need to move her three children from Curtis if James is not part of the 'top' groups. The teachers opt to avoid conflict and put James in the 'top' sets.

What is the effect of this? What advantage does James gain? How does this decision disadvantage other children? What would be the effect on the school if they lost Ms Johnson, her three children and other similar parents? What about the ethics involved in reaching this decision?

This example also demonstrates the role of teachers in the interpretation of policy and therefore in the process of ensuring a socially just education system. First, if the teachers opt to avoid conflict and put Ms Johnson's son in the 'top' group, they are likely to have to deny another child a place that could be more suited to their needs. Second, to succeed in the 'high-ability' group, Ms Johnson's son may require extra support that will draw teacher time away from other children with similar or even greater needs. The teachers in this case are required to consider all the children, evaluate their needs and attempt to do the best they can to work in a fair and equitable manner.

Teachers in all schools face these sorts of tensions on a regular basis as they attempt to decide how to interpret policy in the best interests of the majority of their children. Although policy changes impact at a local, school-based level, teachers are the people who translate policy into action on the ground. Issues of social justice therefore are not solely the responsibility of policy-makers, although they do bear the ultimate responsibility. They are also the responsibility of headteachers and teachers within primary schools themselves. In the urban primary school, where resources may be reduced and where the local community may be less able to raise additional funding for the school, rationing education provision and rationing any additional resources is likely to have more deep-seated consequences in terms of social justice and fairness. Schools with more advantaged intakes will be able to afford support for more, if not all, of their children, because of their enlarged fundraising capacity and extended budget. More privileged children in these primary schools will, in any case, have extended access to out of school enrichments, activities and educational support within their families (Crozier and Reay 2005).

Individual needs and the common good

Our second social justice policy issue in education relates to the tensions between individual needs and those of the wider community – the common good. In this section, we want to explore a hypothetical issue related to individual choice and staffing issues in the urban primary school. In the UK, there has been a tradition of individual teachers' choosing which school to work in. This is less the case in some other national settings. For example, in Japan teachers are assigned to schools. In Australia, incentives are offered to try to ensure that rural and indigenous schools are staffed by well-qualified teachers. Yet, some schools in urban areas regularly experience difficulty in recruiting and retaining their teaching staff. Newly qualified teachers and even the more experienced teachers often choose not to work in challenging schools (Menter et al. 2000). One way forward has been to advocate offering additional incentives to individuals who 'choose' to work in urban schools (Johnson 2003).

> Holly has graduated from college and has been offered a job by Curtis Primary School where she did her final block of teaching experience. She is a very good teacher. She knows the school is tough and would be extremely challenging. She has also been offered employment in Maryland Gardens Primary School, which is located in a more privileged area where the SATs results are excellent and behaviour is commonly known to be less difficult. What might be the effects of her choosing Maryland Gardens Primary School for the staffing of Curtis Primary School?

While Holly might choose the 'easier' school in which to complete her first few years of teaching, there are some possible consequences of this choice for Curtis Primary School. The 'good' school may improve still further while Curtis Primary School may have to rely on temporary short-term supply cover until they are able to find a suitable teacher. One solution could be to pay Holly more for working in Curtis Primary School. However, although schools are permitted to pay teachers more in urban settings, they do not receive additional funding for this. If they offer points for recruitment and retention, the money has to come from the school budget. Should teachers be appointed in a more socially just manner that considers the needs of the whole school community, the common good, rather than the choices of individual teachers, whose training has been subsidized by the state? Consider the following scenario.

> Curtis Primary School's local education authority (LEA) has suggested a scheme to alleviate teacher shortages and inequalities in staffing. The LEA has decided that all new teachers should be allocated to schools based on their teaching practice profiles. Students with excellent practice profiles will be sent to the most challenging schools while competent students will be placed in settings that are less challenging. This will support struggling schools while simultaneously ensuring that human resources (teachers) are more evenly distributed. Curtis Primary School is perceived by the LEA as a 'coping' school and therefore would receive a newly qualified teacher who was competent but perhaps not outstanding. The teachers and headteacher are not fully behind the idea but can see the benefits to the authority as a whole. Is it fair to restrict teacher choice for a few years after graduation if the overall effects for the common good are generally positive? Are there any other ways of supporting 'less popular' schools in their attempts to recruit staff?

On the surface, this solution towards staffing problems might seem socially just – the most needy schools get the better new teachers from college while the less confident new teachers get to develop their skills in schools in less challenging circumstances. However, a related point is that social justice, as a principle through which we ensure fairness throughout the education system, does not limit itself to what happens with individual schools, although that is important. There is a need to consider the needs of all children. Where schools exist that find it harder to recruit good teachers due to the high cost of housing or the challenging behaviour of children, radical solutions might be necessary. Directing newly trained teachers to the more challenging schools is one such solution but others could include additional incentive payments or accelerated progress up the pay scale. The question of directing teacher placement would be a thorny issue (where the choices of individuals were set against the needs of a wider constituency) and could deter some from entering the profession. Nevertheless, alternative staffing strategies certainly deserve consideration.

Fairness and recognition in centralized systems

Our third social justice policy issue relates to fairness and recognition in centralized systems of educational provision. Here we are referring to the centrally planned and controlled National Curriculum, the introduction of the national strategies for literacy and numeracy and nationally set targets for performance management. For all the benefits the curriculum offers, what we are suggesting is that it may well work against many children in our urban areas who have different needs. One fundamental question is whether a National Curriculum, through which all children are exposed to the same content and are expected to reach the same levels, meets the needs of all children. Echoing an earlier point, all children should have 'access to worthwhile knowledge and experiences' (Lawton 1977: 187) but this approach needs to be mediated by the needs (and interests) of the children. The situated vignette we have included here relates to issues of relational or cultural justice.

> The majority of children who attend Curtis Primary School live across the road from the school in the local council estate. The estate has housed many families who have come to the UK as refugees and asylum seekers. Some of these families send their children to Curtis Primary School. The children are aware of some local hostility towards recent arrivals. The National Curriculum does little to provide an opportunity where issues of oppression and the need to seek asylum can be discussed. Yet Mrs Ali, the headteacher, thinks it is important that the school takes a lead and provides knowledge and understandings about the recent movements of peoples. She also wants to assure her local community that racism will be tackled if it occurs. What steps could the staff take to extend their curriculum offer? What can and should urban primary schools do to respect differences in their curriculum offer?

In their study of school exclusion, Wright et al. (2000) argued that, because the success of a school is largely determined by its results, some headteachers might be exercising 'damage limitation strategies' through excluding children perceived as disruptive. These children may then have difficulty obtaining a place at another school because headteachers are well aware of the reasons why they are seeking admission. What follows is a scenario that highlights the dilemmas between social justice for individuals and issues to do with the common good in a setting regulated by centrally determined measures of performance management (Tomlinson 2001).

> Darren attends Curtis Primary School. He has difficulties with managing his temper. He has had anger management sessions with a worker from the school's psychology service. He knows that when he feels he is losing control he must go to Mrs Ali who will keep him until he cools down. However, he has, from time to time, been excluded. Last week he completely lost his temper and hurt a classmate. Mrs Ali has now excluded Darren on a permanent basis. Darren's mother wants him back at school. She cannot cope with him and believes that Curtis Primary School has the experience and expertise to help and support him. The staff believes Darren has overstepped the mark. They are worried about the safety of other children and believe Darren is having a negative effect on the education of other children in the class. They believe classes will be easier to teach without Darren and that, in consequence, more children will be likely to achieve higher marks in their SATs. What social justice claims exist in relation to the different needs of Darren, his classmates, his teachers, and the school community?

What this scenario illustrates is the way in which one policy (here testing and publishing performance details) may have a second-order unintended outcome. That is, it may exert pressure on schools to resort to permanent exclusion for children with challenging in-school behaviours. It is worrying to think that teachers may well feel forced to weigh up the position of a school in a league table of results alongside the education of some of the more challenging children in our society. Equally, it could be the case that the school has reached a decision in respect of the needs of the greater number of children. Whatever the outcome, those responsible in schools for reaching a decision in cases like Darren's will be caught in a conflict between a number of ethical positions in a context where national policy has also to be considered.

So far, we have focused on some of the issues of distributional justice that surround selection and educational rationing (Gillborn and Youdell 1999). We have also briefly explored relational and cultural decision making. One aspect of social justice that we have not directly considered relates to associational justice. In urban primary schools, where the policy imperatives for partnerships are strongly urged, often because of the age of the children, there is a need to develop and extend participation in the life and decision making of the school. However, this might be harder to achieve in the urban primary school. Working-class parents might be less able to become actively involved in the work of the school because of the lack of time and the demands of managing their circumstances. Even when they try to become involved, they may be more prone to being 'fobbed off' by teachers (Reay 1998a: 118) or being regarded as a 'hindrance' rather than as partners (Roffey 2002: 18).

Parents who have EAL might not always be supported to actively participate in decision-making in their children's primary school. Families that are being temporarily housed and who are prone to higher than average levels of mobility may have other pressing priorities.

Conclusion

Since New Labour was elected to office, some attempts have been made to reduce poverty and promote social inclusion, particularly through raising participation levels in employment. As Jones (2003: 146) points out, this 'does not entail a lessening of the advantages of more privileged groups, not an effort to return to the objectives of "equality of outcome" that many social reformers thought possible in the 60s and 70s'. In contrast, in the education sector an increase in hierarchies and selective mechanisms has allowed 'more advantaged social groups differential access to particular forms of provision' (Jones 2003: 146). Somewhat contradictorily, families in urban areas may be in receipt of family tax credits and have a Sure Start provider in their area, but they may have reduced access to targeted provisions like booster classes or 'gifted and talented' supplements.

From our 'case study' of Curtis Primary School, it seems that 'social justice has a variety of facets ... [and] these facets might sometimes be in tension with one another' (Cribb and Gewirtz 2003: 18). Tensions exist in making decisions that have different consequences for individuals and institutions, for example, when reaching exclusion decisions. Potential conflicts exist between different forms of cultural justice and distributional justice. For instance, boy-friendly reading support might sideline the needs of some girls who also need additional support (Hey et al. 1998). There are also tensions because of the differential power that exists between and among people.

We have highlighted some of the 'practical difficulties teachers have to face in trying to implement socially just practices' in the urban primary school (Cribb and Gewirtz 2003: 16). Decisions about socially just practices are often left to small groups of teachers, in their own school settings, sometimes in their own classrooms. In some urban settings, the primary school might represent the major local investment by the state. In some urban locations, the local community might have a much reduced capacity to supplement the basic education provision. In a competitive market-driven environment, where resources will be rationed out and where 'success' is rewarded and 'failure' punished, implementing socially just decisions will be a complex proposition indeed:

> In a political culture of relative private interest a growing number of citizens reject the legitimacy of action in support of the disadvantaged (who are seen to be responsible for their own problems) and support policies designed to enhance their own interests. (Grace 1994: 53)

Whether the focus is on distributional, cultural or associational social justice, without the political will for a change in the political culture, urban primary teachers might be left struggling to work towards social justice in overwhelmingly challenging circumstances.

Questions

1. What could be done in the urban primary school to broaden alliances and strengthen associational forms of justice?
2. Would it be fair or socially just to place all newly qualified teachers in their first appointments according to the needs of local schools?
3. What additional policies could be implemented to promote social justice in urban primary schools?

A US PERSPECTIVE

This chapter explores some major trends in urban education policy and practice in the USA with a specific focus on elementary schooling (primary education). The chapter is divided into the following sections: understanding the US urban context; a historical overview of US urban school reforms; research into educational activities and programmes in urban US communities; and, finally, a consideration of some contemporary initiatives that have been introduced to manage and support urban elementary school education in the USA.

Introduction

The UK and the USA have had a well-established academic and empirically focused concern with urban development and with urban education. The USA has generally taken the lead in this area of enquiry: 'Desegregation of the school system, the whole civil rights movement, the start of the capital flight, white flight and economic decline of many major industrial cities [led] to a growth in educational concern for the children within inner city schools' (Bash et al. 1985: 44). In the UK, similar changes in production modes and in the requirements of the labour market, coupled with population shifts, have underpinned intellectual enquiry into the so-called urban 'crisis'. In both settings social, cultural and economic changes have impacted on educational provision. Specifically in terms of education policy and practice, it is useful to explore US-based approaches and provision because the two systems are sufficiently alike so that ideas could be interchanged relatively easily between the two nation settings (Corner and Grant 2004). For instance, the UK (and more specifically England) has frequently looked towards the USA and earlier approaches towards urban underachievement have been 'borrowed' and inserted into forms of compensatory education (Bash et al. 1985).

One distinction needs to be acknowledged at the start of this chapter. In the USA, public education is a function of the state and, in each state, resources are devolved to the school district in which the schools are located. These districts respond to their state legislature, rather than the nation, in the administration of local public (state) schools. Instead of a 'national curriculum', each state in the USA has its own curriculum. However, 'despite decentralisation and the consequent diversity of values, resourcing and provision, there is a fair measure of overall consistency in the [US] education system's structure' (Alexander 2000: 103).

Both England and the USA are relatively affluent, highly industrialized nations with densely populated and complex cities and with large numbers of poor and marginalized groups living mainly in the inner cities. Kozol (1991, 1995) has demonstrated in his studies of American inner cities that the conditions of life for poor children and inner city families are particularly harsh. In *Amazing Grace* (1995: 3) he describes an elementary school in the South Bronx, where: 'Only seven of 800 children do not qualify for free school lunches. "Five of those seven," says the principal, "get reduced-price lunches, because they are classified as only 'poor,' not 'destitute'. In what follows we consider the policy responses towards the US urban school. Our intention is that this work will provide an additional perspective through which to consider policy and practice in the UK urban setting.

The US urban context

There has been a growth in social and economic polarization as well as the geographic isolation of urban populations and communities in the USA. This polarization has been fuelled by a major shift in the modes of production (Castells 1989). In particular, the emergence of new urban-based information technology economies has impacted on the labour market:

> The bulk of new jobs pay lower wages and enjoy less social protection . . . At the same time, to fill jobs a new supply of workers is also changing the characteristics of labor, generally making workers more vulnerable to management requirements in terms of their social characteristics, along the lines of gender, race, nationality, and age discrimination in society at large. (Castells 1989: 202)

Information technology industries emphasize the need for workers with a higher level of education and the complex skills that are needed to fill knowledge-intensive jobs. Traditional manufacturing and manual jobs are being phased out as a consequence of de-industrialization and globalization (Bettis and Stoeker 1993). While most highly paid jobs are to be found in metropolitan areas: 'The majority of the resident population of inner cities cannot match the skill requirements of the new labour market because of the inefficiency and segregated nature of the public school system' (Castells 1989: 204). This gap in skills looks set to widen because of disparities in funding that mean that some schools are less well resourced to support a technology-rich pedagogy.

In 1977 Castells argued that a contradiction existed between the provision of services and the economics of the city. His point was that where the increasing demands for urban welfare services were seen as unprofitable and unsustainable for capital to fund, they were resisted by financial corporations and neo-liberal economic policies (Hutton 1995). The consequence was that many states in the USA made extensive cuts to their social programmes, to avoid fiscal crises and maintain financial credibility. Castells (1998: 161) claims that the USA is characterized by 'a sharp divide between valuable and non-valuable people and locales'. He refers to this overall urban policy trend as denoting the *dual city*.

The consequences of the dual city coupled with shifts in production modes have outcomes for the lives of children in the poorest neighbourhoods who often attend run-down inner city schools (Anyon 1997). Urban school systems in the USA have to cope with the effects of families who experience high levels of poverty, housing problems, crime, vandalism, drug and alcohol abuse, child abuse and neglect, gang fights and unemployment (Doherty 1998). The students who currently live and attend schools in US inner cities are from 'a highly culturally, ethnically, and socioeconomically diverse population' (Brown 2004: 285) with a disproportionate number of them coming from low socio-economic households and minority groups. As Kozol informs us:

> Even with a genuine equality of schooling for poor children, other forces would militate against their school performance. Cultural and economic factors and the flight of middle-income blacks from inner cities still would have their consequences in the heightened concentration of the poorest children in the poorest neighbourhoods. (1991: 123)

In terms of economic factors, inadequacies in public funding have compounded the difficulties in urban schools. In the USA, as well as federal (national) and state government funding, local property taxes have historically been used as a mechanism for funding public schools. In richer districts, property is more highly valued and therefore property taxation produces higher levels of finance through which to fund public schools. Urban districts are disadvantaged as property is less valuable and, thus, less tax can be raised for local schools. A landmark lawsuit occurred in 1981 (Abbott v Burke) when the Education Law Center filed a case on behalf of urban school students in New Jersey. The result of the case was that the New Jersey constitution was amended to establish a more equitable system of funding schooling and to raise the level of spending on students in poorer districts to match that spent per student in wealthier districts. In 1990 the case of Abbott and Burke was in court again in New Jersey. The court now ruled that funding needed to be focused on schools in the poorest districts, providing additional, rather than equal assistance.

There has been a raft of legislative changes in the USA that have attempted to provide support as well as reduce inequality in urban schools. However, arguments in support of these legislative changes have frequently been conducted in a policy environment that has sought to understand the 'causes' of the urban problem. In the USA, as in the UK, a search for someone to 'blame' for failures in urban education, whether students, teachers, parents or administrators has been widespread (Doherty 1998). One approach, 'that "if classrooms are run properly, student achievement will improve" highlights teachers as the central problem' (Doherty 1998: 231). Staff shortages and inexperienced and unprepared teaching staff have been blamed for the problems of urban schools. This particular emphasis has resulted in calls for greater accountability and increased monitoring of teachers' performance. As a result, there are pressures to recruit and retain staff in urban schools.

In American urban schools, teacher turnover is high and retention rates have dropped to an average of three years (Adams and Adams 2003). Urban schools and those with relatively high populations of minority and low-income students face the greatest shortage of teachers (Murphy et al. 2003). In terms of addressing teacher retention in urban schools, Adams and Adams (2003) suggest that the following matters need to be considered: mentoring new teachers in urban districts; job sharing to help teachers feel less overworked and stressed; better teacher training programmes for graduates who want to be successful in the urban context; focused financial incentives such as increases in salary and support for urban leadership.

Urban teachers face distinctive challenges in their schools. They may sometimes experience a sense of isolation and may sometimes lack parental and community support for their schools (Stone 1998; Fisher and Frey 2003). Adams and Adams (2003: 3) illustrate some of the complexities involved in urban teaching:

> It is hard being a teacher, and even harder being an urban teacher. There are no typical days but lots of unpredictable ones. Dealing with students from different backgrounds, making immediate decisions, balancing several tasks at once, and continuing to labour at a thankless and very public job can be overwhelmingly stressful. Having few resources and little control over curriculum and pedagogical decisions, and working in dilapidated buildings with mould, leaking water, no air conditioning and, in some cases, no heat – these circumstances can take a toll.

However, the most central and enduring educational urban issue relates to reduced levels of academic achievement in urban schools. Sometimes lower achievement rates have been 'blamed' on reduced expectations, on the lack of a demanding curriculum as well as ineffective instructional practices (Doherty 1998). As a result, there have been calls for curricular reforms and an increase in pressure to improve results. As with some of the urban policy approaches in the UK, there has been an emphasis in the USA on in-school features rather than wider structural issues such as poverty and disadvantage:

> The fact that many urban children show no marked differences from others when they enter school but increasingly fail in comparison after each year of attendance (Feldman 2001) turns the attention to school and community structures (that is, policies and practices) and away from a pessimistic deficit view of and expectations for urban children. (Fisher and Frey 2003: 3)

Therefore, standardized testing has become a key factor in US education (Ravitch 2000). Assessment results in the USA are being used in some states to assess the 'success' of schools and school districts and to identify 'badly' performing schools. In some school districts, the advent of standardized testing has been accompanied by a skills-based and test-focused curriculum. Such a 'one size fits all' approach runs contrary to a view that recognizes the realities of variation and differentiation in the lives of children:

> We do not confront abstract 'learners' ... instead, we see specific classed, raced and gendered subjects, people whose biographies are intimately linked to the economic, political and ideological trajectories of their families and communities, to the political economies of their neighbourhoods. (Apple 1986: 5)

Not surprisingly, urban schools have tended to fare worse in testing regimes and some schools have had funding constraints placed on them as a result. However, echoing a 'success against the odds' UK perspective (Maden 2001), Stone notes:

> In a diverse society where people are spatially differentiated by income, class, ethnicity, race, and religion, particular school districts and individual schools inevitably march to different drummers. Despite the general failures of urban school systems, some city schools do a much better job of educating disadvantaged children than others. (1998: 294)

Thus, while there are some differences in the US urban setting, notably the extremes of urban poverty and a much reduced welfare safety net (Anyon 1997), it is also possible to see some convergences between policy approaches to the 'crisis' of the urban school in the UK and the USA.

Overview of urban school reforms in the USA

This section will briefly review the key policy phases of school reforms in the USA that successive administrations have introduced since the 1980s until the present day. As with reforms in the UK, there is a degree of continuity over time in terms of reforms focusing on 'failing' schools. The policy emphasis is with discourses of urban school failure and governmental responses to this.

In the early 1980s during the Reagan administration (1981–9), a commission was set up to look at the quality of education, as it was reported that education in the USA was inferior to that of many other nations. The report, 'A nation at risk' (1983), criticized public education standards and in particular urban public education. In response to the publication of 'A nation at risk' it was agreed that the introduction of more rigorous academic standards for students and more professional standards for teachers would improve the existing educational provision. Urban schools were hit hardest by 'A nation at risk' as they were identified as having the lowest test scores, highest dropout rates, lowest graduation levels and so forth. Reformers wanted to increase accountability among urban schools to pressure them to perform as well as other non-urban schools. Therefore parents were to be given the opportunity to move their children through the introduction of voucher systems, allowing children to attend a school of their choice. However, no extra funding was provided to help with school improvements.

The late 1980s saw a focus on grassroots changes at individual school level. For instance, there was the introduction of greater accountability and school restructuring with an emphasis on site-based management and the involvement of all stakeholders, a focus on teacher empowerment and enhanced professionalism strategies that have continued to the present day. School management approaches were advocated as ways of making urban schools systems more efficient. These initiatives concentrated on centralization, standardization and bureaucratization.

In George H.W. Bush's administration (1989–93), further proposals were made to improve public education. This administration published a key report, 'America 2000'. Contentious proposals in this report included introducing national standards, vouchers and standardized testing. President Clinton (1993–2001) published 'Goals 2000' in the 1994 Educate America Act, which retained most of the America 2000 reforms and supported standardized testing and school choice. Under Clinton's administration, the emphasis for reforming public education took place at school district level. These developments included a number of strategies such as reforms of the school's day and time spent in school; more time for teacher planning and preparation; specific curricular innovations and an increased provision of in-service support. Other tactics included shifting the control of schools further from central administration to the individual school sites. In general, however, there were no specific plans at policy level to reform urban provision as such, although the increase in testing meant that further pressure of accountability was placed on urban schools.

The No Child Left Behind (NCLB) Act (2001) was the centrepiece of George W. Bush's education agenda. In contrast with previous administrations' approach towards education, urban areas and urban levels of attainment were now firmly back on the policy agenda. In law, schools and school districts receiving Title 1 federal funding (distribution of federal funding to disadvantaged areas) were now required to test students annually in Grade 3 (Year 4) through to 8 (Year 9) in mathematics, language, arts, literacy and science, to begin in 2005. The NCLB Act also called for all children to have achieved minimum competency levels by 2014. Failure to achieve 100 per cent proficiency would result in sanctions and 'corrective measures' being introduced (US Department of Education 2002). These were to include greater monitoring at district level, giving parents the option of transferring their children out of failing schools and extreme measures including replacing staff or schools being taken over by a private company. The key goals of the Act are to improve the achievement of all pupils and to analyse and address the achievement gap between disadvantaged students and others. It aims to equalize levels of attainment between urban and non-urban students and aims to increase the English fluency of those students with English as an additional language.

The act encouraged greater accountability. Measures were put in place that aimed to increase the involvement of parents and the promotion of parental choice in their child's education; improve safety in schools and increase financial assistance particularly for disadvantaged schools. Another thrust sought to enhance the quality of teachers and school principals. States were to be allowed to address teacher shortages through implementing alternative/shorter forms of certification than usually required; they could also offer merit pay and help with housing for those teaching in shortage subject areas.

The US Department of Education, the Council of the Great City Schools and some school superintendents have reported some early evidence that NCLB is helping to raise student academic achievement in the major cities at elementary school level. The Council of the Great City Schools stated that the largest urban public school systems have shown improvement in reading and maths scores in the first year under the NCLB law (Casserly 2004). However, not all public educators are convinced that NCLB is workable. The National Education Association – the largest professional educational employee organization in the USA – claims that it costs more to educate children in urban schools than elsewhere and points out that the vital issue of under-funded mandates has not been resolved by NCLB. Critics of NCLB also argue that telling educators what, when, where, why and how to teach is misguided (see Peterson and West 2003). It has also been suggested (Moscovitch 2005) that the adequate yearly progress (AYP) target is unrealistic and unworkable for all schools, while the testing and accountability-linked sanctions could mean that some schools previously considered successful may well be identified as underachieving if their contextual background is not taken into consideration (Linn 2003).

Hess (1999: 9) claims that: 'Critiques of urban schooling almost invariably begin with the presumption that urban public school systems are in a state of crisis.' He argues that because of this assumption, policies are frequently produced that deal with the symptoms of the 'crisis' rather than addressing more fundamental causes. For example, as Stone (1998: 295) argues:

> Should Americans concur that every child must be enabled to reach some minimal level of educational accomplishment, then national standards and a new set of nationally shared educational practices will be needed. In the end, practices are more important than standards, since the goal is to improve education rather than to provide a national scorecard that will presumably underscore what we already know – that city school districts, schools, and students perform poorly in contrast to most other schools.

In this section, we have argued that efforts to improve education in urban areas have continued intermittently and successive federal administrations have continued to tackle the urban 'crisis'. However, in these policy approaches there is a fundamental contradiction: 'Since support for public schools is shallow, reforms that fail become further evidence of the inadequacy of the system' (Doherty 1998: 225). Furthermore, the introduction of policy after policy has, according to Hess (1999), hampered the embedding of reforms and their potential success in practice: 'The key to improving teaching and learning through new initiatives is through implementation and cultivation of expertise. These are difficult tasks in the best of circumstances, and urban school districts do not present the best of circumstances' (Hess 1999: 157). One tension is that the policy thrust is a top-down bureaucratic response that frequently sidelines the perspectives of those who are the intended focus of the reforms: 'A shared definition of the issues surrounding education, and the establishment of common goals among reformers, may be at least more promising than efforts built only on a shared distain of the current system' (Doherty 1998: 244) and this effort ought to focus on the needs of children.

Educational activities and programmes in urban communities in the USA

In this section, we explore some examples of educational activities and programmes conducted in urban settings in the USA to bring about change and improve the educational experiences of urban students. Strategies to tackle the achievement gap for urbanized groups have included the provision of extra classes; additional individual tutoring programmes, increased accountability at state and local levels; improved professional development for educators; changes in federal economic policy; a reduction in class sizes and improved preparation of students in school for entering college.

One notable example that addresses the educational experiences of poor, urban students of minority heritage is the Comer School Development Program, named after the child psychiatrist, James Comer. It originated in inner city elementary schools in the late 1960s and was developed to improve the education of students through building relationships between all members of the local school community. It had a particular emphasis on developing home–school relationships to improve academic achievement (Comer 1988). In many ways this approach was a precursor to later attempts, both in the UK and USA, to enhance social capital. Evaluations of the programme found that it improved social skills and raised achievement and attendance levels (Coulter, Office of Research, 1993).

There have been other success stories in urban schooling. For instance, E.J. Scott Elementary School is located in a poor neighbourhood of Houston, Texas, where:

> A majority of the boxy, one-storey frame houses are well kept, but others are in bad shape, with their foundations sagging, shingles missing, and trash strewn about the yards. Many have bars on the windows. The only businesses nearby are bars, a small grocery, and a couple of fast-food restaurants. (Miller 1998: 2)

The school population comprises about 60 per cent Hispanic and 40 per cent black children, with over one-third of the children at an early stage of English acquisition. However, according to Miller: 'The school is in most ways a model of the kinds of initiative and attitudes that researchers say are common to high poverty urban schools that succeed against the odds' (1998: 2). She reports that many students achieve 'exemplary' high standards, through staff teamwork, a clear educational purpose and emphasis by all on achievement and success combined with effective leadership.

Some urban elementary schools, such as New Stanley Elementary School in Kansas City have been experimenting for some time with extending the school year, having a longer school day with before- and after-school programmes and keeping the same teacher with the same students for several years. Such initiatives were found to be successful in ensuring that children progressed to middle school at or above average grade level (Prisoners of Time 1994).

In one small-scale longitudinal study, Davis (1999) described collaboration between an inner city elementary school and a university in Virginia that provided opportunities for professional development activities with the aim of improving child-focused teaching and learning. Davis (1999) highlighted the time-consuming, slow process and complexity of change and the many demands and pressures on the school and university involved. Davis concluded that in order for such collaborations to work and for school change to occur, it was critical to provide adequate resources and staff development. In terms of associational justice forms, the study argued that parents and carers needed to be empowered to take ownership of the restructuring and change process.

A study of 13 Chicago elementary schools undertaken by Diamond and Spillane (2004) explored different schools' responses to high-stakes accountability policies. These policies emphasized 'managerial' and 'professional' accountability and required teachers to be more answerable for their practice and performance through strengthening in-school mechanisms for learning. The responses from schools depended on whether the school was a 'low-' or 'high-'performing school. The 'low-'performing schools had a narrower focus on standardized test materials in order to 'comply(ing) with policy demands, focusing on improving performance of certain students with benchmark grades, and in certain subject areas' (Diamond and Spillane 2004: 2). As working-class, minority students tend to go to the lower-performing schools, the findings suggest that using standardized test materials might restrict their access to the wider forms of knowledge (and cultural capital) available in the high-performing schools, therefore contributing to the maintenance of class-based educational inequalities (Ladson-Billings 1995). As Ravitch (2000: 15) comments on these sorts of curriculum 'alternatives':

> Curricular differentiation meant an academic education for some, a non-academic education for others; this approach affected those children – mainly the poor, immigrants and racial minorities – who were pushed into undemanding vocational, industrial or general programs by bureaucrats and guidance counsellors who thought they were incapable of learning much more.

A three-year research study of two districts in a midwestern US city and an eastern seaboard city with large numbers of children from poor neighbourhoods and on free school meals was undertaken by Corbett et al. (2002). The researchers were interested to see if the teachers' assumptions about their students as learners impacted on what took place in the classroom. Most of the teachers adhered to the often quoted school mission statement that 'all children can learn and succeed in school' but they qualified this by stating that without the support from home and effort by the students there was only so much they could do. Other teachers refused to accept lack of parental support or lack of student motivation to be reasons for them not succeeding. On the contrary, these teachers saw it as part of their job to ensure that their students succeeded.

Corbett et al. (2002) explored the impact of the 'it's my job' and 'no excuses' philosophies and campaigns supporting better education for the poor by educators taking responsibility for their students' success. They studied schools and classrooms where students who had previously performed poorly were now succeeding and making good progress. These teachers and schools raised the performance of their students by:

> Quite simply ... refus(ing) to accept any excuses for students performing poorly in school. Instead, they took it upon themselves as their jobs to supply all the support necessary for students to complete assignments at an acceptable level of quality. We argue that there was no recipe for doing this and adamantly avoid extracting any categories of actions and/ or programs that would promote success for all. (Corbett et al. 2002: 9)

These successful teachers were found to be extending their students' learning and competency well beyond the basic skills. There was a greater emphasis on what the students were capable of achieving, rather than on what they were unable to do. This perspective reflects earlier discussions in this book about a 'cultural deficit' perspective (which implies that it is the students and their home backgrounds that prevent their success). In order to succeed, Corbett et al. (2002) concluded, educators need to recognize and value student diversity, establish links between home and school, adjust the school to support students' needs and crucially to recognize and believe that students are capable of success. At the same time, they insist that a 'myopic' approach towards poverty is unproductive – it exists and presents the students with a number of obstacles.

Corbett et al. (2002) found that most of the teachers in their study did not appear to believe that urban students could succeed. One upshot of such findings could be that teachers might now be blamed for not believing enough. Corbett et al. (2002) recommended that there needed to be fundamental changes in beliefs about urban schooling, in particular a need to examine teachers' beliefs about the nature of successful pedagogies. They identified a need to develop sets of shared beliefs that, with the right support structures, could shape classroom practice. Furthermore, these researchers argued that support and policies were needed to assist the efforts of the schools in working towards student success.

Another study conducted by Hess (1999) examined the nature of school reforms among 57 urban school districts during 1992–5. He concluded that: 'The vigilant search for the right "silver bullet reform", the one that will serve urban education, is distracting and unproductive'. He added that the search for 'quick fixes wastes resources even as it fosters apathy, cynicism and disillusionment among veteran teachers' (1999: 191). Hess maintained that in order to help urban students, the greatest emphasis needed to be placed on the performance, not of the students, but of the policymakers and administrators. He saw reform most urgently needed at school district rather than at individual school level: 'This spinning of wheels has aggravated the sad plight of urban education' (Hess 1999: 177). Hess called for policymakers and administrators to be held accountable for their results and actual achievements, rather than rewarding them for what they promise to achieve. 'The professional and political interests of urban school leaders need to be hitched to the long-term performance of urban schools' (1999: 181).

Contemporary initiatives to support urban elementary school education

Educationalists who consider that educational change is achievable:

> Bring resources to ideas, ideas to actions, and actions to outcomes, whether they are involved in building new schools from the ground up with widespread community partnerships or in aggressively challenging traditional tracking, testing, curriculum, or pedagogy. (Fisher and Frey 2003: 3)

It is often grassroots initiatives that have had most success in urban locales. Such initiatives have managed to make positive alliances between the different groups that support urban schools (Grace 1994), such as students and their parents, teachers and school administrators. The initiatives that will now be explored in this section reflect this approach.

Full Service Schooling emerged in the USA in the 1970s and 1980s with the recognition that there was a need for health and welfare support services to contribute towards maintaining a child's learning. These programmes involve schools and community agencies, incorporating health and social services, working collaboratively rather than in isolation, to form a system of support and intervention services for children and their families. They aim to provide quality educational activities and increase the chances of school attendance and encourage students and their families to get more involved in the life of the school. Dryfoos (1994), one of the leading advocates of Full Service Schooling, maintains that this development amounts to a 'revolution' in health and social services and offers benefits to all stakeholders.

The model for full service schooling is that most of the services are located on the school site. This approach is sometimes referred to as 'one-stop shopping' and is viewed as providing a number of advantages for urban communities in terms of access to healthcare, career and employment advice, housing support and welfare services during the school day and before and after school, as well as during the weekends and holidays. However, some criticisms have been expressed. These concerns have focused on practical questions such as who would be in charge and manage the provision; how would collaboration between agencies work and would there be any tensions, particularly between new arrivals and already existing support staff? Concerns have also been raised about the possibility that the school, rather than more community-based programmes could become the main focus and beneficiary of any additional resources. Furthermore, close association with the school might put some people off utilizing the services (Smith 2001).

Another initiative is the charter school movement. It aims to form small and intimate school communities that are not under the same central control, regulations or constraints of conventional state schooling. This shift towards smaller schools is in response to the view that larger public school bureaucracies and particularly urban schools, have become an 'obstacle to high quality education'. They are seen as being unwieldy, impersonal and students get 'lost' in the system (Doherty 1998: 230). Various stakeholders have been involved with the formation and management of such schools, such as parents, teachers, community and business leaders.

Charter schools have emerged in many urban areas where the need to reform education due to lack of resources and overcrowding of state public schools has been identified. The reduced size of the charter school student population means that there is supposedly less anonymity between children and staff. Some charter schools have focused on the requirements of urban minority/multilingual students, through utilizing culturally appropriate materials and curricula and including cultural events and activities to promote and support the cultural heritage of the school population. Proponents of charter schools maintain that the choice to attend is open to any child. Critics of the movement have suggested that there are hidden factors such as transportation costs and that those children who are easiest to teach have been admitted to these schools.

There has also been strong and trenchant opposition to the charter school movement in the USA. In their critique of the insertion of a competitive market into education, Apple and Bracey (2001) claim that charter schools are neither innovative nor diverse and that the movement has been hijacked by middle-class, moral majority parents (conservative, fundamentalist Christian groupings). Furthermore, they claim that:

> While a few children may be helped by vouchers, there may be even less financial support for inner city schools in the long run, leading to fewer resources for those parents who 'choose' to keep their children in underfunded schools because, notwithstanding vouchers, they cannot avail themselves of private education. (www.asu.edu/educ/epsl/EPRU/documents/)

Some charter schools are non-profit-making while others are for-profit organizations. There have been examples of private corporations taking over individual schools and even whole school districts, in a bid to reform the education systems and simultaneously make a profit; consequently prioritizing private benefit, taking funds out of the state sector and breaking down the public purpose of equality in state education (Kuehn 1995; Apple 2001). As these schools are 'chartered' by either school districts or the state department of education they are able to receive public funding for their function, yet have the freedom to run themselves. However, they need to demonstrate to the chartering authority that they are successful in improving student achievement. Adams and Adams (2003: 55) claim that: 'As of 2003, charter schools have shown no improvement over urban public schools in terms of academic achievement.' If this be the case, they are not fulfilling their mission.

There are, in addition, many examples of partnership programmes in the USA created to tackle specific issues in urban education, such as teacher shortages in urban schools. For instance, in order to address recruitment, some urban districts 'grow their own' teachers through programmes providing local people with the opportunity and support to train as teachers. Other initiatives have included the 'Troops to Teachers' programme for military personnel to begin a new career as teachers in public schools and 'Teach for America', where well-qualified individuals commit for two years to teach in low-income rural and urban communities.

Various partnership schemes have been introduced in higher education to increase the number of student teachers preparing to teach in urban areas, with urban teacher training programmes and internships often guaranteeing employment for graduates. The State University of New York Urban Education Teacher Center (SUTEC) opened in 2001 with the aim of preparing student teachers who wanted to work in an urban setting and, in particular, New York City schools. A partnership has been developed between SUTEC and the NYC Department of Education to provide a supportive environment and access to resources for student teachers. For instance, the student teachers are provided with a SUTEC support team that includes experienced teachers and administrators who provide various workshops throughout the year. There is a shortage of teachers in New York City, so there are many job opportunities when student teachers have obtained their New York state teaching licences. There are funding and housing opportunities for those qualifying teachers who are prepared to commit themselves to working in a high-need school.

One established programme, the Urban Education Partnership, was founded in Los Angeles in 1984. It is an independent, non-profit-making organization, relying on contributions for its support. It currently works in four states, 14 school districts and more than 300 schools. It aims to tackle the most difficult problems and issues in urban education using pioneering approaches: 'To help students in high-need schools increase their academic achievement by partnering with educators, parents and the community' (Urban Education Partnership 2003: 1). It focuses on strategic leadership – improving training and development for leaders in urban education; transforming schools; restructuring schools to create more effective teaching and learning environments and connecting parents and communities to schools. According to the Urban Education Partnership, its urban learning centres initiative has received national recognition for raising and sustaining student achievement. Testimonies from school principals and teachers provide evidence of their success in supporting low-achieving schools, partnership building with families and communities and changing beliefs among all those responsible for improving academic achievement in high-need urban schools.

Conclusion

This chapter has demonstrated that in the USA there has been a lack of agreement about how to improve education for urban communities. From the brief historical overview, it seems that there is no simple quick-fix formula for successful educational reform through the introduction of new policies and initiatives and such efforts seem to proceed on tenuous ground (Hess 1999). However, there are some examples of elementary school-based reforms and state–district initiatives that have made a difference. In this chapter, a number of policy initiatives in the US setting have been explored, with the intention of providing a contrasting account of the complexities and tensions that impact urban education. What has emerged is the need for a flexible, nuanced and localized response towards issues in urban education. An understanding of how these issues have been addressed elsewhere could potentially enhance our capacity to address similar challenges in the UK.

Questions

1. How can an understanding of other urban education systems and policies support and develop your understanding of urban education in your own country?
2. What are the arguments for and against full service schooling?
3. To what degree is it useful for UK policymakers to 'borrow' urban policies from the USA?

11 UNDERSTANDING THE URBAN PRIMARY SCHOOL

This chapter will consider what the discussions in the foregoing chapters have to offer to an understanding of the urban primary school. It will revisit the main purposes of the book, namely, to articulate a more complex picture of the urban primary school that goes beyond some of the stereotypes that still dominate urban policy; to explore some of the challenges of learning and teaching in urban settings; and to reassert some critical urban educational concerns. Finally, it will offer some comments about urban policy and urban primary schools in terms of the private and public good.

The main themes of this book

As we have argued in this book, too often government urban education policymaking is couched in 'deficit' terms that marginalize and disregard the wider social setting and that 'blame' individual children, their parents, their schools and teachers for any 'failure' in achievement. Garcia and Guerra (2004: 151) claim that 'school reform efforts stall or fail because deficit beliefs become a filter that blocks educators' abilities to examine their assumptions and to look beyond traditional solutions for real and meaningful change'. Thus, the first purpose we had in writing this book was to theorize urban primary schools in a way that engaged with the wider social issues of structural disadvantage, poverty, oppression and exclusion.

In a competitive environment, the more privileged in society enjoy increased 'access' to social advantage (Pahl 1970) and are better at gaining benefits for their families (Ball 2003a). When less privileged families are trapped in low wages, poor housing and have limited access to social welfare, it is not surprising that their children fare less well in school. Urban education theory involves a recognition that 'urban problems and crises' are not failings in people or institutions, rather they occur as symptoms of the wider contradictions of capitalism (Grace 2005). Urban theory offers an insight into the broader contradictions that shape the educational world of the urban child:

> Urban schools are at the center of the maelstrom of constant crises that beset low-income neighborhoods. Education is an institution whose basic problems are caused by, and whose basic problems reveal, the other crises in cities: poverty, joblessness and low-wages, and racial and class segregation. Therefore, a focus on urban education can expose the combined effects of public policies, and highlight not only poor schools but the entire nexus of constraints on families. (Anyon 2005: 177)

The second purpose of this book was to explore the challenges of teaching and learning in the urban primary school. We have argued that the children who attend these schools need access to the same curriculum that is offered to more advantaged children. In addition, children in urban primary schools need to understand and have access to the cultural capital of dominant, more powerful groups in society (Bourdieu 1986). This is a rights entitlement in any democratic society (Delpit 1997). Children in urban primary schools also need the capacity to interrogate and critically engage with the curriculum (Ladson-Billings 1995). Ladson-Billings (1992) argues that a culturally relevant curriculum should explore and extend children's own experiences. Through this curriculum children can come to critically engage with dominant cultures to reveal the distortions and bias that exist. Children growing up in urban areas have the right to see their own experiences reflected in the school's curriculum. They have the right to a curriculum that includes diverse cultural and social values, different histories and literatures and that deploys 'narrative materials and styles like those used in the local community' (Corson 1998: 136). Children who attend urban primary schools need to be taught in a way that respects and recognizes their capacity to achieve and supports their progression in a culturally sensitive way. Teachers in urban primary schools still have some capacity to challenge socially divisive policies through their organizations at a local level. In their classrooms and schools they still play a part in mediating education policy and in struggling to enact socially just decisions.

In the UK, the study of urban education and urban schooling has been neglected for some time. So, the third purpose of this book was to assert the distinctiveness of urban primary schools in theory, practice and policy decisions. Teachers in urban and non-urban primary schools face some similar pressures, such as the need to meet targets and raise standards. What is distinctive in the urban context is the catastrophe of poverty that shapes urban settings and the schools in these areas. Rather than an education policy that simply exhorts the urban primary school to emulate its more privileged neighbour, there is a need to recognize the broader socio-economic contradictions that impact on the urban primary school: 'The urban context remains a challenging one. It is time to re-assert the positive features of cities as learning environments' (Menter 1998: 23).

Moving forward

'Society needs to be clearer about what schools can and cannot be expected to do and what support they need' (Whitty 2002: 124). Urban policymaking, urban pedagogy and teacher education need to directly acknowledge the impact of the urban crisis. As Jones (2003: 172) claims, focusing on raising standards without recognizing contextualized factors 'may well give rise to misdirected pressures, demanding too much of schools, and planning too little for wider sorts of social change'. Just as importantly, there is a need for a politics of education reform that will recognize and respect difference, offer all children the life chances that come with educational success and promote inclusion and the common good rather than private advantage.

In some ways, this is a pessimistic book. The structural and material disadvantages that surround and shape the urban primary school cannot be overcome by educational reform alone or by individual schools and teachers. They cannot be overcome without policy reform or the support of schools and teachers either. And no change can take place without the political will and desire for reform:

> In a political culture of relative public good, a significant sector of citizens accept the legitimacy of political action taken in support of disadvantaged citizens as a practical expression of commitment to ideas of social justice, equality of opportunity and equity in society. In a political culture of relative private interest a growing number of citizens reject the legitimacy of action in support of the disadvantaged (who are seen to be responsible for their own problems) and support policies designed to enhance their own interests. (Grace 1994: 53)

In the survey and interviews we conducted with teachers and headteachers in urban schools what came across powerfully was their commitment to the children they worked with and their desire to 'make a difference'. In a period where 'the need to give consideration to the fate of others has been lessened' (Ball 2003a: 179), the ethical integrity of those who work and stay working in challenging circumstances needs more recognition. These educators could go to 'easier' schools but they stay where they believe they can make most impact. They also stay where they know they are needed. All those who work in primary schools face tensions between their ethics of care (Nias 1989) and policies that they do not always recognize as pedagogically appropriate. In the urban primary school, these tensions make even greater demands on the professional repertoires of all those working to educate young children in settings of higher than average levels of social and economic disadvantage.

Our intention is not just to argue for more resources for urban primary schools, a more appropriate curriculum or greater responsiveness and respect for those who learn and teach in urban primary schools. Even if these proposals were enacted, a hierarchical and class-based system would still deliver advantage to some and disadvantage to others. What is needed is a political commitment to eradicate social inequalities and injustices in education. In his book, *The Courage to Teach*, Palmer (1998) acknowledges that challenging social conditions and the power and resistance of institutions to change may lead to a sense of despair and pessimism. In contrast, he claims that 'only in the face of such opposition has significant social change been achieved. If institutions had a capacity for constant evolution, there would never have been a crisis demanding transformation' (Palmer 1998: 165). Palmer argues that those who have transformed society (and he cites the civil rights movements in the USA) 'found sources of countervailing power' outside of formal institutional settings and 'consolidated that power in ways that eventually gave them leverage on the structures themselves'. He identifies a way forward through building social movements and making common cause with others who work to 'make a difference' in education.

In this book, we have highlighted the ways in which teachers and headteachers talked about the challenges and the rewards of working in urban primary schools. As Donnelly (2003: 14) claims, 'the greatest challenges in life bring the greatest rewards'. Working with children who sometimes make it 'a triumph of will over adversity that they get to school in the first place' (Brighouse in Riddell 2003: x) is emotionally costly, but professionally satisfying. Rather than seeing urban schools and children who attend them as 'deficient', the best urban primary schools are able to realize their children's experiences as 'assets rather than problems' to be drawn on as powerful resources for teaching and learning (Menter et al. 2000: 227). The dilemma for the urban primary school teacher is to be able to recognize the impact of the wider social context and draw on its cultural resources without losing their belief in the power of education to promote and sustain social transformation.

BIBLIOGRAPHY

Adams, D. and Adams, K. (2003) *Urban Education: A Reference Handbook*. Contemporary Education Issues. Santa Barbara, CA: ABC Clio.

Adler, M., Petch, A. and Tweedie, J. (1989) *Parental Choice and Educational Policy*. Edinburgh: Edinburgh University Press.

Alexander, C. (2002) *The Asian Gang: Ethnicity, Identity, Masculinity*. Oxford: Berg.

Alexander, R.J. (2000) *Culture and Pedagogy: International Comparisons in Primary Education*. Oxford: Blackwell.

Angotti, T. (1993) *Metropolis*. London: Routledge.

Anning, A., Cullen, J. and Fleer, M. (eds) (2004) *Early Childhood Education*. London: Sage.

Anyon, J. (1997) *Ghetto Schooling: A Political Economy of Urban Educational Reform*. New York: Teachers' College Press.

Anyon, J. (2005) *Radical Possibilities. Public Policy, Urban Education and a New Social Movement*. New York and London: Routledge.

Apple, M. (1986) *Teachers and Texts: A Political Economy of Class and Gender Relations in Education*. New York: Routledge.

Apple, M. (2001) *Educating the 'Right' Way: Markets, Standards, God, and Inequality*. New York: Routledge/Falmer.

Apple, M. and Bracey, G. (2001) *School Vouchers*. http://www.asu.edu/educ/epsl/EPRU/documents/cerai-00-31.htm (accessed 23 December 2004).

Archer, L. (2003) *'Race', Masculinity and Schooling: Muslim Boys and Education*. Maidenhead: Open University Press.

Archer, L., Hutchings, M. and Ross, A. with Leathwood, C., Gilchrist, R. and Phillips, D. (2003) *Higher Education and Social Class*. London: Routledge/Falmer.

Auld, R. (1976) William Tyndale Junior and Infants School Public Enquiry. A Report to the Inner London Education Authority. London: ILEA.

Baker, C. (2001) *Foundations of Bilingual Education and Bilingualism*. Clevedon: Multilingual Matters.

Balfanz, R. (2000) Why do so many urban public school students demonstrate so little academic achievement?, in M.G. Saunders (ed.) *Schooling Students Placed at Risk*. London: Lawrence Erlbaum Associates, pp. 292–319.

Ball, S.J. (1990) *Politics and Policy Making in Education.* London: Routledge.

Ball, S.J. (1994) *Education Reform: A Critical and Post-structural Approach.* Buckingham: Open University Press.

Ball, S.J. (2003a) *Class Strategies and the Education Market: The Middle Classes and Social Advantage.* London and New York: Routledge/Falmer.

Ball, S.J. (2003b) The teacher's soul and the terrors of performativity, *Journal of Education Policy*, 18(2): 215–28.

Ball, S.J., Maguire, M. and Macrae, S. (2000) *Choice, Pathways and Transitions Post-16.* London: Routledge/Falmer.

Barber, M. (1996) Creating a framework for success in urban areas, in M. Barber and R. Dann (eds) *Raising Educational Standards in the Inner City. Practical Initiatives in Action.* London and New York: Cassell, pp. 6–26.

Barber, M. (1998) The dark side of the moon: imagining an end to failure in urban education, in L. Stoll and K. Myers (eds) (1997) *No Quick Fixes: Perspectives on Schools in Difficulties.* London: Falmer Press, pp. 17–33.

Bash, L., Coulby, D. and Jones, C. (1985) *Urban Schooling: Theory and Practice.* Eastbourne: Holt, Rinehart & Winston.

Bashi, V. and Hughes, M. (1997) Globalization and residential segregation by 'race', *Annuls of the American Academy of Social and Political Science*, 551: 105–20.

Beck, U. (1992) *Risk Society; Towards a New Modernity.* Newbury Park, CA: Sage.

Bell, D. (2003) Access and achievement in urban education: ten years on. Speech to the Fabian Society by Her Majesty's Chief Inspector of Schools, London, 20 November. London: Ofsted.

Bell, L. (1999) Primary schools and the nature of the education market place, in T. Bush, L. Bell, R. Bolam, R. Glatter and P. Ribbens (eds) *Educational Management: Redefining Theory, Policy and Practice.* London: Paul Chapman, pp. 59–74.

Benn, C. and Chitty, C. (1996) *Thirty Years On: Is Comprehensive Education Alive and Well or Struggling to Survive?* London: David Fulton.

Beresford, E. and Hardie, A. (1996) Parents and secondary schools: a different approach, in J. Bastani and S. Wolfendale (eds) *Home-School Work in Britain.* London: David Fulton, pp. 139–51.

Bernstein, B. (1971) Education cannot compensate for society, in B. Cosin, I.R. Dale, G.M. Esland and D.F. Swift (eds) *School and Society. A Sociological Reader.* London: Routledge & Kegan Paul in association with the Open University Press, pp. 61–6.

Bernstein, B. (1990) *The Structuring of Pedagogic Discourse: Class, Codes and Control, Vol. 4.* London: Routledge & Kegan Paul.

Bettis, P. and Stoeker, R. (1993) New urban sociology and critical education theory: framework for urban school reform in an era of deindustrialisation. Paper presented at the American Educational Research Association, Conference, Atlanta, GA, April.

Black, M.S. (2000) Using your city as a multicultural classroom, *Teaching Education*, 11(3): 343–51.

Blair, M. (2001) The education of black children: why do some schools do better than others?, in R. Majors (ed.) *Educating our Black Children. New Directions and Radical Approaches.* London: Routledge/Falmer, pp. 28–44.

Blair, M. and Bourdillon, H. (1997) The implications of partnership for equal opportunities, in M.I. Fuller and A.J. Rosie (eds) *Teacher Education and School Partnerships.* Lewiston: Edwin Mellen Press, pp. 61–74.

Boaler, J. (1997) Setting, social class and the survival of the quickest, *British Educational Research Journal*, 2(5): 575–95.

Bonnet, A. and Carrington, B. (2000) Fitting into categories or falling between them? Rethinking ethnic classification, *British Journal of Sociology of Education*, 21(4): 487–500.

Bourdieu, P. (1986) *Distinction: A Social Critique of the Judgement of Taste*. London: Routledge.

Bourdieu, P. and Boltanski, L. (2000) Changes in the social structure and changes in the demand for education, in S.J. Ball (ed.) *Sociology of Education: Major Themes, Vol. 2*. London: Routledge/Falmer, pp. 895–923.

Boyson, R. (1974) *Oversubscribed*. London: Ward Lock.

Brown, D.F. (2004) Urban teachers' professed classroom management strategies. Reflections of culturally responsive teaching, *Urban Education*, 39(3): 266–89.

Brown, M. (2003) Poverty: the issue, *TES*, 21 March.

Brown, P. (1997) The 'third wave': education and the ideology of parentocracy, in A.H. Halsey, H. Lauder, P. Brown and A. Stuart Wells (eds) *Education, Culture, Economy, Society*. Oxford: Oxford University Press, pp. 393–408.

Burn, E. (2001) Battling through the system: a working class teacher in an inner-city primary school, *International Journal of Inclusive Education*, 5(1): 85–92.

Burr, V. (1995) *An Introduction to Social Constructionism*. London: Routledge.

Burrows, R. (1999) Residential mobility and residualisation in social housing in England, *Journal of Social Policy*, 28(1): 27–52.

Butler, T. and Robson, G. (2003) *London Calling: The Middle Classes and the Re-Making of Inner London*. Oxford: Berg.

Butler, T. and Savage, M. (eds) (1995) *Social Change and the Middle Classes*. London: University College Press.

Bynner, J. (2003) *Changing Britain, Changing Lives*. London: Centre for Longitudinal Studies, Institute of Education, University of London.

Byrne, D. (1998) *Complexity Theory and the Social Sciences*. London: Routledge.

Byrne, D. (2001) *Understanding the Urban*. London: Palgrave.

Campbell, R.J and Neill, S.R. (1994) The use of primary teachers' time: some implications for beginning teachers, in J. Bourne (ed.) *Thinking Through Primary Practice*. London: Routledge, pp. 67–84.

Carlyle, D. and Woods, P. (2002) *The Emotions of Teacher Stress*. Stoke-on-Trent: Trentham Books.

Carrington, B. and Skelton, C. (2003) Re-thinking 'role models': equal opportunities in teacher recruitment in England and Wales, *Journal of Education Policy*, 18(3): 253–65.

Carrington, B., Bonnett, A., Demaine, J., Hall, I., Nayak, A., Short, G., Skelton, C., Smith, F. and Tomlin, R. (2001) Ethnicity and the professional socialisation of teachers. Report submitted to the TTA.

Casserly, M. (2004) *Big-City Schools Begin to Ascend in Achievement*. Council of the Great City Schools. http://www.cgcs.org/about/onissues/oped081604.html (accessed 5 April 2005).

Castells, M. (1977) *The Urban Question: A Marxist Approach*. London: Edward Arnold.

Castells, M. (1989) *The Informational City*. Oxford: Blackwell.

Castells, M. (1997) *The Power of Identity*. Oxford: Blackwell.

Castells, M. (1998) *End of Millennium*. Malden, MA, and Oxford: Blackwell.

Centre for Contemporary Cultural Studies (CCCS) (1981) *Unpopular Education: Schooling and Social Democracy since 1944*. London: Hutchinson.

Cicirelli, V.G. (1972) Education models for the disadvantaged, in J. Raynor and E. Harris (eds) *Schooling in the City*. Glasgow: Ward Lock Educational in association with the Open University Press, pp. 253–62.

Clark, D. (1996) *Urban World: Global City*. London: Routledge.

Clay, M.M. (1982) *Observing Young Readers*. Exeter, NH: Heinemann.

Cockburn, A.D. (1996) *Teaching Under Pressure. Looking at Primary Teachers' Stress*. London: Falmer Press.

Cohen, L., Manian, L. and Morrison, M. (2000) *Research Methods in Education*. London: Routledge.

Cohen, N. (2005) Going to war in the classroom, *The Observer*, 24 July.

Coles, B. and Kenwright, H. (2002) Educational achievement, in J. Bradshaw (ed.) *The Well-being of Children in the UK*. Plymouth: Save the Children Fund, pp. 231–49.

Colley, H. (2003) *Mentoring for Social Inclusion: A Critical Approach to Nurturing Mentoring Relationships*. London and New York: Routledge/Falmer.

Comer, J. (1988) Educating poor minority children, *Scientific American*, 259(5): 42–8.

Common, J. (1951) Kiddar's luck, in D. Hargreaves, (1982) *The Challenge for the Comprehensive School: Culture, Curriculum and Community*. London: Routledge & Kegan Paul, pp. 75–6.

Connolly, P. (2003) The development of young children's ethnic identities: implications for early years practice, in C. Vincent (ed.) *Social Justice, Education and Identity*. London: Routledge/Falmer, pp. 166–84.

Connor, C. with B. Lofthouse (eds) (1990) *The Study of Primary Education: A Source Book. Vol. 1: Perspectives*. London: Falmer.

Corbett, D., Wilson, B. and Williams, B. (2002) *Effort and Excellence in Urban Classrooms*. New York: Teachers' College Press.

Cork, L. (2005) *Supporting Black Pupils and Parents*. London: Routledge.

Corner, T. and Grant, N. (2004) Comparing educational systems, in D. Matheson (ed.) *An Introduction to the Study of Education*. London: David Fulton, pp. 65–78.

Corson, D. (1998) *Changing Education for Diversity*. Buckingham: Open University Press.

Coulson, A.A. (1986) *The Managerial Work of Primary School Teachers*. Sheffield: Department of Education Management, Sheffield Polytechnic.

Coulter, P. (Office of Research) (1993) *The Comer School Development Program* http://www.ed.gov/pubs/OR/ConsumerGuides/comer.html (accessed 3 August 2004).

Cox, C.B. and Dyson, A.E. (eds) (1969) *Fight for Education*. Critical Quarterly Society. Hull: Hull Printers.

Cox, T. (ed.) (1999) *Combating Educational Disadvantage. Meeting the Needs of Vulnerable Children*. London: Falmer Press.

Cribb, A. and Gewirtz, S. (2003) Towards a sociology of just practices. An analysis of plural conceptions, in C. Vincent (ed.) *Social Justice, Education and Identity*. London and New York: Routledge/Falmer, pp. 15–29.

Croll, P. (ed.) (1996) *Teachers, Pupils and Primary Schooling: Continuity and Change*. London: Cassell.

Crozier, G. (2000) *Parents and Schools: Partners or Protagonists?* Stoke-on-Trent: Trentham Books.

Crozier, G. (2005) Beyond the call of duty: the impact of racism on black parents' involvement in their children's education, in G. Crozier and D. Reay (eds) *Activating Participation: Parents and Teachers Working towards Partnership*. Stoke-on-Trent: Trentham Books, pp. 39–56.

Crozier, G. and Reay, D. (eds) (2005) *Activating Participation: Parents and Teachers Working towards Partnership*. Stoke-on-Trent: Trentham Books.

Dale, R. (1989) *The State and Education Policy*. Milton Keynes: Open University Press.

Datta, M. (ed.) (2000) *Bilinguality and Literacy. Principles and Practice*. London and New York: Continuum Press.

David, M., West, A. and Ribbens, J. (1994) *Mother's Intuition: Choosing Secondary Schools*. London: Falmer Press.

Davies, B. and Ellison, L. (1994) *Managing the Effective Primary School*. London: Longman.

Davis, M. (1999) The restructuring of an urban elementary school: lessons learned as a professional development school liaison, *Early Childhood Research and Practice*, 1(1): 1–10.

Day, C., Hall, C. and Whitaker, P. (1998) *Developing Leadership in Primary Schools*. London: Paul Chapman.

Day, C., Harris, A. and Hadfield, M. (2001) Challenging the orthodoxy of effective schools, *International Journal of Leadership in Education*, 4(1): 39–56.

Day, C., Harris, A., Hadfield, M., Tolley, H. and Beresford, J. (2000) *Leading Schools in Times of Change*. Milton Keynes: Open University Press.

Deem, R. (1989) The new school governing bodies – are gender and race on the agenda?, *Gender and Education*, 1(3): 247–60.

Delpit, L. (1997) *Other People's Children: Cultural Conflict in the Classroom*. New York: New Press.

Demaine, J. (1999) *Education Policy and Politics*. Basingstoke: Palgrave/Macmillan.

Department for Education (DfE) (1992) *Choice and Diversity*. London: HMSO.

Department for Education (DfE) (1994) *Our Children's Education: The Updated Parent's Charter*. London: DfE.

Department for Education and Employment (DfEE) (1997) *Excellence in Schools*. London: The Stationery Office.

Department for Education and Employment (DfEE) (1998a) *Draft Guidance on Home-School Agreements*. London: HMSO.

Department for Education and Employment (DfEE) (1998b) *Teachers Meeting the Challenge of Change*. London: HMSO.

Department for Education and Employment (DfEE) (1999a) *Ethnic Minority Pupils for whom English is an Additional Language 1996/97: Statistical Bulletins No. 3*, March. London: HMSO.

Department for Education and Employment (DfEE) (1999b) *Sure Start: A Guide for Trailblazers*. London: The Stationery Office.

Department for Education and Employment (DfEE) (1999c) *Excellence in Cities*. London: The Stationery Office.

Department for Education and Employment (DfEE) (2005) *London Schools: Rising to the Challenge*. London: HMSO.

Department for Education and Science (DES) (1985) *Better Schools: A White Paper*. London: HMSO.

Department for Education and Science (DES) (1991) *The Parents Charter*. London: DES, HMSO.

Department for Education and Science (DfES) (2001) *Statistics of Education: Pupil Absence and Truancy from Schools in England, 2000–2001*. London: HMSO.

Department for Education and Science (DfES) (2002) *Teachers in Service and Teacher Vacancies: January 2002 (revised) SFR 18/2002*. London: HMSO.

Department for Education and Science (DfES) (2003) *National Curriculum Assessment for Key Stage 2 and Key Stage 1 to 2 Value Added Measures for 11 Year Olds in England for 2002/2003 SFR 33/2003*. London: HMSO.

Department for Education and Science (DfES) (2004) *National Curriculum Assessments of 7 and 11 Year Olds in England 2003: National Statistics*. London: HMSO.

Department of Employment, Training and Rehabilitation (DETR) (2000) *Indices of Deprivation*. London: DETR.

Desforges, C. (2001) *Children's Learning in the Primary School*. London: Routledge/Falmer.

Diamond, J. and Spillane, J. (2004) High-stakes accountability in urban elementary schools: challenging or reproducing inequality?, *Teachers' College Record*, 106(6): 1145–76.

Dillabough, J. (2001) Gender theory and research in education: modernist traditions and emerging contemporary themes, in B. Francis and C. Skelton (eds) *Investigating Gender. Contemporary Issues in Education*. Buckingham: Open University Press, pp. 11–26.

Dobson, J., Henthorne, K. and Lynas, Z. (2000) *Pupil Mobility in Schools. Final Report*. London: Migration Research Unit, Geography Department, University College London.

Doherty, K. (1998) Challenging urban education: defining the issues, in C. Stone (ed.) *Challenging Urban Education*. Lawrence, KS: University Press of Kansas, pp. 225–49.

Donnelly, J. (2003) *Managing Urban Schools. Leading from the Front*. London and Sterling, VA: Kogan Page.

Douglas, J.W.B. (1964) *The Home and the School*. London: McGibbon and Kee.

Draper, J. and McMichael, P. (1998) Making sense of primary headship: the surprises awaiting new heads, *School Leadership and Management*, 8(2): 197–211.

Dryfoos, J. (1994) *Full-service Schools: A Revolution in Health and Social Services for Children, Youth and Families*. San Francisco: Jossey-Bass.

Dyson, A. (2003) *Urban Education: Challenges and Possibilities*. Inaugural lecture, 8 December 2002. Manchester: University of Manchester.

Dyson, A. and Gains, C. (1993) *Rethinking Special Needs in Mainstream Schools: Towards the Year 2000*. London: David Fulton.

Dyson, A. and Robson, E. (1999) *School, Family, Community – Mapping School Inclusion in the UK*. Leicester: Youth Work Press/Joseph Rowntree Foundation.

Echols, F.M. and Wilms, J.D. (1991) Parental choice in Scotland, *Journal of Education Policy*, 5(3): 207–22.

Edwards, T. (2002) A remarkable sociological imagination, *British Journal of Sociology of Education*, 23(4): 527–36.

Egan, K. (2005) *An Imaginative Approach to Teaching*. San Francisco: Jossey-Bass.

Eliott, B. and McCrone, D. (1982) *The City: Patterns of Domination and Conflict*. London: Macmillan.

Ennals, P. (2003) *Child Poverty and Education*. Briefing paper. London: End Child Poverty with the National Children's Bureau.

Epstein, D., Hewitt, R., Leonard, D., Mauthner, M. and Watkins, C. (2003) Avoiding the issue: homophobia, school policies and identities in secondary schools, in C. Vincent (ed.) *Social Justice, Education and Identity*. London: Routledge/Falmer, pp. 120–36.

Espinosa, L.M. and Laffey, J.M. (2003) Urban primary teacher perceptions of children with challenging behaviours, *Journal of Children and Poverty*, 9(2): 135–56.

Feldman, S. (2001) Closing the achievement gap, *American Educator*, 25(3): 7–9.

Fergusson, R. (2000) Modernizing managerialism in education, in J. Clarke, S. Gewirtz and E. McLaughlin (eds) *New Managerialism, New Welfare?* London: Sage, pp. 202–21.

Fidler, B. and Alton, T. (2004) *The Headship Game: The Challenges of Contemporary School Leadership*. London: Routledge/Falmer.

Field, J. (2003) *Social Capital*. London: Routledge/Taylor Francis Group.

Fisher, D. and Frey, N. (eds) (2003) *Inclusive Urban Schools*. Baltimore, MD: Paul Brooks.

Fishman, W. (1988) *East End 1888: A Year in a London Borough among the Labouring Poor*. London: Duckworth.

Flaherty, J., Viet-Wilson, J. and Dornan, P. (2004) *Poverty: The Facts*. London: Child Poverty Action Group.

Flew, A.G.N. (1976) *Sociology, Equality and Education*. London: Macmillan.

Fraser, N. (1997) *Justice Interruptus: Critical Reflections on the Post-socialist Condition*. New York and London: Routledge.

Frey, J.H. and Mertens Oishi, S. (1995) *How to Conduct Interviews by Telephone and in Person*. Thousand Oaks, CA and London: Sage.

Friere, P. (1972) *Pedagogy of the Oppressed*. Harmondsworth: Penguin.

Fullan, M. and Hargreaves, A. (1994) The teacher as a person, in A. Pollard and J. Bourne (eds) *Teaching and Learning in the Primary School*. London: Routledge, pp. 67–72.

Gaine, C. and George, R. (1999) *Gender, 'Race' and Class in Schooling. A New Introduction*. London: Falmer Press.

Gamarnikow, E. and Green, T. (2003) Social justice, identity formation and social capital: school diversification policy under New Labour, in C. Vincent (ed.) *Social Justice, Education and Identity*. London and New York: Routledge/Falmer, pp. 209–23.

Garcia, S.B. and Guerra, P.L. (2004) Deconstructing deficit thinking. Working with educators to create more equitable learning environments, *Education and Urban Society*, 36(2): 150–68.

Gardiner, P. (1984) *The Lost Elementary Schools of Victorian Britain*. London: Croom Helm.

Garreau, J. (1992) *Edge City*. New York: Doubleday.

Gewirtz, S. (2000) Education action zones: emblems of the 'third way'?, in H. Dean and R. Woods (eds) *Social Policy Review 11*. Luton: Social Policy Association, pp. 145–65.

Gewirtz, S. (2001) Cloning the Blairs: New Labour's programme for the re-socialisation of working-class parents, *Journal of Education Policy*, 16(4): 365–78.

Gewirtz, S. (2002) *The Managerial School. Post-welfarism and Social Justice in Education*. London and New York: Routledge.

Gewirtz, S., Ball, S. and Bowe, R. (1995) *Markets, Choice and Equity in Education*. Buckingham: Open University Press.

Gibson, A. and Asthana, S. (1999) Schools, markets and equity: access to secondary education in England and Wales. Paper presented to the American Education Association Annual Conference, Montreal, Canada.

Gillborn, D. (2001) Racism, policy and the (mis)education of black children, in R. Majors (ed.) *Educating Our Black Children. New Directions and Radical Approaches*. London and New York: Routledge/Falmer, pp. 13–27.

Gillborn, D. and Gipps, C. (1996) *Recent Research on the Attainment of Ethnic Minority Pupils*. London: HMSO.

Gillborn, D. and Mirza, H.S. (2000) *Educational Inequality: Mapping 'Race', Class and Gender – A Synthesis of Evidence*. London: Ofsted.

Gillborn, D. and Youdell, D. (1999) *Rationing Education: Policy, Practice, Reform and Equity*. Buckingham: Open University Press.

Ginsburg, N. (1992) Racism and housing: concepts and reality, in P. Braham, A.

Rattansi and R. Skellington (eds) *Racism and Antiracism. Inequalities, Opportunities and Policies*. London: Sage, pp. 109–32.

Gordon, J. (2000) *The Color of Teaching*. Buckingham: Open University Press.

Grace, G. (1978) *Teachers, Ideology and Control: A Study in Urban Education*. London: Routledge & Kegan Paul.

Grace, G. (1984) *Education and the City: Theory, History and Contemporary Practice*. London: Routledge & Kegan Paul.

Grace, G. (1994) Urban education and the culture of contentment: the politics, culture and economics of inner-city schooling, in N. Stromquist (ed.) *Education in Urban Areas. Cross National Dimensions*. Westport, CT and London: Praeger, pp. 45–59.

Grace, G. (1995a) *School Leadership: Beyond Education Management*. London: Falmer Press.

Grace, G. (1995b) Theorizing social relations within urban schooling: a socio-historical analysis, in P. Atkinson, B. Davies and S. Delamont (eds) *Discourse and Reproduction: Essays in Honour of Basil Bernstein*. Cresskill, NJ: Hampton Press, pp. 209–28.

Grace, G. (2005) Urban education: confronting the contradictions. Unpublished position paper for the staff of the London Centre for Leadership in Learning, 16 June.

Grant, V.L. (1993) Parental involvement in urban primary schools. MA in Education in Multicultural Urban Areas. London: Institute of Education, University of London.

Griffiths, M. (1998) *Educational Research for Social Justice*. Buckingham: Open University Press.

Gunter, H.M. (2001) *Leaders and Leadership in Education*. Thousand Oaks, CA and London: Paul Chapman.

Hall, S. (1977) Education and the crisis of the urban school, in J. Raynor and E. Harris (eds) *Schooling the City*. Glasgow: Ward Lock in association with Open University Press, pp. 7–17.

Hall, S. (1991) Old and new ethnicities, in A.D. King (ed.) *Culture, Globalisation and the World System*. London: Macmillan, pp. 41–69.

Hall, S. (1996) Who needs 'identity'?, in S. Hall and P. du Gay (eds) *Questions of Cultural Identity*. London: Sage, pp. 1–17.

Hallam, S., Ireson, J. and Davies, J. (2004a) Primary pupil's experiences of different types of grouping in school, *British Educational Research Journal*, 30(4): 515–34.

Hallam, S., Ireson, J. and Davies, J. (2004b) Grouping practices in the primary school: what influences change, *British Educational Research Journal*, 30(1): 117–40.

Hallgarten, J. (2000) *Parents Exist OK? Issues and Visions for Parent–School Relationships*. London: Institute for Public Policy Research.

Halpern, D. (2005) *Social Capital*. Cambridge: Polity.

Halpin, D. (2003) *Hope and Education: The Role of the Utopian Imagination*. London: Routledge/Falmer.

Halsey, A.H. (1972) *Educational Priority, Volume 1*. London: HMSO.

Hamilton, R. and Moore, D. (eds) (2004) *Educational Interventions for Refugee Children: Theoretical Perspectives and Implementing Best Practice*. London: Routledge/Falmer.

Hargreaves, D.H. (1982) *The Challenge for the Comprehensive School: Culture, Curriculum and Community*. London: Routledge & Kegan Paul.

Harris, R. (1997) Romantic bilingualism: time for a change?, in C. Leung and C.

Cable (eds) *English as an Additional Language: Changing Perspectives*. Watford: NALDIC, pp. 14–27.

Harris, R. (1999) Rethinking the bilingual learner, in A. Tosi and C. Leung (eds) *Rethinking Language Education: From a Monolingual to a Multilingual Perspective*. London: CILT, pp. 70–83.

Harris, R. and Leung, C. (2001) English as an additional language: challenges of language and identity in the multilingual and multiethnic classroom, in J. Dillon and M. Maguire (eds) *Becoming a Teacher. Issues in Secondary Education*, 2nd edn. Buckingham: Open University Press, pp. 203–14.

Harvey, D. (1973) *Social Justice and the City*. London: Edward Arnold.

Harvey, D. (1989) *The Condition of Postmodernity*. Oxford: Blackwell.

Hayden, C. (1996) Primary school exclusions: the need for integrated solutions, in E. Blythe and J. Milner (eds) *Exclusions from School: Inter-professional Issues in Policy and Practice*. London: Routledge, pp. 224–36.

Herman, R. and Stringfield, S. (1995) *Ten Promising Programmes for Educating Disadvantaged Students*. Baltimore, MD: Johns Hopkins University.

Hess, F. (1999) *Spinning Wheels: The Politics of Urban School Reform*. Washington: Brookings Institution Press.

Hey, V., Leonard, D., Daniels, H. and Smith, M. (1998) Boy's underachievement, special needs practices and questions of equity, in D. Epstein, J. Elwood, V. Hey and J. Maw (eds) *Failing Boys? Issues in Gender and Achievement*. Buckingham: Open University Press, pp. 128–44.

Hill, A. (2005) Young children given £27m of free books, *Observer*, 24 July.

Hillman, J. (1996) Introduction. The challenge of disadvantage, in National Commission on Education, *Success against the Odds. Effective Schooling in Disadvantaged Areas*. London and New York: Routledge, pp. 1–13.

Hills, J. (1996) *New Inequalities: The Changing Distribution of Income and Wealth in the UK*. Cambridge: Cambridge University Press.

Hopkins, D., West, M., Ainscow, M., Harris, A. and Beresford, J. (1997) *Creating the Conditions for Classroom Improvement*. London: David Fulton.

Howard, M., Garnham, A., Finnister, G. and Veit-Wilson, J. (2001) *Poverty: The Facts*, 4th edn. London: Child Poverty Action Group.

Hutton, W. (1995) *The State We're In*. London: Cape.

Jackson, B. and Marsden, D. (1968) *Education and the Working Class*. London: Routledge.

Jeffrey, B. (2003) Countering learner 'instrumentalism' through creative mediation, *British Educational Research Journal*, 29(4): 489–504.

Jesson, D. (2004) Free lunch need not be a bad thing, *Times Educational Supplement*, 16 April.

Johnson, J. (1999) *Hope for Urban Education*. University of Austin, TX: Charles Dana Centre.

Johnson, M. (1999) *Failing School, Failing City*. Oxford: Jan Carpenter Press.

Johnson, M. (2003) *Schooling in London: An Overview*. London: Institute for Public Policy Research.

Johnson, R. (1976) Notes on the schooling of the English working class 1780–1850, in R. Dale, G. Esland and M. MacDonald (eds) *Schooling and Capitalism. A Sociological Reader*. London: Routledge & Kegan Paul, pp. 44–54.

Jones, C., Maguire, M. and Watson, B. (1997) The school experiences of some minority ethnic students in London schools during teacher training, *Journal of Education for Teaching*, 23(2): 131–44.

Jones, C., Maguire, M. and Watson, B. (1998) Needed and wanted? The school experiences of some minority ethnic trainee teachers in the UK, *European Journal of Intercultural Studies*, 19(1): 79–91.

Jones, K. (2003) *Education in Britain: 1944 to the Present*. Cambridge and Malden, MA: Polity Press.

Jones, R. and Wyse, D. (2004) *Creativity in the Primary Curriculum*. London: David Fulton.

Jordan, B., Redley, M. and James, S. (1994) *Putting the Family First: Identities, Decisions and Citizenship*. London: UCL Press.

Keys, W., Sharp, C., Greene, K. and Grayson, H. (2003) *Successful Leadership of Schools in Urban and Challenging Contexts*. Slough and York: NFER.

Kinder, K., Harland, J., Wilkin, A. and Wakefield, A. (1996) *Three to Remember: Strategies for Disaffected Pupils*. Slough: NFER.

Kinlaw, D.C. (1989) *Coaching for Commitment*. London: Pfeiffer.

Kozol, J. (1991) *Savage Inequalities: Children in America's Schools*. New York: Crown.

Kozol, J. (1995) *Amazing Grace. The Lives of Children and the Conscience of a Nation*. New York: Perennial.

Krupat, E. (1985) *People on Cities*. Cambridge: Cambridge University Press.

Kuehn, L. (1995) *Ten Problems with Charter Schools*. BCTF Research Report, Section XII, 95-EI-06, pp. 1–5.

Ladson-Billings, G. (1992) Reading between the lines and beyond the pages: a culturally relevant approach to literacy teaching, *Theory into Practice*, 31: 312–20.

Ladson-Billings, G. (1995) Towards a theory of culturally relevant pedagogy, *American Educational Research Journal*, 32(3): 465–91.

Lawton, D. (1977) *Education and Social Justice*. London: Sage.

Lawton, D. (1994) *The Tory Mind on Education 1979–1994*. London: Falmer.

Lightfoot, M. and Rowan, P. (1998) *ILEA: Unsuitable Case for Treatment*? London: Education Reform Group.

Linn, R. (2003) Accountability, responsibility and reasonable expectations, *Educational Researcher*, 32(7): 3–13.

Lucey, H. and Reay, D. (2000) Rationality and mastery: independent special mobility and urban middle class children. Unpublished project paper. London: King's College.

Lucey, H. and Reay, D. (2002) Carrying the beacon of excellence: social class differentiation and anxiety at a time of transition, *Journal of Education Policy*, 17(3): 321–36.

Lynch, K. and Lodge, A. (2002) *Equality and Power in Schools*. London: Routledge/ Falmer.

Lysaght, Z. (1993) Partnership with parents in primary education, *Irish Educational Studies*, 12: 196–205.

Mac An Ghaill, M. (1999) *Contemporary Racisms and Ethnicities. Social and Cultural Transformations*. Buckingham: Open University Press.

MacBeath, J. (ed.) (1998) *Effective School Leadership: Responding to Change*. London: Paul Chapman.

Maden, M. (1996) Divided cities: 'dwellers in different zones, inhabitants of different planets'. The TES/Greenwich Education Lecture 1996. London: University of Greenwich and *The Times Educational Supplement*.

Maden, M. (ed.) (2001) *Success Against the Odds – Five Years On. Revisiting Effective Schools in Disadvantaged Areas*. London and New York: Routledge/Falmer.

Maden, M. and Hillman, J. (1996) Lessons in success, in National Commission on Education, *Success against the Odds. Effective Schooling in Disadvantaged Areas*. London and New York: Routledge, pp. 312–69.

Maguire, M. (1995) Hobson's choice: Kids at the thin edge of the (UK) market wedge. Paper given at BERA, Bath.

Maguire, M. (1999) Hobson's choice: Kids at the thin edge of the (UK) market wedge, *Primary Teaching Studies*, 11(1): 50–6.

Maguire, M. (2001) The cultural formation of teachers' class consciousness: teachers in the inner city, *Journal of Education Policy*, 16(4): 315–31.

Maguire, M., Macrae, S., and Milbourne, L. (2003) Early interventions: preventing school exclusions in the primary setting, *Westminster Studies in Education*, 26(1): 43–62.

Mahony, P. (1998) Girls will be girls and boys will be first, in D. Epstein, J. Elwood, V. Hey and J. Maw (eds) *Failing Boys? Issues in Gender and Achievement*. Buckingham: Open University Press, pp. 37–55.

Majors, R. (ed.) (2001) *Educating Our Black Children. New Directions and Radical Approaches*. London and New York: Routledge/Falmer.

Martin, R. and Rowthorn, R. (eds) (1986) *The Geography of Deindustrialisation*. London: Macmillan.

Massey, D. (1995) *Space, Place and Gender*. Cambridge: Polity Press.

Matheson, J. and Babb, P. (eds) (2002) *Social Trends No. 32*. London: Palgrave/Macmillan.

May, S. (ed.) (1999) *Critical Multiculturalism: Rethinking Multicultural and Antiracist Education*. London: Falmer Press.

McCurdy, B.L., Mannella, M.C. and Eldridge, N. (2003) Positive behaviour support in urban schools, *Journal of Positive Behaviour Interventions*, 5(3): 158–70.

McMahon, A. (2003) Fair Furlong Primary School: five years on, in M. Preedy, R. Glatter and C. Wise (eds) *Strategic Leadership and Educational Improvement*. London: Paul Chapman, pp. 198–212.

McNamara, O., Basit, T., Campbell, A., Marsh, N., Rowley, C., Chidley, P. and Offord, S. (2002) Seminar to identity best practice in teacher induction. Report submitted to the TTA.

McNeish, D. and Roberts, H. (1995) *Playing it Safe*. London: Barnardos.

Menter, I. (1998) Whatever happened to urban (teacher) education?, *Education File*, 2: 17–23.

Menter, I., Cunningham, P. and Sheibani, A. (2000) Safe at last? Refugee children in primary schools, in M. Datta (ed.) *Bilinguality and Literacy. Principles and Practice*. London and New York: Continuum Press, pp. 209–27.

Menter, I., Hutchings, M. and Ross, A. (eds) (2002) *The Crisis in Teacher Supply: Research and Strategies for Retention*. Stoke-on-Trent: Trentham Books.

Midwinter, E. (1972) Teaching with the urban environment, in J. Raynor and E. Harris (eds) *Schooling in the City*. Glasgow: Ward Lock Educational in association with the Open University Press, pp. 110–17.

Miller, J. (1998) *A Model Urban Elementary School*. http://www.edweek.org/sreports/qc98/solutions/so-n3.htm (accessed 10 September 2004).

Mortimore, P. and Whitty, G. (1997) *Can School Improvement Overcome the Effects of Disadvantage?* London: Institute of Education, University of London.

Moscovitch, E. (2005) *Facing Reality: What Happens When Good Schools are Labelled Failures?* Boston, MA. Partners for Public Schools. http://www.masc.org/PDF'S/AYPReportJune05.pdf (accessed 28 July 2005).

Munn, P. and Drever, E. (1995) *Using Questionnaires in Small-scale Research*. Edinburgh: SCRC Publications.

Murphy, P., DeArmond, M. and Guin, K. (2003) A national crisis or localized problems? Getting perspective on the scope and scale of the teacher shortage,

Education Policy Analysis Archives, 11(23). http://epaa.asu.edu/epaa/v11n23 (accessed 13 April 2005).

Myers, K. and Goldstein, H. (1998) 'Who's failing?', in L. Stoll and K. Myers (eds) *No Quick Fixes: Perspectives on Schools in Difficulties*. London: Routledge, pp. 175–88.

National Commission for Education (NCE) (1996) *Success against the Odds. Effective Schooling in Disadvantaged Areas*. London and New York: Routledge.

National Foundation for Educational Research (NFER) (2004a) *Annual Survey of Trends in Education, Digest No. 16*. http://www.nfer.ac.uk/research/surveyof-trends.asp (accessed 9 March 2005).

National Foundation for Educational Research (NFER) (2004b) *Excellence in Cities. The Policies and Programme*. http://www.nfer.ac.uk/research/EIC_asp (accessed 25 February 2004).

National Union of Teachers (NUT) (2002) *Workload, Stress and Bullying: NUT Health and Safety Briefing*. http://www.data.teachers.org.uk/pdfs/work.stress.bull.pdf (accessed 20 November 2004).

Newell, P. (1989) *Children Are People Too: The Case Against Physical Punishment*. London: Bedford Square.

Nias, J. (1989) *Primary Teachers Talking*. London: Routledge.

Nieto, S. (1999) *The Light in their Eyes: Creating Multicultural Learning Communities*. Stoke-on-Trent: Trentham Books.

Oakley, A. (1997) Gender, methodology and people's ways of knowing: some problems with feminism and the paradigm of debate in social science, *Sociology*, 32: 707–31.

Office for Standards in Education (Ofsted) (1993) *Education for Disaffected Pupils 1990–1992*. London: HMSO.

Office for Standards in Education (Ofsted) (2002) *School's Use of Temporary Teachers*. London: Ofsted.

Ogilvy, C., Boath, E., Cheyne, W., Jahoda, G. and Scafler, H.R. (1992) Staff–child interaction styles in multi-ethnic nursery schools, *British Journal of Developmental Psychology*, 10(1): 85–97.

Oppenheim, C. (1993) *Poverty: The Facts*. London: Child Poverty Action Group.

Osborn, M., Abbott, D., Broadfoot, P., Croll, P. and Pollard, A. (1996) Teachers' professional perspectives: continuity and change, in R. Chawala-Duggan and C.J. Pole (eds) *Reshaping Education in the 1990s: Perspectives on Primary Schooling*. London: Falmer Press, pp. 137–53.

Osler, A. (1997) *The Education and Careers of Black Teachers*. Buckingham: Open University Press.

Osler, A. and Vincent, K. (2003) *Girls and Exclusion: Rethinking the Agenda*. London: Routledge/Falmer.

Ozga, J.T. and Lawn, M. (1981) *Teachers, Professionalism and Class*. Lewes: Falmer Press.

Pahl, R. (1970) *Patterns of Urban Life*. London: Longman.

Pahl, R. (ed.) (1968) *Readings in Urban Sociology*. Oxford: Pergamon.

Palmer, P.J. (1998) *The Courage to Teach. Exploring the Inner Landscape of a Teacher's Life*. San Francisco: Jossey-Bass.

Pascal, C. and Ribbens, P. (1998) *Understanding Primary Head Teachers: Conversations in Characters, Careers and Characteristics*. London: Cassell.

Pavlenko, A. and Blackledge, A. (eds) (2004) *Negotiations of Identities in Multilingual Settings*. Clevedon: Multilingual Matters.

Peterson, P. and West, M. (eds) (2003) *No Child Left Behind? The Politics and Practice of School Accountability*. Washington, DC: The Brookings Institution.

Phoenix, A. (2001) Racialization and gendering in the (re)production of educational inequalities, in B. Francis and C. Skelton (eds) *Investigating Gender. Contemporary Issues in Education*. Buckingham: Open University Press, pp. 126–38.

Plowden Report (1967) *Children and their Primary Schools, Report of the Central Advisory Council for Education in England*. London: HMSO.

Pollard, A. (1996) *An Introduction to Primary Education: For Parents, Governors and Student Teachers*. London: Cassell.

Pollard, A. and Bourne, J. (eds) (1994) *Teaching and Learning in the Primary School*. London: Routledge in association with the Open University.

Pollard, A., Bradfoot, P., Croll, P., Osborn, M. and Abbott, D. (1994) *Changing English Primary Schools: The Impact of the Education Reform Act at Key Stage One*. London: Cassell.

Pons, V. (1975) *Imagery and Symbolism in Urban Society*. Inaugural lecture, 21 January 1975. Hull: University of Hull.

Power, A. and Mumford, K. (1999) *The Slow Death of Great Cities?* York: Joseph Rowntree Foundation.

Power, S. and Whitty, G. (1999) New Labours' education policy: first, second or third way?, *Journal of Education Policy*, 14(5): 535–46.

Power, S., Halpin, D. and Whitty, G. (1997) Managing the state and the market: 'new' education management in five countries, *British Journal of Educational Studies*, 45(4): 342–62.

Power, S., Warren, S., Gillborn, D., Clark, A., Thomas, S. and Coate, K. (2002) *Education in Deprived Areas: Outcomes, Inputs and Processes*. London: Institute of Education, University of London.

Pratt, S. and Maguire, M. (1995) Inner-city children and their schooling, *Primary Teaching Studies*, 9(2): 22–8.

Prisoners of Time (1994) http://www.ed.gov/pubs/PrisonersOfTime/Urban/html (accessed 10 September 2004).

Pyke, N. (1997) Billions fail to add up to rising standards, *Times Educational Supplement*, 3 October.

Ravitch, D. (1997) *New Schools for a New Century: The Redesign of Urban Education*. New Haven, CT and London: Yale University Press.

Ravitch, D. (2000) *Left Back: A Century of Failed School Reforms*. New York: Simon & Schuster.

Rawls, J. (1972) *A Theory of Justice*. Oxford: Clarendon Press.

Reay, D. (1996) Contextualising choice: social power and parental involvement, *British Education Research Journal*, 22(5): 581–96.

Reay, D. (1998a) *Class Work: Mother's Involvement in their Child's Primary Schooling*. London: University College Press.

Reay, D. (1998b) Engendering social reproduction: mothers in the educational marketplace, *British Journal of Sociology of Education*, 19(8): 195–210.

Reay, D. (2005) Mothers' involvement in their children's schooling. Social reproduction in action?, in G. Crozier and D. Reay (eds) *Activating Participation: Parents and Teachers Working towards Partnership*. Stoke-on-Trent: Trentham Books, pp. 23–38.

Reay, D. and Ball, S.J. (1997) 'Spoilt for choice': the working class and educational markets, *Oxford Review of Education*, 23(1): 89–101.

Reay, D. and Lucey, H. (2000a) Children, school choice and social differences, *Educational Studies*, 26(1): 83–100.

Reay, D. and Lucey, H. (2000b) 'I don't like it here, but I don't want to live anywhere else': children living on inner London council estates, *Antipode: A Radical Journal of Geography*, 32(4): 410–28.

Reay, D. and Lucey, H. (2003) The limits of 'choice': children and inner city schooling, *Sociology*, 37(1): 121–42.

Reay, D. and Safia-Mirza, H. (2005) Doing parental involvement differently: black women's participation as educators and mothers in black supplementary schooling, in G. Crozier and D. Reay (eds) *Activating Participation: Parents and Teachers Working towards Partnership*. Stoke-on-Trent: Trentham Books, pp. 137–54.

Reeder, D. (1977) *Urban Education in the Nineteenth Century*. Proceedings of the 1977 Annual Conference of the History of Education Society of Great Britain. London: Taylor & Francis.

Rendall, S. (2001) *Factors Relating to School Exclusion: A Systematic Approach*. London: Tavistock Centre.

Riddell, R. (2003) *Schools for Our Cities: Urban Learning in the 21st Century*. Stoke-on-Trent: Trentham Books.

Riley, K.A. (1998) *Whose School is it Anyway?* London: Falmer Press.

Riley, K.A. and Louis, K. (2000) *Leadership for Change and School Reform: International Perspectives*. London: Routledge/Falmer.

Riley, K.A. and West-Burnham, J. (2004) *Educational Leadership in London*. Nottingham: National College for School Leadership.

Robbins, M. (1995) Black students in teacher education, *Multicultural Teaching*, 14(1): 15–22.

Roberts, L., McNamara, O., Basit, T. and Hatch, G. (2002) It's like black people are still aliens: retention of minority ethnic student teachers. Paper presented at the annual BERA conference, University of Exeter, September.

Robinson, P. (1997) *Literacy, Numeracy and Economic Performance*. London: CEP/London School of Economics.

Roffey, S. (ed.) (2002) *School Behaviour and Families. Frameworks for Working Together*. London: David Fulton.

Rogers, B. (2001) Crowcroft Park Primary School, in M. Maden (ed.) *Success Against the Odds – Five Years On. Revisiting Effective Schools in Disadvantaged Areas*. London and New York: Routledge/Falmer, pp. 75–99.

Rose, D. (1988) A feminist perspective of employment restructuring and gentrification: the case of Montreal, in J. Wolch and M. Dear (eds) *The Power of Geography*. Boston, MA: Unwin Hyman, pp. 118–38.

Ross, A. (2001) Towards a representative profession: teachers from the ethnic minorities. Paper presented to the seminar on the Future of the Teaching Profession, 11 December, London. London: Institute for Public Policy Research, University of North London.

Rowe, K.J. (1995) Factors affecting students' progress in reading: key findings from a longitudinal study in literacy, *Teaching and Learning, An International Journal of Early Literacy*, 1(2): 57–110.

Runciman, W.G. (1969) *Social Science and Political Theory*, 2nd edn. Cambridge: Cambridge University Press.

Rutter, J. (1994) *Refugee Children in the Classroom*. London: Trentham Books.

Rutter, J. (2003) *Supporting Refugee Children in 21st Century Britain: A Compendium of Essential Information*. Stoke-on-Trent: Trentham Books.

Rutter, J. (2004) *Refugee Children in the UK*. Milton Keynes: Open University.

Sassen, S. (1994) *Cities in a World Economy*. Thousand Oaks, CA: Pine Forge Press.

Saunders, P. (1981) *Social Theory and the Urban Question*. London: Hutchinson.

Saunders, P. (1986) Comment on Dunleavy and Pretceille, *Society and Space (Environmental Planning D)*, (4): 153–63.
Savage, M. (2000) *Class Analysis and Social Transformation*. Buckingham: Open University Press.
Savage, M. and Warde, A. (1993) *Urban Sociology, Capitalism and Modernity*. London: Macmillan.
Scottish School Census (2002) www.scotland.gov.uk/library5/education (accessed 25 June 2005).
Seddon, T. (2003) Framing justice: challenges for research, *Journal of Education Policy*, 18(3): 229–52.
Sewell, T. (1997) *Black Masculinities and Schooling. How Black Boys Survive Modern Schooling*. Stoke-on-Trent: Trentham Books.
Shain, F. (2003) *The Schooling and Identity of Muslim Girls*. Stoke-on-Trent: Trentham Books.
Sharp, P. (2001) *Nurturing Emotional Literacy: A Practical Guide for Teachers, Parents and Those in the Caring Professions*. London: David Fulton.
Sharp, R. and Green, A. with Lewis, J. (1975) *Education and Social Control*. London: Routledge.
Sikes, P. (2000) 'Truth' and 'lies' revisited, *British Educational Research Journal*, 26(2): 257–70.
Siraj-Blatchford, I. (1993) *'Race', Gender and the Education of Teachers*. Milton Keynes: Open University Press.
Siraj-Blatchford, I. (1994) *The Early Years: Laying the Foundations for Racial Equality*. Stoke-on-Trent: Trentham Books.
Skeggs, B. (1997) *Formations of Class and Gender*. London: Sage.
Skelton, C. and Francis, B. (eds) (2003) *Boys and Girls in the Primary Classroom*. Maidenhead: Open University Press.
Smith, M. (2001) *Full-Service Schooling*. http://www.infed.org/schooling/f-serv.htm (accessed 7 December 2004).
Smith, T. and Noble, M. (1995) *Education Divides: Poverty and Schooling in the 1990s*. London: Child Poverty Action Group.
Smithers, A. and Robinson, P. (2003) *Factors Affecting a Teacher's Decision to Leave the Profession*. Nottingham: DfES.
Solberg, A. (1997) Negotiating childhood: changing constructions of age for Norwegian childhood, in A. James and A. Prout (eds) *Constructing and Reconstructing Childhood*. London and New York: Falmer Press, pp. 126–44.
Southworth, G. (1995) *Looking into Primary Headship. A Research-based Interpretation*. London: Falmer Press.
Southworth, G. (1998) *Leading Improving Primary Schools. The Work of Headteachers and Deputy Heads*. London: Falmer Press.
Southworth, G. and Lincoln, P. (1999) *Supporting Improving Primary Schools: The Role of Heads and LEAs in Raising Standards*. London: Falmer Press.
Spear, M., Gould, K. and Lee, B. (2000) *Who Would Be a Teacher? A Review of Factors Motivating and Demotivating Prospective and Practising Teachers*. Slough: NFER.
Stedman-Jones, G. (1971) *Outcast London: A Study in the Relationship between Classes in Victorian Society*. Oxford: Clarendon Press.
Stoll, L. and Fink, D. (1995) *Changing Our Schools*. Buckingham: Open University Press.
Stoll, L. and Myers, K. (eds) (1998) *No Quick Fixes: Perspectives on Schools in Difficulties*. London: Routledge.
Stone, C. (1998) *Changing Urban Education*. Lawrence, Kansas: University of Kansas Press.

Swift, A. (2003) *How Not to be a Hypocrite: School Choice for the Morally Perplexed Parent*. London: Routledge.

Sylva, K. and MacPherson, K. (2002) *Parents and Parenting in the Early Years: Research Evidence*. Oxford: Department of Educational Studies, Oxford University.

Teacher Training Agency (TTA) (2000) *Raising the Attainment of Minority Ethnic Pupils: Guidance and Resource Materials for Providers of Initial Teacher Training*. London: TTA.

Thomas, A. and Dennison, B. (1991) Parental or pupil choice – who really decides in urban schools?, *Education Management and Administration*, 19(4): 243–51.

Thompson, P. (2000) Move over Rover! An essay/assay of the field of educational management in the UK, *Journal of Educational Policy*, 15(6): 717–32.

Thompson, P. (2003) No more managers-r-us! Researching/teaching about head teachers and 'schools in challenging circumstances', *Journal of Education Policy*, 18(3): 333–46.

Thrift, S. (1997) 'Us' and 'them': re-imagining places, re-imagining identities, in H. Mackay (ed.) *Consumption and Everyday Life*. Buckingham: Open University Press, pp. 159–212.

Thrupp, M. (1998) The art of the possible: organising and managing high and low socio-economic schools, *Journal of Education Policy*, 13(2): 197–219.

Thrupp, M. (1999) *Schools Making a Difference: Let's Be Realistic!* Buckingham: Open University Press.

Tomlinson, H., Gunter, H. and Smith, P. (eds) (1999) *Living Headship: Voices, Values and Vision*. London: Paul Chapman.

Tomlinson, S. (1984) *Home and School in Multicultural Britain*. London: Batsford.

Tomlinson, S. (1990) *Multicultural Education in White Schools*. London: Batsford.

Tomlinson, S. (2001) *Education in a Post-welfare Society*. Buckingham: Open University Press.

Townsend, P. (ed.) (1970) *The Concept of Poverty*. London: Heinemann.

Troman, G. (2000) Teacher stress in the low-thrust society, *British Journal of Sociology of Education*, 21(3): 331–54.

Urban Education Partnership (2003) http://www.laep.org/ (accessed 23 December 2004).

US Department of Education (2002) *No Child Left Behind*. http://www.ed.gov/nclb/ (accessed 3 August 2004).

Vincent, C. (1996) *Parents and Teachers: Power and Participation*. London: Falmer Press.

Vincent, C. (2000) *Including Parents? Education, Citizenship and Parental Agency*. Buckingham: Open University Press.

Vincent, C. (2001) Social class and parental agency, *Journal of Education Policy* 16(4): 347–64.

Vincent, C. (ed.) (2003) *Social Justice, Education and Identity*. London and New York: Routledge/Falmer.

Vincent, C. and Martin, J. (2000) School-based parents' groups – a politics of voice and representation?, *Journal of Education Policy*, 15(5): 459–80.

Vincent, C., Ball, S.J., Kemp, S. and Pietikainen, S. (2004) The social geography of childcare: making up the middle class child, *British Journal of Sociology of Education*, 25(2): 229–44.

Walker, A. and Walker, C. (1997) *Britain Divided*. London: Child Poverty Action Group.

Walkerdine, V., Lucey, H. and Melody, J. (2001) *Growing Up Girl. Psychosocial Explorations of Gender and Class*. Basingstoke: Palgrave.

Wallace, M. and Huckman, L. (1999) *Senior Management Teams in Primary Schools: The Quest for Synergy*. London: Routledge.
Warde, A. (1991) Gentrification as consumption: issues of class and gender, *Society and Space*, 9(2): 223–32.
Weeks, A. (1986) *Comprehensive Schools. Past, Present and Future*. London: Methuen.
Wellington, J. (2000) *Educational Research*. London: Continuum.
West, M., Ainscow, M. and Stanford, J. (2005) Sustaining improvement in schools in challenging circumstances: a case study of successful practice, *School Leadership and Management*, 25(1): 77–98.
West-Burnham, J. (2003) *Leadership for Learning*. London: Routledge/Falmer.
White, J. (ed.) (2004) *Rethinking the Curriculum: Values, Aims and Purposes*. London: Routledge/Falmer.
Whitty, G. (2002) *Making Sense of Education Policy*. London: Paul Chapman.
Whitty, G. and Mortimore, P. (2000) Can school improvement overcome disadvantage?, in T. Cox (ed.) *Combating Educational Disadvantage. Meeting the Needs of Vulnerable Children*. London: Falmer Press, pp. 156–76.
Whitty, G., Aggleton, P., Gamarnikow, E. and Tyrer, P. (1998) Education and health inequalities, *Journal of Education Policy*, 13(5): 641–52.
Wilkinson, R. (1997) *Unfair Shares: The Effects of Widening Income Differences on the Welfare of the Young*. London: Barnardos.
Williams, R. (1961) *The Long Revolution*. Harmondsworth: Pelican Books.
Willig, C.J. (1963) Social implications of streaming in junior schools, *Educational Research*, 5: 151–4.
Woods, P. and Jeffrey, B. (1996) *Teachable Moments: The Art of Teaching in Primary Schools*. Buckingham: Open University Press.
Woods, P.C., Bagley, C. and Glatter, R. (1998) *School Choice and Competition*. London: Routledge.
Wooldridge, T.P. (1997) 'Now, make your choice'. A study of children choosing their secondary school. Unpublished dissertation, MA in Urban Education. London: King's College London, University of London.
Wright, C. (1992) *'Race' Relations in the Primary School*. London: David Fulton.
Wright, C., Weekes, D. and McGlaughlin, A. (2000) *'Race', Class and Gender in Exclusions from School*. London and New York: Falmer Press.
Young, I.M. (1990) *Justice and the Politics of Difference*. Princeton, NJ: Princeton University Press.

AUTHOR INDEX

INDEX

LEARNING WITHOUT LIMITS
Susan Hart, Annabelle Dixon, Mary Jane Drummond and Donald McIntyre.

This book describes and explores the importance of using ways of teaching that are free from determinist beliefs about ability. It draws on a partnership research project, based at the Faculty of Education, University of Cambridge, which involved case studies of nine teachers' classroom practice.

From these case studies the authors have constructed a model of pedagogy based on the principle of transformability: the principle that children's futures as learners are not fixed or pre-determined, since teachers can act to remove the limits on learning created by ability-focused teaching. The authors show how transformability-based teaching could play a central and critical role in the construction of an alternative improvement agenda, offering a focus for school and curriculum development that is rooted in teachers' own values, commitments and aspirations.

The book will appeal to teachers, lecturers and policy makers, and to everyone who has a stake in how contemporary education and practice affect children's future lives and life chances.

Contents:

296pp 0 335 21259 X (EAN: 9 780335 212590) Paperback
0 335 21260 3 (EAN: 9 780335 212606) Hardback

SES Awards 2005: Second Prize

TEACHERS AND ASSISTANTS WORKING TOGETHER
Karen Vincett, Hilary Cremin and Gary Thomas

"Few areas of education can equal the growth rate of that for teaching assistants over the past seven years, doubling to more than 133,000 in England between 1997 to 2004. TAs are vital in the development of inclusive education, yet their status, pay, conditions, qualifications and their relationship with classroom teachers are all of deep concern in the majority of cases. This excellent, practical book is a welcome and much-needed authoritative study of the all-important relationship between TA and teacher." Mark Vaughan OBE, Founder and Co-Director, Centre for Studies on Inclusive Education

This book is for teachers and teaching assistants seeking to improve the ways in which they work together to meet the needs of children in their classes. It outlines the thinking behind the employment of teaching assistants in the classroom and spells out some of the teamworking opportunities and problems that can arise. Drawing on research, it explores ways in which teachers and teaching assistants can work together to support children's learning and examines different models of working together.

This unique book provides:

- Highly effective models for working together, tried and tested in schools
- A practical section with activities, hand-outs and resources that teachers can use to develop these models in their own schools

This is a key text for classroom teachers, teaching assistants, trainee teachers and postgraduate education students, and those studying foundation degrees for teaching assistants. It is also of use to parents, headteachers, educational psychologists, and other support personnel.

Contents:

192pp 0 335 21695 1 (EAN: 9 780335 216956) Paperback
0 335 21696 X (EAN: 9 780335 216963) Hardback

MAKING FORMATIVE ASSESSMENT WORK
Effective Practice in the Primary Classroom
Kathy Hall and Winifred Burke

- What does formative assessment look like in practice?
- How are formative assessment and learning connected?
- What are the issues involved in implementing formative assessment?

This book explains and exemplifies formative assessment in practice. Drawing on incidents and case studies from primary classrooms, it describes and analyses how teachers can use formative assessment to promote learning. It argues the case for formative assessment with reference to sociocultural perspectives on learning, and examines this in the context of current assessment policy.

Themes addressed include feedback; the power and roles of learners and teachers in formative assessment; self and peer assessment; and sharing success criteria with learners. Individual chapters explore formative assessment across the curriculum, including literacy, numeracy, art, science, and history. In addition there are two chapters on formative assessment in the early years.

Making Formative Assessment Work provides teachers, student teachers, teacher educators and researchers with a sophisticated grasp of issues in formative assessment, and how they relate to the improvement of pupil learning.

Contents: Introduction / Learning and Assessment / Formative Assessment and Official Policy: Issues and Challenges / Formative assessment: What are teachers doing? / Feedback, Power and the Roles of Teachers and Learners in Formative Assessment / Helping Learners Understand How Their Work is Judged / Formative Assessment and Literacy / Formative Assessment and Numeracy / Formative Assessment and Science / Art and Design and Formative Assessment / Formative Assessment and History / Assessing What We Value:Learning Dispositions in the Early Years / Playful Learning, Learning Stories and Making Assessment Visible in the Early Years / Level Descriptions and Opportunities for Formative Assessment (with Austin Harding) / Conclusion.

184pp 0 335 21379 0 (EAN: 9 780335 213795) Paperback
0 335 21380 4 (EAN: 9 780335 213801) Hardback

Education in an Urbanised Society
SERIES EDITORS: GERALD GRACE, MEG MAGUIRE AND IAN MENTER

REFUGEE CHILDREN IN THE UK

Jill Rutter
London Metropolitan University, UK.

Asylum migration causes intense media and political debate. However, little attention has been paid to how forced migrants can rebuild their lives in the UK or elsewhere. This timely book analyzes the social policies that impact on refugee children's education, and:

- Provides the background to the migration of refugees
- Explores how dominant discourses about trauma homogenise and label a very diverse group of children
- Examines how policy towards refugees is made, and how it relates to practice
- Offers alternative visions for refugee settlement

Drawing on case studies of the experiences of refugee children, *Refugee Children in the UK* brings a much-needed insight into the needs of refugee children. It is valuable reading for academics, policy makers, students of education, sociology and social policy as well as education, health and social work professionals.

Contents: Part One: Introduction / Introduction / Global overview / **Part Two: Refugee Policy** / Refugee settlement in the UK: history repeats itself / The creation of non-citizens: today's asylum policy / The integration agenda / The influence of Europe / Researching refugees / **Part Three: Refugee Children** / The under fives / The education of asylum-seeking and refugee children: policy / The education of asylum-seeking and refugee children: unresolved issues / Unaccompanied children / Healthcare / Alternative visions.

0 335 21373 1 (EAN: 9 780335 213733) Paperback
0 335 21374 X (EAN: 9 780335 213740) Hardback

Education in an Urbanised Society

S EDITORS: GERALD GRACE,MEG MAGUIRE AND IAN MENTER

IPROVING URBAN SCHOOLS
eadership and Collaboration
Mel Ainscow and Mel West (eds)

Issues related to poverty create particulardifficulties in urban schools, and the emphasis on market-led improvement strategies has tended to add to these challenges. In addition, strategies for 'raising standards', as measured by aggregate test and examination results, can result in marginalisation or exclusion of some groups of learners.

Drawing on research evidence, Improving Urban Schools addresses the question of how primary and secondary urban schools can be improved in a more inclusive way. The authors argue that urban schools and their communities have within them expertise that tends to be overlooked, and latent creativity that should be mobilised to move thinking and progress forward. They show that new approaches to leadership, various forms of collaborative school-to-school partnerships, and major changes in national policy development are needed to make use of this untapped energy.

The book includes vivid accounts of these activities to shed light on what really happens in urban schools, and presents practical strategies for school leaders and practitioners who want to make a difference in urban schools.

Contributors: Mel Ainscow, D.A. Dyson, Samantha J. Fox, Helen Gunter, Andrew J. Howes, Andrew Morley, Maria Nicolaidou, Jacqueline Stanford, David Tweddle, Mel West. Contents: The challenge of urban school improvement / The experience of failure in urban schools / The role of the Headteacher in schools facing challenging circumstances / Leading developments in inclusive practices: barriers and possibilities / Achieving sustainable improvements in urban schools / Moving leadership practice in schools forward / Achieving educational equity in practice: stories from a metropolitan local educational authority / Putting heads together: a study of school-to-school cooperation / Moving practice forward at the district level / Collaborating to improve secondary education / Urban schools and community regeneration / Drawing out the lessons: culture and leadership/ Index.

160pp 0 335 21911 X (EAN: 9 780335 219117) Paperback
0 335 21912 8 (EAN: 9 780335 219124) Hardback

Since escaping the East Midlands to find his fortune in the big city, Adrian Harvey has combined a career in and around government with trying to see as much of the world as he can. He lives in North London, which he believes to be the finest corner of the world's greatest city; *Being Someone* is his first novel.

URBANE